OGONI'S AGONIES

OGONI'S AGONIES: KEN SARO-WIWA AND THE CRISIS IN NIGERIA

EDITED BY
ABDUL-RASHEED NA'ALLAH

Africa World Press, Inc.

P.O. Box 1892
Trenton, NJ 08607

P.O. Box 48
Asmara, ERITREA

Africa World Press, Inc.

P.O. Box 1892
Trenton, NJ 08607

P.O. Box 48
Asmara, ERITREA

Copyright © 1998 Abdul-Rasheed Na'Allah

First Printing 1998

Cover design: Jonathan Gullery

Library of Congress Cataloging-in-Publication Data

Ogoni's agonies : Ken Saro-Wiwa and the crisis in Nigeria / edited by Abdul-Rasheed Na'Allah.
       p   cm
   Includes bibliographical references and index.
   ISBN 0-86543-646-0 (hb). -- ISBN 0-86543-647-9 (pb)
   1. Saro-Wiwa, Ken, 1941- 2. Ogoni (African people)--History.
3. Ogoni (African people)--Crimes against. 4. Ogoni (African people)--Government relations. 5. Saro-Wiwa, Ken, 1941--Assassination. 6. Saro-Wiwa, Ken, 1941--Political and social views. 7. Genocide--Nigeria. 8. International business enterprises--Nigeria. 9. Nigeria--Politics and government--1984-
10. Nigeria--Social conditions. 11. Nigeria--In literature.
   I. Na'allah, Abdul Rasheed.
DT515.45.O33048   1998   98-22493
966.905' 3--dc21   CIP

FOR

Ken

all Ogoni

suffering Nigerians

Nigeria.

Government is [meant] to protect the rights [of its people] and the creations of God... Giving responsibility (of leadership) to irresponsible persons is a sin.

Abdullahi Dan Fodi in *Diya al-siyasat* (The Light of Politics), 1819

Abu Sayyid reported that the Prophet said: "The best Jihad (Holy War) is that of one who speaks a true word to a tyrannical ruler."

(Ibn Majah, Tirmizi, Abu Daud)

CONTENTS

Poetry:

IV. LAMENT, STRUGGLE

ACKNOWLEDGEMENTS

The idea that gestated into the birth of Ogonis Agonies originated from a meeting between my friend Adebayo Toyo and I sometimes toward the end of 1994. Bayo soon afterward moved from Edmonton and could not be part of the process that made this plan a reality, but I would like to recognize Bayo's friendship and encouragement. I am also indebted to my professors at the University of Alberta, Milan V. Dimič, George Lang and Stephen Slemon, for their constant advice throughout the cause of putting this book together. Jonathan Hart and Stephen Arnold also deserve recognition for their support. The Department of Modern Languages and Comparative Studies and the University of Alberta made it possible for me to coordinate contributions for this book by providing many campus resources. In particular, I would like to thank Kwame Anthony Appiah, the Harvard Professor of Afro-American Studies and Philosophy, and Biodun Jeyifo, Professor of English at Cornell University, for taking time to write the Preface and Foreword respectively to this book, despite their other numerous engagements.

I cannot miss the opportunity to thank the University of Alberta International Centre, as well as Nancy Hannemann, its Global Education Coordinator; Rowena Pugh and all those from within and without the Centre who helped in typing and proof-reading the manuscripts. To my intimate friends in Nigeria, Britain and Canada, Bilyamin Ajewumi Raji, Muhammad Adeniyi Kamal (Baba Habibu), Lukman Adam, Abdul-Razaq Abdullahi, Abubakar Aliagan, Richard Solly, Sanjit Singh Bakshi, Amritha Fernandes, Paul and Mona Martin, also profound gratitude.

Of course I cannot forget my darling wife Rahmat, and my beloved daughter Saratu Asabi, born in 1996 when the compilation of this work was reaching its peak, for their patience and understanding. I thank Allah Subuhana Ta'ala for bringing this project to fruit.

Finally, this book was conceived as a part of a commitment to non-silence against the national and multinational forces of death in Nigeria. It is my wish that Nigeria, for which it is written, shall overcome its postcolonial tragedy and emerge a resounding success.

Abdul-Rasheed Na'Allah
Edmonton
March 1998

PREFACE

The hanging of Ken Saro-Wiwa came as an enormous shock to many of us. His fellow writers and many human rights and environmental activists in Africa and around the world mounted the sort of campaign in his defense that has worked in other countries; Nelson Mandela placed the power of his enormous moral prestige and his considerable diplomatic skill in the balance; along with him, the Commonwealth's leaders worked to persuade their Nigerian counterparts that they were taking the wrong path; and, until the last moment, writers, activists, diplomats, politicians all found it hard to believe that the Nigerian government would put its prestige and the fate of the Nigerian economy at risk under the cover of a process as obviously flawed as the 'trial' that led to his hanging. Whether or not we knew him, whether or not we agreed with him about this or that question in the long struggle in Ogoniland for justice for the people and respect for the natural environment, many of us, in and out of Nigeria, saw in the death of Saro-Wiwa and the eight activists who were killed with him, a reflection of so many failures: the collapse of the rule of law; the betrayal of the vision of resolution through dialogue; the long history (going back to the colonial period) of the Nigerian state's lack of concern for Ogoni people; the environmental irresponsibility of oil companies and of governments.

I myself was reminded of a passage from Margery Perham's biography of Lord Lugard, the British colonial official who played the largest role in creating Nigeria, in which she quotes an appalling letter, written to Lady Lugard:

> This evening late I hear the Ogonis are up. Moorhouse came to tell
> me and read the telegram that they have eaten two persons. "What
> sort of persons," I asked, "were they Govt. employees?" He said, oh
> no they were no one in particular. Then let them eat some more, I
> said. If Ogoni eats Ogoni, my withers are unwrung.

If Nigerian postcolonial government, civilian and military, have
done little to carry out the environmental rehabilitation of the desecrated landscape that is the Ogoni homeland, they have surely
been treading in the footsteps of their colonial predecessors.

Even if — as some in the families of the four chiefs for whose murder Saro-Wiwa was held responsible believe — Saro-Wiwa had, in
fact, done everything the Nigerian government claimed, his trial
would, of course, have been a travesty. But he himself would have
wanted us to focus not on his own individual suffering, and the loss
to his family and friends and to African literature, but on the terrible assaults on the Ogoni people and the land that nurtures them
materially and is their spiritual home. We should remember not
only those who died with him, assassinated under color of law, but
all those whose bodies, spirits and way of life have been corrupted
by the physical pollution of the oil spills and the spiritual division
that a cruel state and an uncaring oil industry have brought to the
Ogoni people. Whatever else we may disagree about, every person
of good will must agree that something terrible has happened to
the Ogoni people; and that the Nigerian government and the oil
companies, Shell chief among them, have played a part in it. It
would be wrong to deny that there are those in Ogoniland who
have played a villain's role in this tragedy; but there is blame
enough to go around.

This collection displays in the diversity of its origins — in and
out of Nigeria, in and out of Ogoniland; writers, scholars, activists;
Muslim, Christian and neither; strangers, friends and enemies of
Ken Saro-Wiwa — and in the diversity of its forms (both poetry and
prose) the extraordinary range of responses to the Ogoni question
that the execution of Ken Saro-Wiwa has occasioned. And we are
privileged to hear his own voice as he speaks of the struggle of the
Movement for the Survival of the Ogoni People and its meaning for
him. But this book also provides the materials for reflection on the

complexity of the issues that went into the struggle that eventually consumed his life. And we can do him no greater honor than to reflect (as this collection enables us to do) on what has happened to the people of his native land — what they have done and what has been done to them — and to commit ourselves, each in our own way, to the struggle for justice, for his people and all people, and for the precious earth that is the mother of us all.

Kwame Anthony Appiah
Boston, Massachusetts
January 1998

FOREWORD
Ken Saro-Wiwa and the
Hour of the Ogoni

The madness of the brave is the wisdom of life.

Maxim Gorky

The struggle was impossible and for that reason it took place.

Jorge Santiago Perednik

vo·lun·ta·ri·sm: a theory that conceives will to be the dominant factor in experience or in the constitution of the world.

Webster's Third New International Dictionary

van·guard·ism: the attitudes, ideas or activities of persons regarding
themselves as members of a vanguard.

Webster's Third New International Dictionary

Since the most obvious historical fact about the act of putting
together and publishing this book may, because of the very
fact of this 'obviousness', escape notice, permit me to point to
it as my opening gesture in this short Foreword to the collection.
This is the fact that the publication of this book constitutes the very
first time in African postcolonial history that an international gathering of poets, essayists and scholars have come together in one volume to endorse the struggle of what is, first and foremost, an *ethno-
national* liberation movement. Indeed, it may very well be a first in
postcolonial history worldwide. And I say this without having suf-

fered temporary amnesia about the worldwide support of the East
Timorese in their struggle against Indonesian 'occupation' colonialism, or similar support for the cause of the Tibetan people against
Chinese usurpation of their political, cultural and religious rights,
or in a wider arc of contemporary global politics, the depth of international feelings and actions in support of the Palestinians, the
Kurds, and the Armenians. What distinguishes the worldwide support for the Ogoni cause — of which this book is a fitting harvest of
the most eloquent supporters and the most perceptive analysts — is
the fact that in none of these other cases, with the possible exception of the Palestinians, is the principle of solidarity with an oppressed people raised to the level of a categorical imperative *within a
situation which is not one of unambiguous occupation by another country*. At any rate, the publication of this book marks the very first
time in African postcolonial history that a liberation movement
that relates to a specific ethno-nationality is able to garner such a
magnitude of African and worldwide support and endorsement.
Again, let us be absolutely clear about the historical significance of
this event: the support that the struggle of the Ogoni enjoys worldwide today is of the same ideological and categorical legitimacy
that 'national liberation', as the mark of the aspirations of colonized people everywhere, enjoyed for decades from about the end
of World War I. This, in simple but quite historic terms, means that
the basic unit for conceiving the most oppressed, the most downtrodden as a social aggregate is no longer the nation-state; rather, it
is what we might call the true communities of suffering and resistance, and they exist on all the five continents, and within, and
sometimes between, the boundaries of the existing nation-states of
the world. Indeed for some time now, it has become a truism of radical democratic possibilities worldwide that it is the liberation of
these communities which will be the benchmark of the prospects
for the liberation of all exploited, dominated groups and individuals everywhere. The editor and the publisher of this book thus deserve our gratitude for having the acumen to perceive this political-
ideological seismic shift in the struggles of the late 20th century for
the political, cultural, economic and ecological survival of most of
the people of our common earth.

In my remarks in this Foreword, I would like to reflect briefly on
some of the ramifications of this event. Using illustrations mostly

from Nigeria — since that is the primary theater of the agony of the Ogoni — I shall in effect be arguing that though the oppressions and injustices of our present age are often as naked and brutal as those of the opening decades of this century, only to the extent that we leave room in our actions and discourses for the ambiguities and complexities which inflect the stark realities of these oppressions and injustices, only to that extent will we be able to grasp the real import of what, for want of a better formulation, I call the hour of the 'Ogonis' of Africa and the developing world.

Prior to the intervention of Ken Saro-Wiwa and MOSOP on the stage of African postcolonial history, it had all but been impossible to win moral and ideological legitimacy for any liberation movement defined in ethnic, or even regional or subnational terms; more pointedly, it had proved impossible to win wide, unambiguous support for such a movement on the continent of Africa itself, and more generally within the international community. For the spectre of secessionism, of fragmentation and the naked play of narrowly chauvinistic ethnic politics has fairly or unfairly haunted all such claims and movements. This is why even in cases of the movements and struggles of dominated communities and groups that were patently just and irreproachably progressive — like the struggles of the EPLF and the Eritrean people and the SPLM and the Southern Sudanese peoples — this spectre unfairly constrained the scope of the solidarity that the movements could generate on the African continent. It is thus the supreme achievement of Ken Saro-Wiwa and MOSOP that they have shaken off this ideological odium and have given unquestionable moral and ideological force to their insistence on the specific plight of the Ogoni while at the same time recognizing that the Ogoni are not alone, that other communities and individuals also suffer from the same chain of linked local, national, and global exploitative and repressive forces.

Thus, we have much to learn from the legacy of Saro-Wiwa and MOSOP. We have, for instance, to learn that it is not enough to experience domination and unspeakable injustice as a distinct community; even though its human and moral validity is without question, such experience of suffering can only have effective moral and ideological legitimacy if it resonates powerfully with the experience of domination and injustices suffered by other communities and individuals. This is a lesson that Nigeria in particular, and other nation-states in Africa and the developing world can ill afford to ignore, but do not seem, at least for now, able and ready to absorb. This is because the very factors which give this sort of exemplary resonance to the plight of an ethno-nationality like the Ogoni are cloaked with ambiguous, ironic truths which activists, militants and advocates of civil and political rights are not always willing, or even able, to recognize, let alone assimilate into their actions and discourses. Permit me to briefly expatiate on this point.

Out of many others, one way to obtain an adequate grasp of the complexity of this matter is afforded by Wole Soyinka's theorizations, in his book *The Open Sore of a Continent*, on what he calls "the spoils of power," thereby signifying contrastively on the more common term, "the spoils of office". It is important to grasp the difference between these two terms, as well as the relevance of this difference to the present discussion on how only a few communities of suffering and resistance in Africa like the Ogoni have achieved the moral and ideological legitimacy which eludes other such communities.

In the operations of the 'spoils of office', the whole apparatus of office-holding and incumbency, from the humblest village or local council employees to the upper echelons of autocratic rulership in the inner core of Abacha's Provisional Ruling Council, exists solely as a means of self-enrichment that is so naked, so remorseless that it has become the constitutive *ethos* of governance. The political elites of all groups and communities participate, and are complicitous, in the pursuit of the 'spoils of office', although the political elites of the major, or larger ethno-national groups constitute the 'big league' of its beneficiaries. There is indeed a more or less effective *naturalization* of this ethos in the way that the non-elite sections of the population act as participants in the political economy of the 'spoils of office' in the manner in which they celebrate the loot cornered by their elites as booty brought from war. More than thirty years ago, Chinua Achebe explored the operation of this ethos in his novel, *A Man of the People*, when he observed wryly that thieving public officials who would face instant justice if they stole from their own local community, say a local church or mosque, or a local school, are celebrated as heroes when they empty the coffers of the state or regional government, or of the nation itself. In other words, this persuasive, naturalized corruption that is 'the spoils of office' operates throughout the length and breadth of the land; it cuts across all ethnic groups even though, as a system, it is especially beneficial to the political elites of the major ethnic groups. It is thus, rather perversely, a 'democratic' and all-inclusive system. And it is precisely on account of the perverse nature of the mode of 'inclusiveness' inherent in the operations of the 'spoils of office' that in Nigeria in the last two decades, more states have been created than in any other nation in the world, as more and more communities, through their political elites, have been brought into the orbit of the glad-rags of the 'spoils of office'. The house maketh the feasters merry; it is emptied out.

The 'spoils of power', as theorized powerfully and persuasively by Soyinka in *The Open Sore of a Continent*, operates far more selectively and lopsidedly, and with a relentless logic of exclusion which cannot even brook the mere possibility of significant or meaningful sharing of power, let alone think of relinquishing power, as an act of political grace and maturity, or in deference to popular electoral sovereignty. This means in effect that there is a crucial distinction to be made between holding office and exercising effective power, since all office-holders, local, state or national, have some measure of power, including the power to embezzle public funds, or, through nepotism and ethnic cronyism, to enrich one's friends and relatives, or members of one's ethnic group. But there is power and there is *power*. In *The Open Sore of a Continent*, Soyinka deploys this notion of the 'spoils of power' primarily in terms of the capacity of a tiny group of Northern military officers and civilian politicians, administrators and diplomats to enjoy, whether or not they are in office, exemptions, rights and privileges that other political actors and the rest of the population don't enjoy. We need to amplify the range of the abuses and corruptions of power covered by this term. Like the power to detain people without having to show cause why they are being detained and for how long; the power not to have to explain why, and for how long, you will hold and exercise power; the power to have exclusive and unchallengeable right to decide who shall be the head of state, and from what part of the country he shall come from, or, conversely, *not* come from; and above all else, the power of life and death over all the citizens of the country.

These are the faces and expressions of the 'spoils of power' which give concrete reality to an otherwise nebulous concept. It is only to the extent that we grasp the essence of the distinction between the 'spoils of office' and the 'spoils of power' that we can understand why, even though members of the political class from all ethnic groups have participated in the operations of the 'spoils of office', there has been such a widespread, consuming public debate in Nigeria in the last two decades on the ethnic, regional or religious identity of the head of state, on *where* he shall come from (it goes without saying that nearly all discussants have presumed that it can only be a *he*, not a she): from the Hausa-Fulani, the Igbo, the Yoruba or a 'minority' ethnic group; from the communities of Muslims or of Christians; from the 'South' or from the 'North'; and now more than ever, from the civilian population at large or from the ranks of the leadership of the military. This reification of the office and person of the head of state is the ultimate mark of the reality of the 'spoils of power' as the determinant in the last instance of every aspect of the corporate political existence of the country.

In *The Open Sore of a Continent*, Soyinka argues that the historical roots of this phenomenon of the 'spoils of power' goes back to the divide-and-rule machinations of the British in colonial Nigeria, especially as they began to plan their departure from the country and started supervising the creation of their legatees in the postcolony of Nigeria. This is somewhat problematic; I think it is more convincing to locate the inception of the system in the second coup of 1966 and, correspondingly, to see its ultimate culmination in the Babangida-Abacha annulment of the June 1993 presidential elections. For at that point, the underlying equation of this nepotistic and fascist reification and monopolization of power became clear:

1. It is only by the use of naked military force can you insist that, whatever happens at the polls, the head of state cannot come from certain sections of the country;
2. That being the case, it is logical and more expedient to have the military more or less permanently *directly* exercise that power.

Most of the leading groups and individuals in the Nigerian pro-democracy movement, from all parts of the country, are driven by resolute opposition to the politics of both the 'spoils of office' and the 'spoils of power'. But without question, for most, the overriding concern is with the ramifications and effects of the politics of the 'spoils of power'. The general thinking seems to be that the corrupt, laissez-faire politics of the 'spoils of office' is the lesser evil, the lesser problem, and it will be easily resolved once the far more desperate and tragic politics of the 'spoils of power' is resolved 'once and for all'. This is without doubt an obsession, a very understandable obsession, but an obsession all the same, and the Nigerian pro-democracy movement bears all the marks of the distortions caused by this obsession. I suggest that Ken Saro-Wiwa and the Ogoni movement, by their radical indifference to both the politics of the 'spoils of office' and the 'spoils of power' and the difference between them have provided an extremely productive legacy of perspectives which have the potential to take us beyond these distortions caused by obsession with the reification and monopolization of power. Before I come to this point in my closing, critical commentary on this legacy, I wish to dwell briefly on some of the problems and dilemmas generated by these distortions.

One of the most telling expressions of these distortions is the fact that it is often virtually impossible to unpack the political sentiment and attitudes which inform the actions and thinking of individuals and groups in the pro-democracy movement and, consequently, to establish an ordering of these sentiments and attitudes based on their relative mobilizational and ideological effectiveness. For instance, in any one individual or group, the sentiments and attitudes which fuel the democratic, patriotic passions and objectives may include some or all of the following:

- bitter, uncompromising rejection of the nullification of the June 1993 presidential elections and the continued incarceration of the winner of the elections, M.K.O. Abiola, a Southerner, a civilian politician, and a Yoruba;
- indignation at the fact that the whole country is now more or less a vast prison, caused by the extreme arbitrariness and arrogance in the exercise of power generally, and specifically in the unrelenting harassment, detention or physical elimination of dissidents and opponents of the regime;

- outrage at the insecurity caused by the ever-worsening quality of life for the general populace, especially as manifested in the virtual collapse of public utilities and services like hospitals, schools, water and electricity supply,and safety of life, limb and property;
- revulsion toward realities and actions which produce and perpetuate the image of the country in the world today as both a pariah nation and one place in the world to avoid at all cost if one has no pressing need to go there;
- determined opposition to the relentless and rapacious plundering of the nation's wealth and resources by a tiny group of military and civilian power and influence peddlers and their expatriate and international partners and associates.

Let us call this compendium of sentiments and attitudes the National Reconstruction Credo. Any of these sentiments and attitudes constitutes a sufficient basis for meaningful and honorable opposition to Abacha's military dictatorship in particular, and to military rule in general; indeed, any one of them may in fact ultimately lead to the removal of the dictatorship. But NONE, by itself, can be generalized to produce an articulation of the experience of suffering and exploitation in Nigeria today which will resonate with all communities throughout the country, not to speak of the continent and the world at large. Furthermore, NONE of these emotions and attitudes will, by itself, suffice to generate the reconstruction of the country and the West Africa region on a solid democratic foundation in a post-military Nigeria.

Let us be completely frank with ourselves on this point: many pro-democracy activists and militants in Nigeria will have to accept that some of the actions and policies of the dictatorship which have provoked their most uncompromising determination to end the political life of the junta do not produce the same responses throughout the country and in the world at large. This applies particularly to the annulment of the June 12, 1993 presidential elections and the continued incarceration of the winner of the elections, Bashorun M.K.O. Abiola. In principle, this ought to have such an effect throughout the country since it strikes at the heart of the reification and monopolization of power and exposes the bared, putrefied entrails of the politics of the 'spoils of power'. But it quite simply doesn't. Other more unsavory and reprehensible factors aside, the primary reason for this is precisely because indignation at the annulment of the June 12 mandate cannot itself escape the extremely reified and divisive reduction of the fate of democracy in Nigeria to the ethnic, regional or religious origins or identity of the head of state of the country. But having said this, it needs to be stated very clearly that if outrage at the cancellation of the June 12, 1993 mandate cannot be generalized to resonate with the experience of suffering and injustice throughout Nigeria and Africa, this should neither lead to dropping it from a central place in the compendium of sentiments and attitudes that we have identified here as the National Reconstruction Credo, nor to bitter resentment toward those in Nigeria who do not feel particularly animated by that act of disenfranchisement of the Nigerian people. What is required is that we do an ordering of the stock of sentiments and perspectives in the National Reconstruction Credo such that what we do and say about suffering and injustice in Nigeria today will not only have a resonance throughout the country, but will also connect with what other communities and individuals in Africa and elsewhere feel and think about suffering and injustice in their particular contexts, and in the world today at the close of this century and this millennium.

This is indeed what Ken Saro-Wiwa and MOSOP, in the way they have waged the struggle of the Ogoni against their local and foreign expropriators and oppressors, have to teach us; this is the legacy of the struggle they have been waging from about 1990. For it was from around this period that Saro-Wiwa and MOSOP began to move decisively and irrevocably beyond and outside of the framework of both the politics of the 'spoils of office' and the 'spoils of power'. It was from around this period that they came to the revolutionary realization that neither of these two 'politics', singly or together, in their complementarity or their difference, fundamentally addresses the crucial link between the monopolization of power through military or civilian dictatorship and the international and global currents and forces of naked, amoral and anti-people super-exploitation represented in Nigeria by Shell and Chevron. From all indications, prior to the very early 1990s, the Ogoni movement could easily have been bought off by giving them a state of their own, or a state in which the Ogoni political elites would have been the dominant power and influence peddlers. This would have effectively brought the Ogoni elites more securely within the blessed firmament of the politics of the 'spoils of office' and everybody would have been happy — the Ogoni elites themselves, the executives of Shell and Chevron, the oligarchs of the Nigerian 'spoils of power' machinery of state. That is to say everybody but the wretched of Ogoni. From around the early 1990s, Saro-Wiwa and MOSOP sealed their fate with the fate of these 'Ogoni' bottom heap of a ravaged country and continent. This is why from that moment, they were on an inevitable collision course with both the Nigerian military *reich* and the local and global propaganda networks of the oil conglomerates, a collision course on which the last word is yet to be written. And this is also why their legacy is today at the forefront of democratic possibilities in Nigeria and Africa.

If I have said little here about the limits and contradictions of the legacy of Ken Saro-Wiwa and MOSOP, it is not because there aren't any to identify and ponder, even as we acknowledge and celebrate their achievements. It is largely because that sort of accounting belongs elsewhere, and is at any rate broached by other contributors to this collection. Indeed, I would like in this respect to point out that all the four epigraphs to this Foreword testify to how so intertwined are the achievements and the limitations of Saro-Wiwa and MOSOP. In another context, I shall expatiate more fully, critically and fraternally on these points. I have thought it more appropriate in the present context to concentrate on what I regard as perhaps the most remarkable aspect of the legacy of Saro-Wiwa and MOSOP. This is the fact they have managed, against all odds, to eloquently clarify the conditions under which the endorsement of an *ethno-national* liberation movement can be unambiguously progressive, ethically compelling, and vital to the prospects for democratic renewal. This message is relevant to all the five continents, but none more so than the continent of Africa.

Biodun Jeyifo
Ithaca, New York
January 1998

I

Introduction

Introduction

Precisely one year after 'A Call for Poems' for this anthology went out, asking for poems in honor of Kenule Saro-Wiwa and the Ogoni people, four Ogoni Chiefs were killed under cloudy circumstances: Samuel Orage, Theophilus Orage, Alberta Badey, Edward Kobani. The leader of the Movement for the Survival of the Ogoni People (MOSOP) was hanged along with eight other Ogonis after a special government tribunal found them guilty for killing, or for inciting the killing of the four Ogoni Chiefs. Many poems poured in, and I became very busy selecting and editing the poems, and discussing with other writers what to include in the anthology.

Bronwyn Mills, an American who described himself as a student of one of the gurus of contemporary African literature, Ngũgĩ wa Thiong'o, sent me an e-mail, which captures the torture and the loss of breath the world went through following the unbelievable death sentence carried out on Saro-Wiwa and the eight Ogoni environmentalists. "Dear Abdul-Rasheed," Mills wrote,

> I was in Ngũgĩ wa Thiong'o's office when the news of Saro-Wiwa's pending execution — then pending came through. A student came in to tell Ngũgĩ that the government was going to execute Saro-Wiwa.
>
> Ngũgĩ just put his head in his hands for a moment and then looked away for a moment.
>
> "Well have you called Amnesty?"
>
> "Yes."
>
> "What about..."

"Well let's call them."
I was struck by the fact that this was both a horror and a familiar one. So they killed him?
I don't have a poem, just more questions, more bewilderments; your idea is a noble one.

For days everyone wished it was only a bad dream, but alas the Nigerian junta's blood theater had played again, and the Nobel Peace Prize nominee and eight others were gone. What is left for us are questions and bewilderments.

This book is to assuage these thirsts, and to engage the world in a dialogue about the diabolical regime, and destruction of human lives and resources in postcolonial Nigeria. As a departure from the many reports on the Ogoni of Nigeria, this book offers literary and scholarly approaches to the Ogoni saga. Critical essays have here converged to beat the membrane of the Ogoni drum. They let us enter into the historical, cultural and social realities of the Ogoni question. The book offers strong insights into the issues of Nigerian oil money and the pact between military government and multinational companies. The articles represent all sides of Nigerian problems. The Ogoni question is therefore a metaphor and a rallying point for discussion of all the cankerworms of postcolonial Nigeria. The deaths of Saro-Wiwa and others have become a watershed in the struggle for the emancipation of the Nigerian downtrodden. This book pays tribute not only to the late Saro-Wiwa but also to the Ogoni people for the many rivers they have crossed and are yet to cross.

The writing styles in this book are as diverse as the cultural backgrounds of the writers. I have intentionally allowed both the British and the American spellings to stay as originally written by the authors. I make bold to say that what we have here is a world in discussion. This project broadens Spivak's (1990) negotiation theory where she asks the Third World academic in the diaspora to discuss issues germane to the liberation of the Third World in their writings and teachings. She says that they must negotiate with the structures of oppression in the postcolonial space by engaging the citizens of the imperial nations (whom they teach) in a discussion and a search to end the imperialists' structures of violence. I agree that

Third World scholars in the diaspora, having mastered Western traditions, have a fundamental duty to strike the bell for the end of the systematic destruction of the developing nations by the imperialist powers. However, everybody in the world has both a right and a duty to unite to wipe out neocolonial tendencies anywhere in the world. The solution to the problems of our globe is the revitalization of the world's multiculturalism as celebrated in this volume: a world where everybody is concerned with the problem of everybody, a world in which critical minds converge in attacking and eliminating every injustice. This is what Niyi Osundare envisions when he insists in his article in Section Three of this book that the Nigerian problem is not an 'internal affair'. As we enter into the twenty first century, we have a responsibility to usher in greater convergences in the cross-cultural discussions of the world's problems. It should be a century where we all are our brothers' and sisters' keepers. That is the appropriate definition of 'the world as a global village'.

This is intended to be a book that truly reaches across cultures. It demonstrates how rich a language becomes when it attains a position of a multicultural medium. The English in this volume breathes Euro-American as well as African cultures. The article by Adotei Akwei, in Section Two, brings an important dimension to the debate on postcolonial Nigeria. It discusses what he calls 'the two faces of Nigeria'. The first face is the progressive, anti-apartheid, oil-rich country whose cough caused imperial nations around the world to catch cold: a nation that "mobilized, funded and almost single-handedly manned a peacekeeping force in Liberia" (Akwei in Section Two), a country with the most independent press in Africa. Akwei says in his piece that this great story which Nigeria had to tell attracted Amnesty to Nigeria, to show the world what an exemplary nation it was. This Ghanaian writer, who is also the USA Amnesty International representative in Africa, explains with a clearly tragic tone how this once shining nation suddenly turned into a pariah nation, where torture, imprisonment, murder, and all forms of political persecution are the order of the day. Amnesty International saw and covered every phase of the Saro-Wiwa trial. Akwei's paper is a thorough account proving what the Hausa calls *Gani ya fi ji*, meaning 'to see is greater than just to hear'.

Desmond Orage's article, 'The Ogoni Question and the Role of the International Community in Nigeria', has been included in this book for many reasons. One is that, as Mr. Orage himself agrees in a letter, his paper is a 'Pro-Shell, Pro-Government' piece. It contributes a different opinion on the complex Nigerian issue. Mr. Orage himself is in grief and thus he is highly emotional. His father Chief Samuel Orage was one of the four Ogoni Chiefs for whose murder Saro-Wiwa was tried and killed. His paper, therefore, is useful to students of language as an excellent example of writing in fury and grief. In a way, Mr. Orage brings to this book an anger with, and a condemnation of, Saro-Wiwa, the youth wing of MOSOP, and the international community. His narration presents a pattern of passion to convince the readers, using words and phrases more powerful and emotional than are normally allowed in scholarly writing. In complete contrast to popular opinions around the world, he qualifies MOSOP, Saro-Wiwa, and the international community as the culprits responsible for the atrocities committed in Ogoniland. The following is a summary of Mr. Orage's indictment:

> Everyone that opposed Mr. Ken Saro-Wiwa's new found militant methodology was labeled a 'vulture' who has been bribed to destroy the Ogoni revolution and therefore must be killed. Ogoni youths at this stage listened to no one else but Mr. Ken Saro-Wiwa who got his instructions from UNPO of which he was a paid Vice-Chairman. The stage was now set for the most sophisticated propaganda in modern history. Environmental degradation was at the heart of his propaganda to win the support of environmentalists in the West. With financial support pouring in from the West and the Nigerian police and Shell sent packing from Ogoni, our fathers were now at the mercy of Mr. Ken Saro-Wiwa and his hoodlums. Increasingly with every brazen act, Mr. Ken Saro-Wiwa believed he was now above the Nigerian law.

Although I trust the readers' eyes to see far beyond today's obscure paintings on the Ogoni's masques, one must also ask people to further lower their gaze so that they can see their own noses.

Ken Saro-Wiwa has responded directly and indirectly to all of Orage's contentions in his interviews reprinted in this book.

Readers thus have the opportunity to hear directly from the horse's mouth. Much evidence shows that Saro-Wiwa was a humble, peaceful and responsible leader of his people. For example, it was his emphasis on peaceful strategies in the Ogoni's struggle that got him a nomination for the Nobel Peace Prize. Conversely, the current Nigerian military government achieved world-notoriety for suppressing the genuine struggle of the Ogoni people and for sending in members of the armed forces to 'waste' any person that frustrated the operation of Shell oil company in Ogoniland. The documentary, *Delta Force*, largely recorded by the Ogoni themselves, serves as a good education for the international community. Before the murder of the four Ogoni Chiefs, the Ogoni community had become a military zone. The people were terribly devastated: houses burnt, women raped, several men, women and children murdered, a few among those who managed to survive had their hands cruelly amputated. This evidence discredits the theory that the oppressed Ogoni condoned violence or that MOSOP was ordering the cannibalism of fellow Ogoni. Yet, the issue of who killed the Ogoni women, children, and the four Chiefs is still greeted with denial upon denial.

Before we read the living attestation of William Boyd, the British novelist whose article follows Orage's paper, we might consider a word from Funsho Aiyejina, another person who had close dealings with Saro-Wiwa. His poetry collection was published by Saros International Press: the first book written by another person to be published by Saro-Wiwa's company. Aiyejina, in an article in the *Trinidad Guardian* (December 19, 1995: 45–48), gave testimony about the peaceful stance of Saro-Wiwa. He remembered a conversation he had in 1987 with Saro-Wiwa at the National Theatre, Lagos, when some Nigerians violently protested then President Babangida's repressions. Saro-Wiwa, said Aiyejina, condemned the protest, saying "Violence is not an option" (1995: 47).

Furthermore, a well researched write-up in *Worldwatch* (1996: 10–21) by Aaron Sachs puts the blame for the violence in Ogoniland squarely on the doorstep of the Nigerian government. Sachs insists: "there were many eyewitnesses who attested to the military's role in the attacks ... The incidents were documented by several international human rights organizations which had no reason to favor the rights of one ethnic group over those of any other" (p. 18). Sachs cites other incidences where Amnesty International and a number of other foreign organizations carried out a detailed investigation and came out with reports that indicted the Nigerian regime:

> In late July and early August 1993, for instance, a series of attacks allegedly by the neighbouring Andoni people, a tiny community of fishers, killed about 200 Ogonis and completely destroyed the village of Kaa, including the market where the Andoni traditionally sold their fish. The automatic weapons, grenades, mortars, and dynamite used in the attacks "were clearly beyond the means of a fishing community" noted a report by the Unrepresented Nations and Peoples Organization (UNPO), a human rights group based in the Netherlands. An immediate on-site investigation by Amnesty International concluded that there had been "no obvious cause for dispute. Soldiers were said to have instigated and assisted the attacks and then followed the attackers into Ogoni villages." (p. 18)

Perhaps the most practical steps taken by Ken Saro-Wiwa to show that he never condoned violence were when he himself mounted campaigns against vigilante groups in Ogoniland, and went so far as to ask the local administration authority to arrest anyone among the Ogonis engaging in acts of violence. MOSOP, according to Sachs, issued a press release disassociating itself from vandalism. Saro-Wiwa frequently visited parts of Ogoniland to campaign against violence (see Sachs p. 19).

The trial of Ken Saro-Wiwa and eight other Ogonis has thus been described as a theater of illusion. The *ALA Bulletin*, an official publication of the African Literature Association, reproduced the testimony of two former prosecution witnesses who said that the military authority coerced and bribed them to implicate Saro-Wiwa:

> Naayone Nkpa, 27, was a member of MOSOP's youth wing and was at the scene of the murders. "After the killings the police took us to give statements," he said. "My statement did not name any person. After some time we were called by the state government to come and change our statements. They covered the paper and told us to

sign. We said we would not sign until we could see what it said. They brought us money — $345 US — and promised us a job. Then they threatened we would be accused as well. Afterwards we signed."

Charles Danwi, 35, is a musician from Bera. He too was picked up as a witness. He says his statement did not satisfy the police and a few days later he was taken to the military governor's lodge. For the next five hours he was encouraged to implicate Saro-Wiwa and others.

"They promised me musical instruments and a contract to play music and become a very rich person. After I signed, every Tuesday we were taken back to the lodge for meetings with prosecutors and other witnesses. They put us together and told us what to say so that we all said the same thing. When we could not answer well they told us to answer like them." (*ALA Bulletin*, 21. 2: 33–4)

Regardless of the mountain of evidence to prove the 'peaceful Saro-Wiwa' side, the other side, represented in this book by Desmond Orage, insists, like the Nigerian military government does, that Saro-Wiwa planned and ordered the murders of the four Ogoni Chiefs. Aiyejina and many other observers, however, described this assertion as the desperation of the pro-government side to 'stop at nothing' to crush Ogoni's backbones, by shedding the blood of their leader. As Aiyejina puts it:

Saro-Wiwa was not even present at the rally during which, in the course of a mob action, the unfortunate deaths of the four pro-government Ogoni chiefs, for which he was sentenced to death, took place. And the government knew that for a fact; its security agents were the ones who detained and prevented him from attending and addressing that rally in his capacity as the President of the Movement for the Survival of the Ogoni People (MOSOP) which organised it. During the trial itself, six prosecution witnesses confessed that they had been bribed to testify against the accused. In addition, Saro-Wiwa's team of lawyers, which included Gani Fawahinmi and Femi Falana, two front-line pro-democracy lawyers, was constantly harassed and denied access to him. On one occasion, Femi Falana was detained without charge on his way to court and prevented from going to discharge his duty to his client. Out of frustration and in fairness to their client, the entire defense team resigned. Saro-Wiwa subsequently refused to talk to a tribunal-appointed lawyer. He insisted on his own lawyers but the tribunal ignored his demand. In essence, Saro-Wiwa was tried and convicted without the benefit of legal representation. (p. 45)

In Desmond Orage's opinion, the blade of the butcher's knife fits the neck of the world's own immaculate pigeon. He still strongly argues that there is no justice greater than the violent death meted out on Ken Saro-Wiwa, the Nobel Peace Prize nominee.

William Boyd's paper, written in flowing Queen's English, exploits modern writing techniques of contemporary British culture. It starts in a moving tone, presenting an emotional but factual picture of Saro-Wiwa's personality, and the government's drastic hunt for his blood. He gives a summary of Ken's life history, most especially his writing career. A bosom friend of Saro-Wiwa, Boyd relates to us how the late writer's resentment of the Dutch/British Shell Oil and the Nigerian government's atrocities in Ogoniland led him to his grave. The article joins in defending Saro-Wiwa against the assertions we read in Orage's paper. In a clear summary that captures the whole episode from Saro-Wiwa's arrest to his eventual conviction, Boyd says:

Ken was arrested and, with several others, was accused of incitement to murder. The fact that he was in a car some miles away going in the opposite direction made no difference. He was imprisoned for more than a year and then was tried before a specially convened tribunal. There was no right of appeal. This 'judicial process' has been internationally condemned as a sham. It was a show trial in a kangaroo court designed to procure the verdict required by the government.

This piece is particularly striking because of the writer's regular references to his personal encounters with Saro-Wiwa. He cites examples from letters the slain author wrote to him from prison.

Ato Quayson's very brilliant paper, 'For Ken Saro-Wiwa: African Postcolonial Relations Through a Prism of Tragedy', traces the

Nigerian crisis to the question of class conflict and the struggle for the control of productional resources of the country, and the state power. It adds a new dimension to the discussion of the Ogoni problem. Quayson conducts a re-reading of the events leading to Saro-Wiwa's death, viewing them from both a perspective of a literary tragedy and that of everyday suffering of the Ogoni people. Quayson demonstrates a clear understanding of Nigeria and its politics by reaching out to all sources of information and examining all implications of issues that led to Saro-Wiwa's tragic end. He brings some newness into the Ogoni story. As you read his paper you almost believe that you are hearing the story for the first time. Addressing those who still strongly think "Saro-Wiwa is partly responsible for creating the environment in which the four Ogoni chiefs were vilified," especially Chris McGreal who in his article, 'A Tainted Hero', published in *The Guardian Weekend* (March 23, 1996: 25–8), tenaciously holds that Saro-Wiwa was morally guilty, Quayson explains how such an argument detaches moral responsibility from "the governing political ethos and onto the individual." Says Quayson, "What McGreal fails to take account of, in deploying a largely liberal humanist understanding of 'personal moral responsibility', is the extent to which the environment in which the Ogoni leadership operated was itself heavily overdetermined by the ethos of Nigerian politics itself." Quayson's well-researched explanations on this ethos are as valid as they are compelling.

All of the poems in Section Two pay tribute to Saro-Wiwa and the Ogoni people, and they all condemn the inhumanity of the multinational oil companies and the Nigerian military regime.

Niyi Osundare's paper, in Section Three, adds more color to Boyd's and Quayson's descriptions of the Nigerian catastrophe. By painting a vivid picture of the pitiable state of Nigeria, Osundare shows how some "African brothers" he met in Britain agonized about the calamity befalling Nigeria, which they saw as a shame for Africa. Here, Osundare locks horns with the military junta, who claim that the world's demand for justice was an interference in Nigeria's internal affairs. Osundare asks, "which Nigeria?" And he asserts, "Except by the perverse logic of some antediluvian hell-hole where state cannibalism is a hallowed practice, there is no way the barbarious hanging of Ken Saro-Wiwa and others can be passed off as the internal affair of any country."

Wumi Raji's paper, 'Oil Resources: Hegemonic Politics and the Struggle for a Re-invention of Post-Colonial Nigeria', examines how oil, 'the national cake', turns out to be a curse for the environment and for the people of the oil producing areas of Nigeria. Citing freely from the Nigerian National Award winner, Claude Ake's studies, from Ken Saro-Wiwa's interviews, and from many other highly reliable sources, Raji gives dates and figures to show how the oil resources became a political hegemony in Nigeria. Raji is not one to shy away from truth and critical convictions as he insists that the Nigerian government is clearly fraudulent in its dealings with the oil producing areas of the nation. Citing a former Nigerian Oil Minister, Raji reacts:

> Lest we be misunderstood, let it be stated categorically that the Nigerian problem has a nationality dimension. Jubril Aminu, as oil minister in 1990 contends that the Niger Delta remains underdeveloped because of the "very harsh" terrain. "Transportation is difficult", he says, "because the creeks are difficult." This is after 32 years of oil exploration. Well, we may need to ask Aminu whether the areas, in any way, are more difficult than Lagos. The former capital city of Nigeria, in spite of its many creeks, its marshes and swamps and even the lagoon and the Atlantic Ocean can, guardedly, be described as having a fine network of roads.

Yet, the article finds fault with Saro-Wiwa for his perception of the Hausa/Fulani as the main ethnic group exploiting the nation's resources. I shall allow readers to explore on their own Raji's authoritative submissions. I must say, however, that it is not uncommon for a few Nigerian writers to lump blame on the Hausa/Fulani, or by implication on Islam or the Muslims in Nigeria, for the woes of the nation. After all, most of the Nigerian Presidents since independence were Muslims: Tafawa Balewa, Murtala Mohammad, Shehu Shegari, Muhammad Buhari, Ibrahim Babangida, Sani Abacha. Wumi Raji's reaction to Saro-Wiwa's condemnation of Hausa/Fulani is applicable to the similar perspective taken by these writers. In Soyinka's songs, *Unlimited Liability Company*, apart from characters' names, the author shows ethnicity through accent and mannerisms: the Hausa/Fulani character is the obliterator of the second republic. By any standard, the blame Soyinka passes on other ethnic groups is very mild (see also Soyinka, 1996). While I do not condone corruption from any quarters, I refuse to accede to the assertion that the second republic was brought down mainly by the ineptitude of Shehu Shagari and Umaru Dikko. What about those who publicly celebrated their entry into the billionaire club and ordered a special gin to be made from overseas in their names? Neither will I leave unchallenged any implication of Islam (or any religion) in the rottenness of the Nigerian leadership. The point I am making is that all ethnic groups in Nigeria, particularly the major ones, share in the gradual degradation and destruction of our nation.

Rather than showing this reality, however, some Nigerian writers have been behaving according to what a Yoruba adage describes as a case of a mad person who is given a hoe to cultivate a piece of land. Even with his mental disorder, he will till the land towards himself. Those who still claim that art is like a photograph, where a person appears exactly as he or she is taken, have missed the point. Contemporary technology already exposed the error in this assertion. Photographs can be easily doctored during printing so that a person can appear where he or she had never been in his or her life. It is sad that some Nigerian writers are like the mad person bearer of the hoe in the Yoruba adage. Blaming a section of Nigeria or a religion for the crisis of the entire nation is like becoming a postindustrial photographer who doctors the picture to produce people's images where he/she wants them rather than where they actually are sited.

Chinua Achebe's (1983) *The Trouble with Nigeria* is more practical in its analysis of the 'tribe' issue. The Nigerian leadership and the elite, without recourse to language, religion or place of origin, perpetuate the discriminatory tendency for selfish ends. Says Achebe:

> In recent years an editorial in *New Nigerian* could write mockingly about "God-knows-what-merit." Ironically it is our new "intellectual" elite who today debunk merit for immediate sectional advantage, just as some "nationalist" leaders in the 1950s forsook nationalism in favour of the quick returns of tribalism. But whereas

tribalism might win enough votes to install a reactionary jingoist
in a tribal ghetto, the cult of mediocrity will bring the wheels of
modernization grinding to a halt throughout the land.

Whoever is out to fight discrimination or enthnicism and corruption in Nigeria must, therefore, address his/her writings against the
'intellectual and nationalist elites' from all parts of the nation. The
larger majority of Nigerians in different parts of the country move
freely among themselves. In a small town called Bagudo in Kebbi
State of Nigeria or in Nsukka, Enugu State or at any village or hamlet in Nigeria, Hausa, Ibo, Yoruba peoples and the minorities live
together peacefully, and without rancour or what is today an epi-
demic of elitist ethnicism. Unfortunately, by selecting a section of
Nigeria for blame for the nation's failures and using a wide slate to
cover up the share of one's own ethnic group's contribution to this
malady, Nigeria may never approach let alone reach the end of its
problems. Even if the Northerners are expelled from Nigeria as
those military boys who masterminded the 'Orkar Coup' tried to do
once, the poor people who buy from local markets or send their
kids to public schools will continue to suffer in whatever remains of
Nigeria as long as the elite continue to leave leprosy aside to apply
medication on a tinea-capitis.[1] Whoever chases about a shadow
instead of the actual body of the Nigerian predicament is treating
tinea instead of the leprosy that may deform and kill Nigeria. When
I heard Major Orkar in his broadcast talk about cutting away main
parts of the North from Nigeria, and saw some Nigerians jubilating,
I felt very sorry for Nigerians. I realized that the elite again wanted
to sidetrack the Nigerian people so that elite savings abroad could
continue to swell. The large number of ethnic groups in Nigeria has
nothing to do with the Nigerian problem. The real victims of the
Nigerian political system's callousness are, in fact, the poor people
who have not thrown their indigenous language competence in
the bin. Nigerians in villages, hamlets and farms who toil daily
from morning to night to increase the nation's productivity but yet
neither enjoy good water nor electricity. Achebe's wording perhaps
presents these downtrodden people better, when borrowing from
Frantz Fanon, he describes them as the "wretched of the earth":

These are the real victims of our callous system, the wretched of the earth. They are largely silent and invisible. They don't appear on front pages; they do not initiate industrial actions. They drink bad water and suffer from all kinds of preventable diseases. There are no hospitals within reach of them; but even if there were they couldn't afford to attend. There may be a school of sorts which their children go to when there is "free education" and withdraw from when "levies" are demanded. (1983: 24)

It is shameful that more than a decade after Achebe wrote the above words, nothing has changed for the better in Nigeria. In 1983, Achebe puts the equivalent of 150 pounds sterling as 180 Nigerian naira (see p. 41). The Nigerian currency was much stronger than the American dollar. In 1997, however, a dollar fetched 83 Nigerian naira. Achebe devotes almost a chapter in *The Trouble* to lamenting about the disintegrating Nigerian roads. Ironically, almost a decade later, Achebe all but lost his life on the same road network. He is today permanently confined to a wheelchair. Nigerian oil money, instead of saving Nigerian lives through good roads, jobs and well-equipped schools, is enriching the few people at the helm of the affairs of the country.

Andrew Apter's article on 'Death and the King's Henchmen: Ken Saro-Wiwa and the Political Ecology of Citizenship in Nigeria' in Section Three defines the nature of Ken Saro-Wiwa's struggle in Nigeria, and how the combination of Shell, the military regime, the three major language groups (Hausa, Igbo and Yoruba) played different roles to frustrate Saro-Wiwa's efforts. The way Apter explains the internal postcolonial politics in Nigeria, and the power with which be declares his facts, could not have come from a person of less scholarly talent. Using freely a number of Ken Saro-Wiwa's books: *Genocide in Nigeria, A Month and A Day, On a Darkling Plain,* and several other credible sources, Apter shows how Saro-Wiwa uses his literary skills to picture the atrocities on Ogoniland for the entire Nigerian nation and the world to see. The paper is comprehensive, and discusses every issue: Shell and other multinational corporations in Nigeria, Nigerian internal ethnicity politics, the military, oil money, corruption and mismanagement of the Nigerian economy, the Ogoni struggle, Ken Saro-Wiwa, Nigeria's future, and other burning matters are addressed with vivid material support. Apter shows how the Nigerian leadership rapaciously destroyed the vision and broke the feather of an up-coming Nigeria. He opens for whoever cares to see the ringworms of Nigeria's intestines, documenting both the colonial and the postcolonial exploitation of the giant African nation.

The poems in Section Three discuss issues of the military in Nigerian politics and the role of the multinational corporations, especially Shell, in the devastation of the resources of the country. From the use of metaphorical drum in Hart's 'The Lie', the adoption of Hausa pop song, in my 'Daga ni sai kai', to the various kinds of invocations by other poets, all the poems in this Section continue the discussion of the internal and external collaborators to the Nigerian problems.

Tayo Olafioye's 'The Ken Saro-Wiwa Echo', in Section Four, exposes the follies of the Nigerian government in its defence of the murder of Saro-Wiwa and the eight other Ogonis. Citing from his and Tanure Ojaide's poems in this book, Olafioye evokes the indignation that greeted Nigeria's murder of its own citizens from peoples and governments around the globe. Olafioye's rock-rolling words add special strength to his insistence that the world must make Shell oil company and the Nigerian military government dance to their own music of death. Turning especially to Shell he says:

> All they needed to do was to threaten withdrawal and exposition to force the oligarchy to behave in a civilized manner. But the lure of billions of dollars in oil revenue was too strong to resist. After all, the Ogoni people and their welfare were too insignificant to wretch the conscience of oil magnates. The oil company needed only to cushion the pockets of power to gain compliance in eliminating the enemies — the crooked woods that destabilize the hearth of raging specks of fire.

With similar anger, Tayo Oloruntoba-Oju's 'The Writer and the Junta' spits fire over how the military junta reduces the Nigerian writer to prey. While using Ken Saro-Wiwa's one time title of an article, 'The Odd, the Odious and Our Very Odia', where he took up issues with a Nigerian poet, Odia Ofeimun, Oloruntoba-Oju says that "the anti-writer, anti-intellectual stance of the Nigerian military is a mere strain of a grand anti-logic." Asserts Oloruntoba-Oju:

> The greatest oddity, reminiscent of classic dog wagging tail absurdity, is that the soldier should rule over the writer in the first place. If a choice were to be made, freely, the writer is arguably more suitable to the leadership of a nation. When in hubristic agony a General Babangida (immediate past Nigerian military dictator) cries out: "We are in power and with power," the writer, amongst other profound elements of society, responds with a knowing smile —broader still when the man fell from power soon after the utterance—that power and holding of it is all too transient. The writer is in knowledge and with knowledge, the lasting legacy.

In this very interesting piece, the writer argues that it is abnormal for the military to govern. He says it is like asking a civilian "without requisite training or orientation to run a battalion." The Nigerian military, he declares, have compromised their professionalism. The article also takes on the Nigerian politicians and writers who compromise their callings to conspire with military dictatorship. The force in Oloruntoba-Oju's raging words and the power in his pen show that as Secretary General of a branch of the Association of Nigerian Authors, he speaks the anger of other Nigerian writers on the murder of their former national President. This article, though short, rings loud and clear that the Nigerian writers, despite the death of Saro-Wiwa, will not give up what it describes as "the constant obligation ... to write them [the military] off the corridors of governance."

Bernth Lindfors's article presents the man Saro-Wiwa, his writing career and his struggle against the destruction of the Ogoni environment. The short but detailed piece shows how Saro-Wiwa, whom Orage portrays as a demon, lived his life for peace, justice, people's happiness and society's progress:

> In his writing, in his politics, in his impulses, Saro-Wiwa was truly a man of the people. But unlike Chief Nanga, he was also, first and

foremost, a man *for* the people. He writes to move people — to make them laugh, think, protest, act. And in his political work he moved to help people, defending them from injustice by pleading their case in the most conspicuous public arenas. In word and deed he had excelled as a champion of the little man and as an advocate of human rights for all people, regardless of size and stature.

Again, the poems in Section Four continue the lamentations we read in Section Three. These poems clearly show that the struggle for a just and better Nigeria persists despite the Nigerian soldier's gun and the multinational company's might.

Harry Garuba's paper in Section Five examines the issue of minority discourse in what he calls the "postmodern world of multinationals, communications and commodities." Using Ken Saro-Wiwa's *Sozaboy*, he develops a theoretical treatise about the situation of minority discourse in Nigeria and the world. The paper recounts *Sozaboy*'s story of how the central hero, Mene, survives the war, faces the threat of being buried alive, and finally exits into exile. He says that his life summarizes the three stages that "constitute the inexorable logic of minority discourse." According to him, Saro-Wiwa's life thus becomes the metaphor in Mene, the character he created. Because Ken Saro-Wiwa refuses exile, he is "buried alive." Harry Garuba gives us, in this article, a fruitful analysis of *Sozaboy* and theoretical insight into Saro-Wiwa and the Ogoni's struggle.

Eckhard Breitinger's paper is an added piece of food for the hungry mind. It discusses Ken Saro-Wiwa's experiences as a writer and television producer, and accents the uniqueness of his works compared with those of other contemporary African writers. The paper features Saro-Wiwa's confrontation with the impossible publishing world, and how, as a publisher of his own works, he "tried to combine the production quality of the multinationals and the low prices of the local publishing industry." Describing Ken Saro-Wiwa's concept of a modern urban popular culture in Africa, Breitinger explicates Saro-Wiwa's television play, *Basi & Company*, published later by the author as *Basi and Company: A Modern African Folktale* (1987), discussing the narrative structure, characterization, and the parallels between what he calls "the old-time oral popular literature and the modern urban popular culture." Without leaving out any detail of the development of Saro-Wiwa as a writer, the article honors him as a person who attained distinction in many aspects of cultural work and organization.

Abiola Irele's paper, 'Ken Saro-Wiwa', makes a very significant addition to this book; without the dimension it introduces, this collection's literary and historical analysis of postcolonial Nigeria would be incomplete. Irele introduces the question of the Nigerian civil war in which Saro-Wiwa not only played a strong role but on which he also wrote his accounts in his popular novel, *Sozaboy*. In his characteristic flowing style, which Wole Soyinka describes elsewhere as a "lyrical delicacy" (Soyinka, 1988: 136), Irele captures the place of civil war literature in the Nigerian national literary assets. He identifies the thrust of Saro-Wiwa's *Sozaboy* as different from the perspective adopted by the Igbo writers whose works dominate Nigerian civil war literature. Irele continues,

> For one thing, Saro-Wiwa is concerned in this novel primarily with the experience of the common people caught up in the war. His choice of an obscure apprentice driver as the hero of the novel underlines a point that the civil war occasioned an involuntary involvement of the masses of individuals in events of whose drift and meaning they had not the slightest idea.

Irele makes a detailed journey around all aspects of Saro-Wiwa's fiction. He asserts that Saro-Wiwa's writings "represent an advanced stage in the development towards a new realism in African literature," and he describes Saro-Wiwa as a major new figure in Nigerian national literature. In a tone that now sounds ironic after the hanging of Saro-Wiwa in 1995, Irele foretells the greatness that awaits Saro-Wiwa in the literary scene:

> The direction already taken by him [Saro-Wiwa], the resources of the imagination that his work evinces, the skill that he deploys in the crafting of his texts — all these indicate a promise that I have every expectation he will come to fulfil.

Indeed, Ken Saro-Wiwa fulfils Irele's expectations by standing vigorously by the common people of his Sozaboy to his death. His spirit still fights on from the pit where he and eight Ogoni environmentalists were dumped.

The poems in this Section represent the draconian situations in Nigeria. Burmeister's 'My Red Beret' is particularly striking in its use of rotten-English in imitation of Ken Saro-Wiwa's novel, *Sozaboy*.

Frank Schulze-Engler's paper on 'Civil Critiques: Satire and the Politics of Democratic Transition in Ken Saro-Wiwa's Novel', in Section Six, is relevant to the recent debates about the democratization of Nigeria, and indeed Third World nations in general. It states that transition to democracy is an unending exercise in Nigeria. Elections that were judged the most free and fair, held in Nigeria in June 1993, were annulled by the military President, Ibrahim Babangida, on the excuse that some cliques in the military were not willing to accept the popularly assumed winner of the presidential poll, Moshood Abiola, who now languishes in jail. Frank Schulze-Engler therefore looks at the politics of democratic transition as projected in the works of Ken Saro-Wiwa. According to Schulze-Engler, Saro-Wiwa's works critique the authoritarian military rulers in Nigeria and the docility with which the Nigerian people resigned their fates to them. He takes Saro-Wiwa's works, *Sozaboy*, *Basi and Company*, *Prisoners of Jebs*, and *Pita Dumbrok's Prison*, and discusses how Saro-Wiwa satirizes and critiques the Nigerian transition to democracy through them. He says:

> All these works, however, are characterized by a sustained involvement in the politics of civil society: they mock the inflated state that seeks to subjugate the whole of society but founded on its own inefficiency, they scorn the culture of violence that has been nurtured by consecutive military regimes, they castigate the systemic violation of human rights and the erosion of the rule of law, they satirize the ignorance, the self-destructive values and the 'culture of cheating' that permeates all layers of society and they deplore the loss of individual initiative and responsibility that constitute the most important resources for an alternative future.

Adetayo Alabi's contribution, 'Saro-Wiwa and the Politics of Language in African literature', discusses how Saro-Wiwa participated in what has been recognized as the most active political issue to date in African literature: language. This has been a notorious post-colonial issue that clearly puts African writers in two camps: those who favor the continued use of colonial languages in African literature and those who believe that every genuine African writer must break away from colonial language and adopt indigenous African languages for creativity and criticism. Saro-Wiwa's experimentation with 'rotten English' in his most popular fiction, *Sozaboy*, shunning both colonial and indigenous languages, introduces a new chapter into the language debate in African writing. 'Rotten English' is made up of elements from the indigenous language, words from standard English and Nigerian pidgin English. By introducing 'rotten English', Saro-Wiwa is not aligning himself with the pidgin English adaptation of Tunde Fatunde. Thus, Alabi gives a detailed historical account of the problem of language in African literature, and analyses Saro-Wiwa's position on this issue. Alabi believes strongly that Saro-Wiwa was not particularly interested in pushing any anti-colonial language position for African writing, not with his use of 'rotten English' in *Sozaboy*. In fact, he says, Saro-Wiwa regarded the colonial languages of English, French and Portuguese as "extra African languages," and saw nothing wrong with African writers writing in them. According to Alabi, Saro-Wiwa was writing a novel in his mother tongue, Khana, before his death. Alabi tells us that Saro-Wiwa insisted that he was not trying to prove any point or support any position, but rather was merely trying to "provide another reading material for his mother who had only the Bible to read in Khana." Alabi, however, argues that whether or not Saro-Wiwa intended it, his indigenous language novel would have advanced Ngũgĩ wa Thiong'o's position that "all these [African] languages are as dynamic and resourceful as any other languages." Unfortunately, Saro-Wiwa was killed before he could finish this novel. Just as he had succeeded in putting his Ogoniland on the world map, the novel would have popularized his Khana language beyond the boundaries of Nigeria and Africa.

Politics and satire are the recurrent themes in the poems in Section Six. Each poem uses poetic fiction to paint pictures of the political and social atrocities in Nigeria. They show how a few Nigerians continue to toy with the lives of the entire population.

Sections Seven and Eight contain Ken Saro-Wiwa's interviews and a paper, 'Ken Saro-Wiwa: A Bio-Bibliography'. The interviews speak for themselves. I reprint them in this book to allow readers to hear directly from Saro-Wiwa's own voice. The last Section is intended to be resource material for anyone who wants to research the life and works of Saro-Wiwa. I give a short biography of the writer and list his numerous publications. The Section ends with a bibliography of critical writings on his works.

Perhaps what most demonstrates the rich cultural diversity in this book is the poetry. Throughout this book, I have included works of poetry that speak directly to the issue of Ken Saro-Wiwa, and Ogonis, and to the political and cultural agonies of the entire people of Nigeria. These poems engage in issues of justice, fair play and social well-being of the people. Most of the poets embraced the African traditional legacy of poetry of engagement by injecting critical feelings into the muscles and veins of their poems. For example, Tanure Ojaide's poem 'Elegy For Nine Warriors', in Section Two, celebrates the spirits of the killed heroes. The 'Elegy', which he wrote in six parts, lambastes the conspirators responsible for the death of Saro-Wiwa and the others. He tells the "hangman," whom he describes as "an old cockroach in the groins of Aso Rock"[2] that it will soon end, and "the General will meet Master Sergeant." In some parts the poet, like an outraged African oracle, resorts to incantations to warn the night marauders, "day shall break over the long night." Parts 2 to 6 are voracious incantations, with the rage of a wounded lion. Pages such as these make me want to forewarn the reader that the present collection is not just another experiment in mere academic ranting. This book is a potent prayer for the emancipation of the Ogoni and the *talakawa* throughout Nigeria. Those who called for 'epe' and 'ase' to fight the drastic Botha/de Klerk regimes in yesterday's apartheid South Africa now have their calls answered in the new fight against draconian Nigerian dictatorship. The poems and essays in this book are pieces of baked clay that our singing birds shall continually drop on the roofs of the knaves of the Nigerian people.

Another example is Niyi Osundare's poem, also in Section Two. His folksong session is evidently one of the richest in this collection, and it demonstrates Osundare's position as a forerunner in the exploration of folk songs and folk narrative technique in modern

African poetry. 'The Man Who Asked Tall Questions' requires heavy drum beats, flutes and dance. The music and the dance accentuate the feeling of overwhelming devastation. The refrain, "The hyena has murdered Thunder's son / An angry fire consumes the land ...," recreates the tragic reality of the murder of the Nigerian people by the military, especially that of Ken Saro-Wiwa for whom he wrote the poem. In other words, Saro-Wiwa is the murdered Thunder's son. Declares the poet in the first stanza:

> A uniformed plague subdues the streets,
> Crimson boots, a cartridge of curses;
> Viper-belts caress their oily waists
> Dreams die in their hands

This is a vivid representation of the tyrannical military regime in Nigeria. The poem, containing five parts, shows how systematically, but without common sense, the "uniformed plague" destroys everything that means much to the Nigerian people: food, free speech, free press, decent environment, education, justice, community development and dreams of greatness. The second refrain that appears in part two of his poem, "These, still, are seasons of omens," clearly captures the atmosphere of mourning and frustration among Nigerians.

As a master of the poetry of commitment, Osundare does not leave out these warnings to the world. He curses the despotic Generals who think living is their sole right:

> A murdered peace bleeds
> A murdered peace bleeds in our frightened land
> The mountain counts its tears
> Rivers are red with rage
> Martyred dreams dangle in our territory of terror
> A medieval darkness descends from a martial sky
> An urgent lightning holds the candle to this gloom:
> Come Thunder: exact your wrath.

Niyi Osundare says it in this poem as African ancestors would say it. He sings it exactly as Sango, the Yoruba god of thunder, would sing it. His poem speaks to everyone whose heart bleeds for Nigeria, and whose eyes water when they see the atrocities of the Nigerian military regime recorded in cinematic words.

In this book, we have some of the finest African poets coming together with contemporary Western writers. The book provides an arena for native English speakers to celebrate the great poetic feats of legendary English writers, and for non-English speakers to demonstrate their creative strategies in a wedding of English and their various native cultures. This book brings to us booming examples of multilingual and multicultural poetry in session. Like a pendulum of an African festival, recitations, drums, flutes, mime, dance and songs, swing from one tradition to another.

Finally, I will comment further on the contention that the Hausa/Fulani [mainly Muslims] are the main internal exploiters of Nigeria's oil wealth, which I had described as a ruse, and the issue of the Nigerian oil wealth as a source of death and destruction rather than one of development and decent living for the people. No single ethnic group is solely responsible for the present state of Nigeria. The Hausa have a proverb, *a shekaran saran ruwa sai tambatse*, meaning 'if one spends a year or years beating water, all he or she will have is water spray'. Making an ethnic group or religion a scapegoat for the ills of Nigeria must end if we are to enable our nation to move forward. Experience has shown that in the complex Nigerian situation we all are losers whenever we exploit ethnic and religious sentiments. Elites from all parts of Nigeria, most especially corrupt military and civilian leaders, are the culprits who have created our mess. These are Muslims and Christians, and adherents of traditional African religions. The point is that, rather than the religions they profess to follow or the languages they claim to speak, the elites themselves are to blame. As a hypothetical example, an erstwhile Nigerian military dictator, a Muslim or Christian, from Jos in the North, Ibadan in the West, or Enugu in the South, spends a total of twenty five years in service, seizes power through a coup to become head of state, spending eight years as President. Towards the end of the eight years, he builds for himself a 50 bedroom duplex of several million dollars in his purported city of origin, where thousands of people are homeless, and a thousand more are unable to feed themselves once a day. How absurd is it to say that the same people, though they belong to the same language group as the General, asked him to be corrupt? Of what benefit is the dictator's corruption to them? Nigeria today has about four hundred languages. In any part of the country, Nigerians buy from the same markets and confront the same biting inflation whether they speak Hausa, Nupe, Yoruba, Edo, Igbo or Okrika. Every corrupt leader in Nigeria serves him or herself, not an ethnic group, not even an extended family of blood relatives. Similarly no religion is to blame for any person's greediness, injustice and blank disregard for the human dignity and welfare, as we have today in Nigeria.

Rather than cowing the victims to look on helplessly while they are being cheated, these religions encourage people to demand justice and to be firm with truth and fairness[3]. An Ilorin oral singer, Alabi Labeka, often sings in his *waka*, an Ilorin oral form that has a strong Islamic root, that every person shall account for his or her actions right here on earth. In one of his public performances, he chants:[4]

Ara to ba wu kaluku koda
Ara to ba wu kaluku koda
B'eda ba n sere
Abo n bo leyin oo
Ara to ba wu kaluku koda
Eni tin sayida, abo n bo leyin oo
Ara to ba wu kaluku koda
"Fa man ya'a mal mithqala dharratin khairan yarahu
Wa man ya mal mithqala dharratin sharran yarahu."[5]
(Public Performance, Ile-Imam, Agbaji, 5 December, 1989)

Whatever manifesto wished by man, let him perpetuate
Whatever manifesto wished by man, let him perpetuate
Whoever perpetuates goodness
God's rewards would soon come up to him
Whatever manifesto wished by man, let him perpetuate
Whoever perpetuates wickedness
Nemesis shall soon catch up with him
Whatever manifesto wished by man, let him perpetuate
"Whoever does good, however small, shall see goodness coming
    after him
Whoever does evil, however small, shall see evil coming after him."

Labeka directs his songs at his Ilorin audience and expects to influence their behavior towards their fellow human beings. Oral performers from all parts of Nigeria embark on the same crusades singing vigorously from the womb of cultural ethics asking Nigerians to be just and good to their fellow human beings. Neither military nor civilian populations of the country can claim ignorance of the social, political, economic and spiritual morality advanced by the traditional oral performers. Instead of heeding these lessons, most Nigerian military and civilian leaders[6] make a mockery of the oral forms and turn many traditional poets into members of welcoming parties at the nation's airports whenever they or foreign heads of state are coming into the country.

Oil becomes a curse for Nigeria because it is an international commodity. Postcolonial Nigeria left one form of bondage to enter into another one, that of the multinational companies. In a way, cheap oil replaces the slaves' cheap labour, the coal, the cocoa, and the peanuts that the British colonialists exploited from Nigeria. The multinational companies replaced colonial power in Nigeria, and indeed in Third World nations as a whole. The imperialist governments, erstwhile slave mongers, now operate from the background by being the father figures for the multinational companies. The theory propounded from many quarters that Shell oil company (or any other oil company for that matter) would refuse to account for its devastation of the Nigerian environment is becoming real. Nothing seems to move Shell after Ken Saro-Wiwa and eight other Ogoni were killed, after many people around the world have demanded justice. Rather than behaving responsibly, the giant Shell went on electronic and print media with its propaganda. Shortly after Saro-Wiwa was hanged, Shell's advertisement titled, 'Clear Thinking in Troubled Times', published in Canada's *The Globe and Mail*[7] of Tuesday, November 21, 1995, claims as follows: "The situation in Nigeria has no easy solutions. Slogans, protests and boycotts don't offer answers. There are difficult issues to consider" (p. A3). Among the 'difficult issues', Shell claims that the world's threats and protests were what hardened the Nigerian military and provoked them to kill Ken Saro-Wiwa and others. It agrees, "there are certainly environmental problems in the area" but that over population, soil erosion and over farming are equally responsible. The same Shell that had announced that it ceased operations in

Ogoniland in 1993, declared that in 1995, "Shell and its partners are spending US $100 million" on environmental development pro-jects. As people continued to protest, Shell embarked on letter writing, and virtually everyone who signed a petition received a letter from Shell's international office in London or from the local headquarters.[8] Shell showed that it started exploring for oil in Nigeria in 1937 and went into actual production in 1958. It said that its production in Nigeria currently came from 94 oilfields spread over the Niger Delta. It claimed it employed half of its Nigerian staff from the Niger Delta and that it built hospitals, schools, roads and water systems. Unfortunately for Shell however, the hard facts that people see in the *Delta Force* documentary made by the Ogoni disproved such claims. Shell made its own documentary where it featured several people to help tell its story to the world. One of the speakers defended Shell so vigorously that she claimed that the Ogoni might not be alive today if not for the generosity of Shell.

Instead of Shell accepting its guilt and taking full responsibility for repairing the damage it had done, the company resorted to insulting the Ogoni and all the concerned peoples of the world who were genuinely calling for justice. History was indeed repeating itself. Slavery was vehemently defended for centuries by those who benefitted from it, exactly as Shell Oil defends its atrocities in Nigeria. International trade is not an aberration. There is nothing wrong with Shell or any international company, from India, Nigeria, Finland, Canada or anywhere, doing business in any part of the world. But when such business is being done as a game of re-enslavement, conscientious peoples of the world, as their brothers' and sisters' keepers must ask questions and insist on answers. That is precisely what this collection of writers in *Ogoni's Agonies* has achieved.

Abdul-Rasheed Na'Allah
University of Alberta
November 1997

NOTES

1   Tinea is a fungal infection and is not likely to kill its victim. In most cases it disappears on its own. However leprosy causes permanent

deformation of its victims, and may lead to death.

2 Aso Rock is the name of the office of the Nigerian military head of state in the new capital city Abuja.

3 Ken Saro-Wiwa ended his closing statement prepared for the Special Tribunal that tried him with the following quotes from the Qur'an (Qur'an 42:41): "But indeed if any do help / And defend themselves / After a wrong (done) / To them, against such / There is no cause / Of blame. / The blame is only / Against those who oppress / Men with wrong-doing / And insolently transgress / Beyond bounds through the land, / Defying right and justice: / for such will be / A Penalty grievous." (Yusuf Ali, *The Holy Qur'an: Translation and Commentary*.)

4 I discussed this and several oral songs of Alhaji Alabi Labeka in 'Waka: The Dialectical Essence of an Ilorin Islamic Oral Genre' given at the 3rd National Conference on Literature in Northern Nigeria, Bayero University, Kano, Nigeria, December, 1990. Translations from Yoruba into English are mine. Abdullahi Dan Fodio made it very unambiguous in his writings and public speeches that leadership in Islam was a trust. He states the consequences of breaking such trusts as many Nigerian leaders do today. Read Shehu Umar Abdullahi, *On the Search for a Viable Political Culture*, Kaduna: New Nigerian Publishing Company, 1984. The late Malam Aminu Kano as a politician and public officer was an excellent example of the Nigerian leaders that demonstrated these Islamic features.

5 He cites from the Qur'an, chapter 99, verses 7 and 8, in the last two lines of his songs so as to give stronger credence to his message with his listeners who are predominantly Muslims.

6 Though military dictatorship is generally distasteful to the Nigerian people, it would not be correct to say that all Nigerian military personnel are corrupt. The largest population of the Nigerian military is the professional low-ranking officers who do not participate in governance. There are (and were) also many selfless top-military officers like Murtala, Buhari and Abdul-Baki Idiagbon who proved to be more prudent with the public treasury when they became leaders. Obasanjo could have been named among them, but he hosted FESTAC '77, and its impact on Nigeria is discussed in this book by Andrew Apter; see also Apter, 1996: 441–66.

7 It was also published in many newspapers in Southern Africa, Eu-

rope and America.

8 One of these letters was written from the Shell International Petroleum Company Limited office, Shell Centre, 2 York Road, London, England, SE1 7NA, in December, 1995. Another letter, written on 26 March, 1996 claims that "Shell, Nelson Mandela and others had adopted an approach of quiet diplomacy — an approach which, we had every hope might succeed — and joined others in asking for clemency," thus fraudulently putting Shell on the same footing with the world revered South African President. The same tactic was used by Shell in its 'Clear Thinking in Troubled Times' advertisements when it compared its statements to those allegedly made by Wura Abiola, daughter of the imprisoned unofficial winner of the 1993 June 12 Nigerian presidential election.

REFERENCES:

Achebe, Chinua. *The Trouble with Nigeria.* London: Heinemann, 1983.

Aiyejina, Funso. "Ken Saro-Wiwa: A Pebble for Our Sling-Shot." *Trinidad Guardian.* December 19, 1995: 45–8.

ALA Bulletin: A Publication of the African Literature Association. 21. 2, 1995: 33–4.

Ali, A. Yusuf. *The Holy Qur'an: Translation and Commentary.* Durban: Islamic Propagation Centre International, 1946.

Mills, Bronwyn. "An E-Mail to Abdul-Rasheed Na'Allah." 27 November, 1995.

Na'Allah, Abdul-Rasheed. "Waka: The Dialectical Essence of an Ilorin Islamic Oral Genre." Paper Given at the 3rd National Conference on Literature in Northern Nigeria, Bayero University, Kano, Nigeria, December, 1990.

Sachs, Aaron. "Dying For Oil." *Worldwatch.* 9. 3, 1996: 10–21.

Saro-Wiwa, Ken. "Closing Statement to the Nigerian Military Appointed Special Tribunal." Not Allowed to Deliver. Distributed throughout the World after the Tribunal Judgement, 2 November, 1995.

Shell International Petroleum Company Limited, London, England. "Clear Thinking in Troubled Times." *The Globe and the Mail.* November 21, 1995: A3–4.

———. "A Letter — Reference PXX (MTW)." 26 March 1996.

———. "An Information Pamphlet." December, 1995.

Soyinka, Wole. *The Open Sore of a Continent: A Personal Narrative of the Nigerian Crisis.* New York: Oxford University Press, 1996.

II

Tribute And Condemnation

And Justice for All?
The Two Faces of Nigeria
Adotei Akwei

In its 37 years of independence, Nigeria has acted out a host of tragedies, triumphs and dilemmas facing Africa. It has suffered a civil war, a seemingly endless procession of military dictatorships and failed enormous economic promise. At the same time Nigeria was one of the leaders of the international effort to rid the world of the racist regimes in Rhodesia (now Zimbabwe) and South Africa. When the nation of Liberia imploded, destabilizing much of West Africa and leaving hundreds of thousands of Liberians at risk, Nigeria mobilized, funded and almost single-handedly manned a peacekeeping force which, while responsible for a host of abuses itself, is credited with saving the lives of thousands. Internally, in spite of hostile governments, Nigeria developed one of the continent's largest and most sophisticated independent press and human rights communities. At the end of 1995 this Jekyll and Hyde dilemma remains the challenge for Nigeria and, increasingly, the international community.

On September 1, 1995 Amnesty International USA (AIUSA) launched a six month campaign against Kenya and Nigeria called 'Freedom in the Balance'. The campaign had several goals, among them; highlighting abuses and restrictions of fundamental civil and political rights, official involvement in investigating ethnic conflict and the sustained undermining of the rule of law. Amnesty International and other human rights groups have become alarmed at trends developing in both countries and the growing potential for violent upheaval.

AIUSA also chose Nigeria because of its vibrant independent press, non-governmental organizations, active professional associations and trade unions, who are struggling bravely to consolidate a conducive political environment for civil society, including the rule of law and respect for human rights. This was particularly important because AIUSA wanted people in the United States to be aware that there were capable Africans leading the fight for fundamental rights, contrary to the images conveyed in the media, and that these individuals are under attack and are increasingly at risk. Finally, the campaign was aimed at convincing policy makers in Washington that supporting these men and women in their efforts now will prevent costly crises later.

The international community had a glimpse of this assault on Nigerian civil society on Friday, November 10, 1995, when the military regime of General Sani Abacha murdered nine environmental and human rights activists of the Movement for the Survival of the Ogoni People (MOSOP). Many may use the term 'execute' but that does not accurately convey the injustice that was done when Paul Levura, Felix Nwate, John Kpuniem, Daniel Gbakoo, Saturday Dorbee, Dr. Barinem Kiobel, Nordu Eawo, Baribor Bera and Ken Saro-Wiwa, all members of MOSOP were hanged. With the killings of the 'Ogoni Nine', Gen. Abacha displayed the full scope of human rights violations being committed by his regime. These include the corruption and crippling of Nigeria's judicial system in the form of the travesty of due process enacted during the Ogoni trial, the assault on civil society and the use of violence, through the security forces or through proxies — in this case ethnic rivals to the Ogoni people.

The challenge before the people of Nigeria is to eliminate the environment that allows a government like that of General Sani Abacha to thrive. The challenge before the international community is to support those efforts in whatever way possible and remain vigilant of the fact. While international attention has understandably focused on the Ogoni tragedy, it is imperative that it be seen for what it is: namely, part of a larger crisis. In the end justice for the Ogoni will demand justice for Nigeria, all of Nigeria.

POLITICAL BACKGROUND

The ongoing human rights crisis in Nigeria underscores the need to focus on enabling environments for accountable governments rather than the specific form of government. Nigeria's ongoing political crisis came to a head in 1993 with the aborting of an eight year, costly, transition program back to democratic rule by the Nigerian army, however the conditions which precipitated the crisis go much further back, beyond the brief scope of this essay. Presidential elections which were to complete the process were held on June 12, 1993. A clear winner had emerged in unofficial results, Chief M.K.O. Abiola. Before these results could be made official, then Head of State Gen. I.B. Babangida canceled the elections, citing fraud and other irregularities. A month later in the face of heavy domestic and international pressure Babangida stepped down, handing power over to an interim government headed by his appointee, Chief Ernest Shonekan.

With the worsening lack of credibility and authority of the Shonekan Administration plunging the country deeper into crisis, Minister of Defense and former Babangida right-hand man Gen. Sani Abacha seized power in November 1993. Since then, despite promises to return Nigeria to civilian rule, convening a controversial national conference to address constitutional reform and other issues involved in a democratic transition, the Abacha regime has enacted a campaign of repression and violence with startling vehemence, eliminating the actors and destroying the environment necessary to even begin creating accountable government. Gen. Abacha's October 1, 1995 announcement of a three year transition did nothing to appease internal and external demands for political reform or convince anyone that the transition would even happen.

THE ASSAULT ON THE RULE OF LAW AND ADMINISTRATION OF JUSTICE

The Abacha regime has retained or has creatively augmented repressive legislation from previous administrations which should be repealed. These include:

The Government (Supremacy and Enforcement of Powers) Decree, No. 12, 1994[1] which removes the jurisdiction of the courts to investigate any action undertaken by members of the federal government.

The State Security (Detention of Persons) Decree, No. 2, 1984 and *Decree No. 11, 1994*[2] which allow for the indefinite detention, renewable every six weeks, of persons considered to be a threat to the security of the state, or if it is believed that they have contributed to the economic adversity of the state. As amended by *Decree No. 11*, the period of detention is now three months and the Chief of General Staff, in addition to the Inspector General of Police, can now detain.

The Public Officers (Protection Against False Accusation) Decree, No. 4, 1984[3] which allows government officials to arrest or detain persons for what they believe to be "false accusations," leaving the burden of proof on the detainees.

The Treasonable Offenses Decree, 1993[4] defines treasonable acts as anything capable of disrupting the general fabric of the country, or any part of it. While this has been suspended it has not been repealed.

The damage done to the rule of law in Nigeria by the government is not limited to the written word. The judiciaries and bar associations have also been direct targets for official repression. The Abacha regime enacted *Decree No. 12*, of 1994, which officially removed the authority of the courts to investigate, let alone challenge, the actions of members of the regime. Even in the cases where the Nigerian court has sought to challenge *Decree No. 12*, or rule on a particular case, military officials continue to simply ignore court judgements. Most sinister has been the creation of a separate system of law accountable to no one and apparently committed to violating all known standards of due process.

Nigeria's use of military tribunals had a long history of due process violations with tragic consequences even before the trail of the 'Ogoni Nine'. Decrees setting up tribunals in the 1970s (the Robbery and Firearms [Special Provision] which resulted in over 500 executions based on its rulings) and the Civil Disturbances (Special Tribunal), set up by *Decree No. 2, 1987*, have consistently failed to meet international standards of due process. In 1993 Major General Zamani Lekwot and at least 16 others were sentenced to death for culpable homicide on the basis of inadequate evidence and glaring violations of due process. The tribunal was created following the ethnic fighting that rocked Kaduna State in Northern Nigeria in 1992.

More recently over 40 people, including ordinary individuals, leading writers, heads of human rights organizations and senior military officers (the only Nigerian Head of State to hand over power to civilian government included) were arrested for involvement in an alleged coup plot and tried before a Special Military Tribunal. The proceedings were held in secret and persons who tried to report about shortcomings of due process were themselves detained and charged before the tribunal with no word of their fate up to this day. On October 1, 1995 after months of rumor, speculation and intense lobbying by domestic and international bodies, the government announced commutations of sentences which had never been publicly announced, again giving scant detail.

ETHNIC VIOLENCE AND THE ROLE OF GOVERNMENT

The Nigerian government has also been implicated in instigating ethnically based violence, which has been concentrated around the turbulent Rivers State oil producing area, home to many of Nigeria's minority groups including the Ogoni. Fighting between the Ogoni and the Ndoki, the Okrika and the Andoni occurred during 1993 and early 1994[5] and reports by human rights groups, both in and outside of Nigeria, soon began to implicate an outside role based on the intensity of the fighting and the sophistication of arms involved in the fighting. In early 1994 the Nigerian security forces became directly involved in some cases following raids by other ethnic groups and razing villages. Their presence and activities intensified following the deaths of the four Ogoni chiefs in May 1994, when the Rivers State Internal Security Task Force was reinforced and over the next several months raided scores of villages. Task Force troops entered towns, shooting indiscriminately, beating villagers, raping women and arresting over 600 men in the process.

Ogoniland remains a volatile region with a massive deployment of soldiers reportedly deployed in the region following the executions of the MOSOP activists. While some may be reluctant to classify the situation as a crisis, they need only remember that the disputed issues between the Ogonis and the other groups had never flared into such levels of violence prior to 1990, the same period when demands for environmental compensation and review of the allocation of oil revenues began to penetrate into the international community and fall on sympathetic ears in other parts of Nigeria.

Concern remains high for the 19 Ogoni activists currently awaiting trial before the same tribunal, on the same charges, based on the testimony of the same key government witnesses and with the same legal shortcomings of the 'Ogoni Nine' trial. Any sign of internal unrest is sure to be met with massive 'pacification' operations from the security forces.

Nigeria can boast of a dynamic civil society in comparison to much of the rest of Africa. The country has several independent newspapers, human rights groups and professional associations. However such analysis belies the conditions and vulnerability of these social movements and most importantly the fact that these movements survive in spite of the government not because of it.

Upon seizing power in Nigeria, Gen. Abacha immediately banned all associations and organizations. In response to labor unrest in August of 1994, demanding that his regime step down, the government promulgated *Decrees 9* and *10* of 1994 which specifically dissolved the national leadership of the Nigerian Labor Congress, the Petroleum and Natural Gas Senior Staff Association of Nigeria and the National Union of Petroleum and Natural Gas Workers. Faced with unflinching criticism from the press on September 5, 1994, *Decrees 5, 6, 7* and *8* were passed banning the *Constitution* newspaper and the Concord, Punch and Guardian Media Groups, all of which individually include several different publications. While the media decrees have been repealed, the Nigerian security forces continue to harass and attack journalists, seize publications and raid media houses.

Human rights groups in Nigeria have often had their publications seized as they were being delivered to the post office. Currently the executives of Human Rights Africa, Tunji Abayomi, the Committee in Defense of Human Rights, Dr. Beko Ransom-Kuti, the Civil Liberties Organization, and Abdul Oroh remain in jail with no official details of their sentences. Their crime: reporting about the trial of the alleged coup plotters. Staff of these groups have also been arrested and assaulted, seminars broken up and on November 10, 1995 General Abacha added murder at the hands of the government to the risks human rights activists in Nigeria face.

CONCLUSIONS

Africa is often portrayed as the continent in crisis with little regard for differentiation among its fifty plus countries. With few exceptions, media coverage has focused on the Liberias, Sudans, Somalias and of course the Congos, Rwandas and Burundis. Such coverage, while factually correct and necessary, has contributed to an attitude of hopelessness about Africa's potential, about its achievements, and the capacity of its people. Amnesty International does not agree with such analysis. When AIUSA decided to campaign against Nigeria, the country was selected because it possesses a dynamic civil society with leadership capacity, because these potential leaders are being steadily attacked and/or eliminated by their government, and finally because Nigeria is precariously poised either to fulfill its potential as an open, rights-respecting society or to deteriorate even further, politically and economically. All would agree that Africa does not need any more states in crisis, especially one as influential as Nigeria. It is essential that the international community shine the spotlight on the Abacha regime and act decisively to help end its human rights abuses.

While the world may be inspired to act because of Ken Saro-Wiwa, his case represents only one of the most prominent points of systematic governmental repression which is robbing the citizens of Nigeria of their rights now, and the next generation of desperately needed leadership in the future. There are hundreds of others, without international name recognition, who are being crushed physically or psychologically by a regime whose only aim appears to be perpetuating itself in power. It is essential that the spotlight now focused on the Abacha government not overlook the scores of others still in jail, the activists and journalists working underground with bounties on their heads.

International pressure has and can continue to play an important role in supporting internal efforts for reform in Nigeria. While it may have failed to save the lives of the 'Ogoni Nine', it did spare the lives of the alleged coup plotters. Similar efforts must be continued and enhanced or we will find ourselves watching a nation with immense potential sink closer and closer toward violent upheaval and chaos, where all are to blame and all ultimately will share the cost of picking up the pieces — rather than preventing the explosion.

NOTES

1   Federal Government Printer, Lagos, Nigeria, 1994.
2   Ibid.
3   Ibid. 1984.
4   Ibid. 1993.
5   See the references after this paper.

REFERENCES

Amnesty International. "Nigeria Military Government Clampdown on Opposition." November 11, 1994, AI Index AFR 44/13/94.

———. "Nigeria: The Ogoni Trials and Detentions." September 15, 1995, AI Index AFR 44/20/95.

———. "Nigeria: A Travesty of Justice, Secret Treason Trials and Other Concerns." October 26, 1995, AI Index AFR 44/23/95.

———. "1996 UN Commission on Human Rights — A Call For Action." January 1996, AI Index IOR 41/02/96.

The Ogoni Question
and the Role of the International
Community in Nigeria[1]
Desmond Lera Orage

On May 21, 1994, Ken Saro-Wiwa's militant supporters, on his instruction and in broad daylight, stormed the palace in Ogoni where Ogoni chiefs were holding a well publicized meeting and gruesomely murdered four prominent chiefs in the most barbaric way imaginable. Several others were also maimed in the process. The murdered chiefs, my late father inclusive, were attending a meeting of the Gokana Council of Chiefs on the invitation of the King of Gokana, a dominant ethnic group within the Ogoni, to plan a reception for two other Ogoni sons who were appointed to high government positions.

Approximately two hours after this meeting began at 10:00 a.m. on Saturday, May 21, 1994, Ken Saro-Wiwa's militant and blood thirsty supporters descended on the King's palace and picked out all those that Saro-Wiwa had always referred to as 'vultures' and who were on their killing list and began torturing them. The ensuing activity that followed after Saro-Wiwa was stopped about 100 yards from the venue of the meeting and escorted from Gokana was the most barbaric action ever witnessed anywhere in our country. My father and three others were beaten with sticks, knives, bottles, stones, machetes and all sorts of crude instruments. The first to die from these punishing attacks that lasted from 12:00 noon to 5:00 p.m. was Albert Badey, a former Secretary to the Rivers State Government who was asthmatic. The next to be killed was my late father, Chief Samuel Orage who, according to eye witness reports, had pleaded with his killers to cut his hands or legs but save his life. When it became obvious to him that they were determined to kill him, he said, "Please deliver my remains to my family if you must kill me." Very unfortunately for my father, his killers never granted him his last wish and I will elaborate on this later.

Upon witnessing these horrible killings, the few supporters of the other targeted vulture, Chief Edward Kobani were able to push him into a nearby room in the palace for temporary safety while my late father's few supporters attempted to whisk his elder brother, Chief Theophilus Orage away from the palace grounds. This daring attempt failed when they were overwhelmed enroute to safety by hundreds of knife wielding militant Ken Saro-Wiwa supporters. What happened thereafter is the most shameful of this horrible tragedy. He was killed and cannibalized. His remains were eaten by these MOSOP barbarians for ritual purposes. At first, I found it very difficult to believe because cannibalism is a rarity in any Nigerian ethnic group. However, this account of events is so true that Saro-Wiwa's MOSOP and most patriotic Nigerians wish it never happened and that we do not discuss it. While we share this concern, we believe that it is a historical part of what happened on that dark Saturday in Ogoniland. They chopped off my uncle's head and took it back to the palace while two of these cannibals made their way to his home in the village which was about two miles away from the King's palace. Upon getting there on a motorcycle covered with blood, they showed my uncle's wife and children their obviously bloodied clothes and some human flesh and said, "You little vultures, do you see this blood on us and this flesh in our hands, they belong to your husband and father. If you want the rest of him, you must hurry to the King's palace now." Upon hearing this, my aunt yelled and cried uncontrollably while her son and daughter got on a motorcycle and rode frantically towards the King's palace.

While this nightmare was unfolding in my uncle's house, Ken Saro-Wiwa's militia meanwhile had succeeded in flushing Chief Edward Kobani out of the room in which he was hiding along with his younger brother, Alhaji Kobani and began torturing him. These blood thirsty killers punished Chief Kobani severely and in his final words, he told his brother that if he could escape, he should go to his house and tell his wife, Rose, what had happened in the palace. No sooner than he said this, according to his brother, the killers smashed his head with a six prong rake that sank into his brain and then drove a spear into his private parts. Alhaji Kobani on the other hand was struck with a bottle. He played dead and later crawled outside into a shrine where he met seventy-two-year-old Chief Francis Kpai also hiding for his life. The senior Kobani on the other hand died instantly from the rake and spear.

As though the dead were not dead enough, these MOSOP killers immediately brought in some of their illegally installed Chiefs, including Dr. Kiobel, one of those executed on November 10, 1995 with Ken Saro-Wiwa, who are now referred to as human rights activists and martyrs, to pray for the dead after which they sang their victory songs. The last instruction was then given to the MOSOP militants to chop off their necks and dispose of the evidence by cremation. Are not these activities barbaric? Having gotten the last instructions, these barbarians proceeded to cut off the necks of my father, Chief Samuel N. Orage, Chief Edward Kobani and Mr. Albert T. Badey and that of my father's elder brother Chief Theophilus B. Orage whose skeletal remains were available after cannibalizing him. They picked up their bodies and put them in a Volkswagen Beetle and pushed the car deep into a nearby forest and burnt it with their bodies. The charred bones that remained were buried in scattered shallow graves that were later recovered by security operatives with the aid of one of the captured killers.

To go back to my uncle's son and daughter (my cousins) who jumped on a motorcycle after being shown their father's flesh and blood, they confirmed that upon approaching the King's palace, they saw hundreds upon hundreds of MOSOP supporters heading towards a huge blazing flame in the nearby bush. They followed the crowd to the location and saw the Volkswagen Beetle burning. Little did they know that my late father and his friends were in it. Unfortunately for them, some of the militant MOSOP supporters recognized them and chased them away. Others caught up with them and assaulted them, stripping my uncle's daughter naked. Some good samaritans immediately came to their rescue and whisked them to safety and provided the lady with a dress. Without knowing that my late father was also in the burning car that they had witnessed, they got into a car which brought them to Port Harcourt, the capital city of our state which is about 40 miles away from the scene of the murders, with the sole intention of telling my dad what happened in the village. Upon getting to our home, my family told them that indeed my father was at the meeting.

So many people have asked if we were sure that Ken Saro-Wiwa was involved in this crime and our answer is absolutely yes. The issue of our fathers' death did not happen spontaneously. It was planned, financed, rumored and executed with unbelievable precision by Ken Saro-Wiwa and his militia. Barely six months before their death, November 13, 1993, in the same palace, Saro-Wiwa sent his henchmen led by one Mr. Celestine Meabe and Mr. Saturday Nwate who took a bottle of whisky to the Chairman of Gokana Council of Chiefs, Chief O.B. Nalelo, and gave notice that because Ken Saro-Wiwa had told the youths that some seven (7) elders had obtained massive bribes running into billions of naira (Nigerian currency) from Shell and the Nigerian government to kill the Ogoni revolution, and because the elders had signed a so-called peace resolution without Ken Saro-Wiwa's authority, and more so because the elders had authorized a publication which is critical of Ken Saro-Wiwa, the vigilante of the National Youth Council of Ogoni People (NYCOP) which is the militant arm of MOSOP had decreed death and destruction of the following:

1. Mr. A.T. Badey
2. Chief Edward N. Kobani
3. Chief Ignatius Kogbara
4. Ms. Priscilia Vikue
5. Chief Samuel N. Orage
6. Dr. Charles Kpakol
7. Dr. Bennett Birabi

This death threat was heard by a stunned full council of Gokana chiefs and elders including the seven individuals mentioned here who protested the threat very vigorously.

In addition to the above, it will interest you to know that the murders of May 21, 1994, were planned very meticulously by Ken Saro-Wiwa and MOSOP. It has also been confirmed that these militant MOSOP supporters spent the weekend of May 13, 1994, consulting oracles and performing rituals in preparation for the May 21, 1994, murderous assault on our fathers. In fact the rumor became so strong that on May 20, 1994, one day before their much publicized meeting of May 21, 1994, the first President of MOSOP Dr. Garrick Leton led a delegation that included Dr. Bennett Birabi, Chief E.N. Kobani and Mr. A.T. Badey to visit the State Governor. During this visit they complained to the Governor that their lives were in imminent danger from Ken Saro-Wiwa's MOSOP and the Governor promised to assist by deploying some security in Ogoniland. Before these security agents were mobilized and deployed, the most gruesome multiple murders in Ogoni history had already taken place.

It is important to point out that our country is comprised of more than 250 ethnic groups. It is therefore common knowledge that from time to time, Nigeria experiences communal clashes. It was at the height of this rash of violent communal clashes which left hundreds of innocent citizens dead that a former Nigerian Head of State decreed the *1987 Civil Disturbances Tribunal Act*. This decree made it very clear that those who incite others to commit criminal offenses are as guilty as those who carried out the crime. This *Civil Disturbances Decree* was among many others reviewed by the original MOSOP leadership before the launching of the organization (MOSOP) in 1990. Ken Saro-Wiwa like other Ogoni leaders was fully aware of these laws but Ken Saro-Wiwa had always believed he was above the law. The United Nations, he told his supporters, will always bail him out.

A BRIEF HISTORY OF THE OGONI STRUGGLE
During the 1980s, the leadership of Ogoni through its oldest and well respected non-violent and non-political apex organization, called Kagote, made a conscious decision to address the environmental degradation and economic inequality in Ogoniland. They decided however, to pursue this objective under a different organization. By August 26th, 1990, the *Ogoni Bill of Rights* was launched in Nigeria by thirty illustrious sons of Ogoni. The objective of MOSOP as a mass movement was to serve as a vehicle to carry out the aims and objectives of the *Ogoni Bill of Rights* which includes,

but is not limited to, the following:

1. Political control of Ogoni affairs by Ogoni people
2. Control and use of a fair proportion of Ogoni economic resources for Ogoni development, and
3. Protection of Ogoni environment and ecology from further degradation.

To the above objectives the elders added the following reassurances in the foreword of the *Ogoni Bill of Rights*, that:

1. We are Nigerians, proud to be Nigerians and would wish to remain Nigerians;
2. We hold no malice to any group or groups in this country and especially the many ethnic groups that comprise Rivers State;
3. We have no affiliation with any organization inside or outside Nigeria; and
4. We speak as loyal and law abiding citizens of Nigeria and are here to fight for our rights, not by force of arm but through dialogue and persuasion.

This last point was emphasized at every meeting and for good measure repeating that we were to fight not with arms but with our heads. "Non violent and passive resistance to all sorts of exploitation" was the motto then.

With the application and acceptance of Ken Saro-Wiwa on September 26th, 1990 as spokesman for the new organization, MOSOP's executive was now fully in place under the leadership of Dr. Garrick Leton, a renowned Nigerian chemical scientist. The new organization resisted all temptations and pursued its agenda nonviolently to the amazement and admiration of most Nigerians. One major concession among others that the organization got from the government was the establishment of the Oil Mineral and Petroleum Development Corporation whereby three percent of all funds accruing from the total sale of Nigeria's crude oil was to be deposited in this private fund. This fund was to be used by entrepreneurs of all the oil producing states. While our elders including Ken

Saro-Wiwa were to begin negotiations regarding an Ogoni State that would comprise 13 local government areas (LGAs), Ken Saro-Wiwa immediately came up with this ridiculous idea from the Unrepresented Nations and Peoples Organization (UNPO) that Ogoni boycott the presidential elections coming up that June 12, 1993.

This action along with numerous others such as the formation of a youth and militant wing of MOSOP, advocating for an Ogoni nation, the production of an Ogoni flag and national anthem, etc. brought serious disagreements between our fathers and Ken Saro-Wiwa. Every effort by our late fathers to persuade Ken Saro-Wiwa to stay within the objectives of MOSOP failed. And so our fathers resigned their leadership of MOSOP that summer of 1993. Their resignation caused Saro-Wiwa to ascend to the presidency of MOSOP and his first action was to declare war between Ogoni and three of our neighbours with deadly consequences. Ogoni suffered untold destruction from these wars even more than we suffered during the Nigerian civil war.

Everyone that opposed Ken Saro-Wiwa's new found militant methodology was labeled a 'vulture' who had been bribed to destroy the Ogoni revolution and therefore must be killed. Ogoni youths at this stage listened to no one else but Ken Saro-Wiwa who got his instructions from the UNPO of which he was a paid Vice-Chairman. The stage was now set for the most sophisticated propaganda in modern history. Environmental degradation was at the heart of this propaganda to win the support of environmentalists in the West. With financial support pouring in from the West and the Nigerian police and Shell sent packing from Ogoni, our fathers were now at the mercy of Ken Saro-Wiwa and his hoodlums. Increasingly with every brazen act, Ken Saro-Wiwa believed he was now above the Nigerian law.

There is therefore a need for a responsible advocacy by international human rights organizations particularly in the Third World countries. This is because the quagmire in Ogoni took a different turn only after Ken Saro-Wiwa unilaterally enrolled the Movement for the Survival of the Ogoni People with the UNPO. It was dumb and irresponsible advice when UNPO instructed Ken Saro-Wiwa to boycott the Nigerian presidential elections in order to bring international attention to the Ogoni plight. People are dying every day fighting for the right to vote and so in 1993, all Ogonis were forcibly denied their right to vote by MOSOP and UNPO.

Amnesty International's declaration of Ken Saro-Wiwa as a 'prisoner of conscience' without a proper investigation or discussion with any other Ogoni leader after the massacre of May 21, 1994, was also irresponsible. The fact that UNPO and Amnesty International abandoned Ogoni leaders that believed in and practiced non-violence in their approach to solving Ogoni problems was irresponsible. It is also irresponsible for Amnesty International to refer to our late fathers as 'pro-government chiefs' simply because they disagreed with Ken Saro-Wiwa over methods. In my opinion, you do not become 'pro-government' simply because you abhor violence. To Amnesty International and UNPO..., thank you but it is over!! We must have human life before human rights. If we do not have human life, we can never have human rights. Perhaps, just perhaps, if these groups had not over influenced my uncle-in-law Ken Saro-Wiwa by holding his intelligence hostage, and if on the other hand my uncle-in-law had cooperated fully with his fellow Ogoni leaders in terms of filtering ideas and policies that are alien to our ethnic, cultural and political composition, it is possible that the 'Ogoni Four' would have been alive today. Consequently, Saro-Wiwa himself would also have been alive today.

Since foreign entities, particularly UNPO and Amnesty International are so interested in Ogoni welfare, I challenge them that rather than engage in smear campaigns, they should join us in bringing peace and stability to the region by asking the Movement for the Survival of the Ogoni People to renounce violence so we can once more begin to address our problems non-violently through dialogue. Amnesty International should ask their future candidate for the 'Prisoner of Conscience Award', Dr. Owens Wiwa, to publicly retract his recent statement that more blood will flow in Ogoniland because we consider that statement to be very provocative.

NOTE

1   This paper was originally given by Mr. Orage at Duke University, Durham, U.S.A., in February 1996 during the African Student Association 1996 Black History Month.

Death of a Writer
William Boyd

He was a nuisance, someone who got in the way of rich men getting richer. So why not kill him?

Ken Saro-Wiwa was a friend of mine. At eleven-thirty in the morning on November 10th, he was hanged in a prison in Port Harcourt, in eastern Nigeria, on the orders of General Sani Abacha, the military leader of Nigeria. Ken Saro-Wiwa was fifty-four years old, and an innocent man.

I first met Ken in the summer of 1986 at a British Council seminar at Cambridge University. He had come to England from Nigeria in his capacity as a publisher and had asked the British Council to arrange a meeting with me. He had read my first novel, *A Good Man in Africa*, and had recognized, despite fictional names and thin disguises, that it was set in Nigeria, the country that had been my home when I was in my teens and early twenties.

Ken had been a student at the University of Ibadan, in western Nigeria, in the mid-1960s. My late father, Dr. Alexander Boyd, had run the university health services there, and had treated Ken and come to know him. Ken recognized that the Dr. Murray in my novel was a portrait of Dr. Boyd and was curious to meet his son.

I remember that it was a sunny summer day, one of those days that are really too hot for England. In shirtsleeves, we strolled about the immaculate quadrangle of a Cambridge college, talking about Nigeria. Ken was a small man, probably no more than five feet two or three. He was stocky and energetic — in fact, brimful of energy — and had a big, wide smile. He smoked a pipe with a curved stem. I learned later that the pipe was virtually a logo: in Nigeria, people recognized him by it. In newsreel pictures that the Nigerian military released of the final days of Ken's show trial,[1] there's a shot of him walking toward the courthouse, leaning on a stick, thinner and aged as a result of eighteen months' incarceration, the familiar pipe still clenched between his teeth.

Ken was not only a publisher but a businessman (in the grocery trade); a celebrated political journalist, with a particularly trenchant and swinging style; and, I discovered, a prolific writer of novels, plays, poems, and children's books (mostly published by him). He was, in addition, the highly successful writer and producer of Nigeria's most popular TV soap opera, *Basi & Co.*, which ran a hundred and fifty-odd episodes in the mid-1980s, and was reputedly Africa's most watched soap opera, with an audience of up to thirty million. Basi and his cronies were a bunch of feckless Lagos wide boys who, indigent and lazy, did nothing but hatch inept schemes for becoming rich. Although funny and wincingly accurate, the show was also unashamedly pedagogic. What was wrong with Basi and his chums was wrong with Nigeria: none of them wanted to work, and they all acted as though the world owed them a living, if that could not be acquired by fair means foul ones would do just as well. This was soap opera as a form of civic education.

Whenever Ken passed through London, we would meet for lunch, usually in the Chelsea Arts Club. His wife and four children lived in England — the children attended school there — so he was a regular visitor. And, though I wrote a profile of him for the London *Times* (Ken was trying to get his books distributed in Britain), our encounters were mainly those of two writers with something in common, hanging out for a highly agreeable, bibulous hour or three.

Ken's writing was remarkably various, covering almost all genres. *Sozaboy*,[2] in my opinion his greatest work, is subtitled "A Novel in Rotten English" and is written in a unique combination of pidgin English, the lingua franca of the former West African British colonies, and an English that is, in its phrases and sentences, altogether more classical and lyrical. The language is a form of literary demotic, a benign hijacking of English, and a perfect vehicle for the story it tells, of a simple village boy recruited into the Biafran Army during the Nigerian civil war. The boy has dreamed of being a soldier (a "soza"), but the harsh realities of this brutal conflict send him into a dizzying spiral of cruel disillusion. *Sozaboy* is not simply a great African novel but also a great antiwar novel — among the very best of the twentieth century.

Sozaboy was born of Ken's personal experience of the conflict — the Biafran War, as it came to be known — and, indeed, so were many of his other writings. Biafra was the name given to a loose ethnic grouping in eastern Nigeria dominated by the Ibo people. The Ibo leader, Colonel Chukwuemeka Odumegwu Ojukwu, decided to secede from Nigeria, taking most of the country's oil reserves with him. In the war that was then waged against the secessionist state, perhaps a million people died, mainly of starvation in the shrinking heartland.

Not all the ethnic groups caught up in Ojukwu's secessionist dream were willing participants. Ken's ethnic group, the Ogoni, for one. When the war broke out, in 1967, Ken was on vacation and found himself trapped within the new borders of Biafra. He saw at once the absurdity of being forced to fight in another man's war, and he escaped through the front lines to the federal side. He was appointed civilian administrator of the crucial oil port of Bonny on the Niger River delta, and he served there until the final collapse of the Biafran forces in 1970. Ken wrote about his experiences of the civil war in his fine memoir, *On a Darkling Plain.*

Ken's later fight against the Nigerian military, as it turned out, was oddly pre-figured in those years of the Biafran War: the helplessness of an ethnic minority in the face of an overpowering military dictatorship; oil and oil wealth as a destructive and corrupting catalyst in society; the need to be true to one's conscience.

This moral rigor was especially apparent in Ken's satirical political journalism (he was, over the years, a columnist on the Lagos daily newspapers *Punch, Vanguard,* and *Daily Times*), much of which was charged with a Swiftian *saeva indignatio* at what he saw as the persistent ills of Nigerian life: ethnic conflict, ignorance of the rights of minorities, rampant materialism, inefficiency, and general graft. Apart from *Basi & Co.*, his journalism was what brought him his greatest renown among the population at large.

In the late 1980s, I remember, Ken's conversations turned more and more frequently to the topic of his ethnic homeland. The Ogoni are a small ethnic group (there are two hundred and fifty ethnic groups in Nigeria)[3] of about half a million people living in a small area of the fertile Niger River delta. The Ogoni's great misfortune is that their homeland happens to lie above a significant portion of Nigeria's oil reserves. Since the mid-1950s, Ogoniland has been devastated by the industrial pollution caused by the extraction of oil. What was once a placid rural community of prosperous farmers and fishermen is now an ecological wasteland reeking of sulfur, its creeks and water holes poisoned by indiscriminate oil spillage and ghoulishly lit at night by the orange flames of gas flares.

As Ken's concern for his homeland grew, he effectively abandoned his vocation and devoted himself to lobbying for the Ogoni cause at home and abroad. He was instrumental in setting up the Movement for the Survival of the Ogoni People (MOSOP) and soon became its figurehead. That struggle for survival was an ecological more than a political one: Ken protested the despoliation of his homeland and demanded compensation from the Nigerian government and from the international oil companies — Shell in particular. (He resented Shell profoundly and, with good reason, held the company responsible for the ecological calamity in Ogoniland.) His people, he said, were being subjected to a 'slow genocide'. But from the outset Ken made sure that the movement's protest was peaceful and nonviolent. The Nigerian leadership today is corrupt and dangerously violent: it was enormously to the credit of the Ogoni movement that it stayed true to its principles. Mass demonstrations were organized and passed off without incident. Abroad, Greenpeace and other environmental groups allied themselves with the Ogoni cause, but, ironically, the real measure of the success of Ken's agitation came when, in 1992, he was arrested by the Nigerian military and held in prison for some months without a trial. The next year, Shell Oil ceased its operations in the Ogoni region.

At that time, the Nigerian military was led by General Ibrahim Babangida. Ken was eventually released (after a campaign in the British media), and Babangida voluntarily yielded power to Ernest Sonekan and General Abacha, a crony. They were meant to supervise the transition of power to a civilian government after a general election, which was duly held in 1993 and annulled by Babangida.

Nigeria entered a new era of near-anarchy and despotism. Things looked bad for Nigeria, but they looked worse for the Ogoni and their leaders. Abacha, meanwhile, removed Shonekan and became the sole authority.

Over these years, Ken and I continued to meet for our Chelsea Arts Club lunches whenever he was in London. In 1992, he suffered a personal tragedy, when his youngest son, aged fourteen, who was at Eton, died suddenly of heart failure during a rugby game. Strangely, Ken's awful grief gave a new force to his fight for his people's rights.

We met just before he returned to Nigeria. From my own experience of Nigeria, I knew of the uncompromising ruthlessness of political life there. Ken was not young, nor was he in the best of health (he, too, had a heart condition). As we said good-bye, I shook his hand and said, "Be careful, Ken, O.K.?" And he laughed — his dry, delighted laugh — and replied, "Oh, I'll be very careful, don't worry." But I knew he wouldn't.

A succession of Nigerian military governments have survived as a result of the huge revenues generated by oil, and the military leaders themselves have routinely benefited from the oil revenues, making millions and millions of dollars. Any movement that threatened this flow of money was bound to be silenced — extinguished. With the ascendance of Abacha and his brazenly greedy junta, Ken was now squarely in harm's way. Even so, he returned to Nigeria to continue his protests. These protests were now conducted in a more sinister country than the one I had known — a country where rapes, murders, and the burning of villages were being carried out as a deliberate policy of state terrorism. There have been two thousand Ogoni deaths thus far.

In May of 1994, Ken was on his way to address a rally in an Ogoni town but was turned back at a military road-block and headed, reluctantly, for home. The rally took place, a riot ensued, and in the general mayhem four Ogoni elders — believed to be sympathetic to the military — were killed.

Ken was arrested and, with several others, was accused of incitement to murder. The fact that he was in a car some miles away and going in the opposite direction made no difference. He was imprisoned for more than a year and then was tried before a specially convened tribunal. There was no right of appeal. This 'judicial process' has been internationally condemned as a sham. It was a show trial in a kangaroo court designed to procure the verdict required by the government.

On Thursday, November 2nd, 1995, Ken and his co-defendants were found guilty and sentenced to death. Suddenly the world acknowledged the nature of Nigeria's degeneracy.

Things did not augur well. But, instinctively wanting to make the best of a bad situation, I hoped that the publicity surrounding Ken's case, along with the timely coincidence of the Commonwealth conference in New Zealand (a biennial gathering of the former members of the British Empire), would prevent the very worst from happening. Surely, I reasoned, the heads of state congregating in Auckland would not allow one of their members to flout their own human rights principles so callously and blatantly? General Abacha, however, did not dare leave his benighted country, which was represented by his Foreign Minister instead.

The presence of Nelson Mandela at the conference was especially encouraging, not only for me but also for all the people who had spent the last months fighting to free Ken. (We were a loose-knit organization, including International PEN, the Ogoni Foundation, Amnesty International, Greenpeace, and others.) We felt that if anything could persuade the Nigerians to think again it would be Mandela's moral authority. We were baffled and confused, though, when Mandela did little more than persistently advocate that we should all be patient, that the problem would be resolved through an easy, low-key diplomacy.

Despite Mandela's advice, there was a clamorous condemnation in the media of the Nigerian military. In response, Abacha's junta released newsreel pictures of Ken's trial to establish the legality of the 'judicial process'. One saw a row of prisoners, still, faces drawn, heads bowed, confronting three stout officers, swaggered with gold braid, ostentatiously passing pieces of paper to each other. In the background, a soldier strolled back and forth. Then Ken addressed the court. His voice was strong: he was redoubtably defiant; he seemed without fear, utterly convinced.

These images both defied belief and profoundly disturbed. If Abacha thought that this would make his tribunals look acceptable, then the level of naïveté, or blind ignorance, implied was astonishing. But a keening note of worry was also sounded: someone who could do something this damaging, I thought, was beyond the reach of reason. World opinion, international outrage, appeals for clemency seemed to me now to be nugatory. Abacha had painted himself into a corner. For him it had become a question of saving face, of loud bluster, of maintaining some sort of martial pride. I slept very badly that night.

The next day, November 10th, 1995, just after lunch, I received a call from the Writers in Prison Committee of International PEN. I was told that a source in Port Harcourt had seen the prisoners arrive at the jail at dawn that day, in leg irons. Then the executioners had presented themselves, only to be turned away, because — it was a moment of grimmest, darkest farce — their papers were not in order. This source, however, was "a hundred and ten per cent certain" that the executions had eventually occurred. Some hours later, this certainty was confirmed by the Nigerian military.

So now Ken was dead, along with eight co-defendants: hanged in a mass execution just as the Commonwealth Conference got under way.

I am bitter and I am dreadfully sad. Ken Saro-Wiwa, the bravest man I have known, is no more. From time to time, Ken managed to smuggle a letter out of prison. One of his last letters I received ended this way: "I'm in good spirits.... There's no doubt that my idea will succeed in time, but I'll have to bear the pain of the moment.... The most important thing for me is that I've used my talents as a writer to enable the Ogoni people to confront their tormentors. I was not able to do it as a politician or a businessman. My writing did it. And it sure makes me feel good! I'm mentally prepared for the worst, but hopeful for the best. I think I have the moral victory." You have, Ken. Rest in peace.

NOTES

1   The military wanted to show the world that Saro-Wiwa and the eight others went through a judicial process before they were hanged. (Ed.)

2   Ken Saro-Wiwa. *Sozaboy: A Novel in Rotten English*. Port Harcourt: Saros International, 1985.

3   The correct number of languages in Nigeria is subject to further research. Some sources claim there are up to four hundred. (Ed.)

For Ken Saro-Wiwa:
African Postcolonial Relations
Through a Prism of Tragedy
Ato Quayson

King rules or barons rule; we have suffered various oppression.

T. S. Eliot, Murder in the Cathedral

And this superiority is not simply that of right, but that of the physical strength of the sovereign beating down upon the body of his
adversary and mastering it: by breaking the law, the offender has
touched the very person of the prince; and it is the prince — or at
least those to whom he has delegated his force — who seizes upon
the body of the condemned man and of the prince; and it is the
prince — or at least those to whom he has delegated his force — who
seizes upon the body of the condemned man and displays it
marked, beaten, broken. The ceremony of punishment, then, is an
exercise of 'terror'.

Michel Foucault, Discipline and Punishment

It is Achille Mbembe (1992) who first shows how literary theory
can be used for the analysis of political ideas in the 'African postcolony'. Drawing on Bakhtinian notions of the banal and the
grotesque, he traces the ways in which there emerges a necessary
'familiarity and domesticity' in the relationships between governments and those they govern in the production and institution of

political 'signs, narratives and symbols' that produce the postcolonial subject as a participant in his own domination. As he points out, "officialdom and the people have many references in common, not least of which is a certain conception of the aesthetics and stylistics of power" (p. 9). He is thus correct in shifting his focus away from the sheer binarisms that proliferate in standard interpretations of domination. Nonetheless, there is a question that Mbembe's model does not elaborate, and that is the question of state violence under totalitarianism and what this implies for the creation of political subjectivity. Though noting the violence that is visited on those who, consciously or otherwise, flout the observances of the state's practices of symbolic self-affirmation, he pays too little attention to the degree to which state violence procures acquiescence in its symbolic self-assertion while simultaneously creating the grounds for its violent reversal and overthrow. It is not only in a rehearsal of the self-validating terms of the state's symbolism that people mime its rationality. Mbembe's emphasis on the 'ludic' and on 'conviviality' as the central means by which people discompose the state's projected grandeur must be set alongside tides of sometimes public, sometimes private civil dissent that continually seek to violently discompose the state. As I shall show later, violence becomes a means by which to visit popular displeasure on those associated with the state, particularly minor officials and those seen as colluding with it. And this becomes heightened during periods of serious civil dissent, as can be shown for the Ogoni case in Nigeria. Thus, any analysis of people's collusion in the state's domination needs to pay attention too to a parallel order of potential violence that subtends and frequently organizes ordinary responses to the state in Africa.

There is another, and highly productive dimension to Mbembe's deployment of literary theory for an analysis of political ideas. It is possible to explore the potential made available not just in literary theory but in certain literary paradigms, such as tragedy, as they provide tools by which to analyse political actions at the dual levels of structure and agency. The death by hanging of Nigerian writer and activist Ken Saro-Wiwa in November 1995 drew a lot of anger from the international community. People expressed shock at the fact that the Nigerian government seemed not to have even token respect for human rights in the hurried way in which it tried and executed Saro-Wiwa. How were the terrible events to be understood in the face of the insulting gesture Abacha made to the gathered heads of Commonwealth governments in New Zealand by hanging Saro-Wiwa at the start of the Commonwealth Conference? As the impact of the news sank in, there was an unconscious attempt to make sense of the events within the available categories offered both by academic and journalistic discourses. One of these, which got to be repeated again and again, was that of 'tragedy'. There were numerous references in the newspapers as well as among academics (in discussions on the Internet, for example)[1] in which Saro-Wiwa's death was referred to as 'tragic'. It is evident that this term was often used in its everyday sense of 'sad' or 'terrible'. But the term also retained a vague ghost of its scholarly, literary dimension. It is at the intersection of the scholarly and the everyday that a re-reading of the events leading to Ken Saro-Wiwa's death may be productively located. This is to attempt a form of translation in which real life events are viewed through the prism of the emotionally and philosophically charged discourse of literary tragedy. Hopefully, such a model would help not only problematize the boundaries that are often implicitly assumed between literary tragedy and everyday suffering but would also arouse a more troubling response to Ken Saro-Wiwa's life and death and open ways in which we, as scholars and observers, can relate with immediacy to the distant events that unfolded in Ogoniland.

The overlap between the ordinary use of the words tragic and tragedy and their more specialist uses have been commented upon by various critics. Raymond Williams (1966) sets this up as the starting point of his nuanced discussion in *Modern Tragedy*. He sees the overlap in terms of a 'crossroads' and pursues the meanings of the term tragedy through a survey of the tradition of literary tragedy and its discussions by literary writers, critics and philosophers. As a consequence of his particular focus, however, Williams remains entirely within the domain of literary theory, and even though he makes frequent references to everyday understandings of tragedy, he inadvertently institutes an uneasy dichotomy between the two. Williams's failure to break from the literary derived from the fact that the key source material for his meditations was literary tragedy itself. He does not establish an equivalent parallel source in the domain of the real world outside the literary by which to test his understanding of tragedy. Like many others, he proceeded by discussing tragedy and tragic theory and then abstracting from these for generalizations about life.

The solution to the problem raised in Williams' methodology does not reside in reversing the procedure by starting from the real world and then moving into the aesthetic domain. Rather, it is preferable to *systematically* blur the distinctions between the two domains by cross-mapping an analysis of real life tragedy with a discussion of categories borrowed from literary tragedy and its theorizations. This is not so much to suggest that real life suffering is infinitely amenable to aestheticization, but rather to link the seriousness and rigour with which literary tragedy is often dealt — its aesthetic, emotional, philosophical, ethical and formal intensities — to an engagement with a specific event in the world.[2]

If the suggestion of the transfer of literary tragedy as a category is to be fruitfully pursued, however, a problem arises about its definition. Tragedy, in the specialist sense, is nothing if not notoriously slippery as a concept. Aristotle offers a classic discussion of tragedy and it is to him that one needs to turn in setting out the ground for any fresh meditations on the subject. There are two things that particularly need to be highlighted in Aristotle's theory. The first is the idea that tragedy is a serious action articulated through a particular formal structuring of incidents. "Plot" is the word Aristotle uses, but his sense of the significance of plot structure is stated in his contention that plot is the "soul" of tragedy. Aristotle ultimately aligns his notion of plot structure to an analysis both of the ideal plots of tragedies as well as to a discussion of the emotional effects that a tragedy can be properly perceived to engender and control.

The very first step in applying tragic categories to real life events would have to be to perceive any such events as enunciating a *form*. In Salman Rushdie's words: "Everything has a shape, if you look for it. There is no escape from form" (*Midnight's Children*: 226). However, the form of real life tragedy is more the expression of history than aesthetics. But history is not an immanent or transcendent category, somehow producing its own essential logic. History resides in the structural and discursive relations between people, events and institutions. The key word here is *relations*. It is the question of discursive and structural relations that allows the deployment of the tragic trope in the first place, because, like literary tragedy, the significance of a real life event may be grasped as inhering in the very constitution and later fragmentation of the cultural, symbolic, personal and political; the 'enunciative modalities' that, in Foucauldian terms, give an event coherence and solidity through time.

Following Hegel, it can also be added that history manifests its essential lineaments in the most important figures of each epoch. The lineaments of history are manifested in the ethical differences between important figures. But important figures are sometimes positioned so as to inspire the confidence of many and to stand as representatives of popularly shared ideals. This is particularly the case in an age where the media magnify and project the ideas of significantly placed individuals. As such, ethical differences are sometimes played out in the relations between individuals, people and institutions so as to open up the potential for change, and, when this is difficult in coming or is resisted, for revolution. Thus it is possible to take exception to Hegel's notion of contradiction as being the working out of the logic of the ideal Spirit. The logic that is worked out is of the reconstitution of society. But whether such a reconstitution is entirely for the better or worse is only partially decided by those who live in the realm of the reconstitution. The value of change is also partly assessed in a future configuration of ethical positions breaking out in conflict in the determination of both past and future.

In the particular case of the African postcolony, Nigeria and Ken Saro-Wiwa, however, a specific conundrum regarding the ethical positioning of key actors needs to be noted. The ethical positioning of Ken Saro-Wiwa and those who murdered him needs to be ultimately linked to the specific question of class conflict in Nigeria. Classes, of course, are here defined not merely as social strata, but as relational entities in competition for the control of productive resources (see Joel Samoff, 1982 and Londsdale, 1981). But, though economistic modes of class analysis are crucial for an understanding of class relations, the crucial thing about African classes is their scramble for control of state power. The control of economic resources is ultimately mediated through the struggle for political authority which is, in the final analysis, the best means for control of economic resources in the African postcolony. This is especially the case because of the size of the public sector (see Richard Sklar, 1979 and M. N. Schatzberg, 1988: 25ff). It becomes quite important to control the state because of its expanded role and its assumption of "a major responsibility not only for insuring the rationalization of production, the mobility of capital and the availability of labor, but, also, in general, for managing the framework for accumulating capital and reproducing capitalist relations," (Samoff, 124–5).

In these struggles for control of the African state, however, it is the military that has shown itself to be at an advantage. I have argued elsewhere, though somewhat lamely, that the military in Africa is the most coherent class grouping that not only shares a particular view of the world but also possesses the means of force by which to ensure the furtherance of its interests (Quayson, 1993). And even though arguments can be marshalled to the contrary to show that like any other class, the military is riddled with internal contradictions that render it not so much a monolithic class but one always in formation, I would like to argue that precisely because they have entered the political domain, they have moulded a rationality that links specifically to the ultimate control of power. In Nigeria, where for thirty of the thirty-seven years of independence the country has been ruled by the military, the interests of soldiers have solidified into a class interest. Thus, what Shivji (1978) terms the "bureaucratic bourgeoisie" in Africa needs to be perceived as primarily aligned to and subserving the interests of the military when in power. It is then pertinent to note with Ebo Hutchful (1991: 185) the central problem for governing soldiers anywhere on the continent: "How to establish general and impartial rules of political procedure in which the subjective interests and preferences of the military are nevertheless embedded — this forms one of the abiding dilemmas of military constitutionalism."

Returning to Aristotle, there is a second thread which is important to highlight. This is his notion of the tragic hero's demise or reversal in fortune as deriving from an error of judgement. The error of judgement defines the ethical quality of the tragedy and simultaneously humanizes the great character thus allowing our identification with the tragic hero (see Jaspers, 1963; Langer, 1953: 351–68; and Georgopoulos, 1993). And yet the specific ethical quality of the error of judgement requires greater specification. For the error of judgement has been expressed in tragedies in relation to different things. In Sophocles' *Oedipus Rex*, for instance, it was an error related to ignorance both about Oedipus's contaminated self and the fate the gods had set down for him. The error of judgement was due to a misapprehension of his own self and of the status of cosmic laws. The entire dramatic action is devoted to slowly peeling off the circumstantial encrustations that prevent him from knowing the truth. This truth, when it comes, is so devastating that he can only blind himself.

Something of the Greeks resides in Shakespeare, but with a number of crucial differences. One key difference between them is the manner in which Shakespeare psychologizes his characters. The error of judgement in Shakespearean tragedy is often correlated to an unfoldment of dramatic structure as linked to psychological understanding. When Lear is exposed to the elements on the heath, it is an extreme psychological crisis that is being tuned by the clashing of the spheres. As he begins to understand the true nature of his folly in allowing himself to be deceived about the nature of Goneril and Regan's filial love, the ravages are foregrounded.

Perhaps the most complex expression of this link between error of judgement, dramatic structure and psychological stress is provided in *Hamlet*. The meandering nature of the play, especially up to the play-within-the-play scene seems to mime the vacillations in the eponymous hero's mind. For Hamlet — suicidal, melancholic, lovelorn and yet intellectually alert — expresses to a certain degree the problem of bringing a fractured consciousness to bear on the enterprise of revenge. Each step of the external circumstances has to be negotiated by Hamlet through critical inquiry. But the critical inquiry is related to stabilizing his own mind. For Hamlet there is no clear error of judgement by which to trace a change in the fortunes of the hero. If he commits any serious error it comes when he misinterprets Claudius's true intentions in inviting him to spar with Laertes. But this misinterpretation comes at the moment when he draws a point of interpretive closure on events in conversation with Horatio, finally deciding that it is "to be damned to let this canker of our nature come/In further evil" (5.2.68–70). It is at precisely the point when he is at one with his own mind, and has consolidated reasons for taking action against Claudius. It is then, and only then, that he commits the error of judgement that costs him his life.

If the notion of error of judgement is going to be useful for application to a real life context, it would need to be even further problematized. The error of judgement of individual actors in the world is often not related solely to a misapprehension of the significance of events, though that can be shown to be quite often the case. In the particular case of Ken Saro-Wiwa, however, another dimension needs to be introduced that would link error of judgement not just to ethical misapprehension, but rather to the misapprehension of historical processes themselves. Again, literary tragedy furnishes interesting examples of the misapprehension of historical process. Consider, for instance, Okonkwo in Chinua Achebe's *Things Fall Apart*. Okonkwko, as has frequently been noted, is a man who lives by the warrior ethic (see, for instance, Irele, 1979). And it is this ethic that seems to him most significant and by which he judges others. It is the ethic for which he himself has been rewarded by his clan. When at the end of the book, he beheads the messenger who comes to break up the clan meeting, he is only asserting this warrior ethic. Unfortunately, he asserts this ethic at a point when, due to the processes of history, his own clan has moved from the assertion of that ethic to embrace a more flexible one. In Raymond Williams' terms, the warrior ethic has become residualized by the processes of history and a new and emergent one has taken its place (1977: 121–7). The emergent ethic is signalled indirectly by references to the new trade in palm products that had brought prosperity into the clan. It is also signalled, crucially, in the flowering of Christianity among the clansfolk. The thing to note, then, is the degree to which Okonkwo misapprehends historical processes and becomes a victim of them. This interpretation of error of judgement, or misapprehension, actually brings the status of the hero closer to the everyday, for which of us can completely comprehend the processes of history as they alter discursive and structural relations? How can we hope to fully control the direction of its flow?

If we recapitulate what we have highlighted about tragedy so far, a number of things emerge: firstly, that tragedy resides in the formal and shifting arrangement of events. This arrangement presents itself as an aesthetic modality in literary tragedy, but as a historical set of discursive and structural relations in real life. The two are not mutually exclusive, and, indeed, literary tragedy often provides instances of such structural and discursive relations. Secondly, tragedy involves an error of judgement. This error of judgement may be grasped in conjunction with psychological processes, or simply in relation to the misapprehension of historical processes. Finally, tragedy always involves a presentation of ethical qualities, which can be grasped either as universals or, as peculiarly related to the specific predicament adduced by the tragedy. To all these, I should add a fourth dimension which is particularly important in relation to the case of Ken Saro-Wiwa. Tragedy often emerges in the assertion of ethical values and of selfhood in the face of forces that would negate them. The assertion of such values is pre-eminently expressed in a will to act in spite of the forces of negation. Sometimes these forces seem so drastically intent on asserting a monologic order of things that they are grasped as versions of a metaphysical evil. At other times they are much more subtle and complex, and are inextricably tied to the very act of asserting the ethical values themselves. As an act of assertion is expressed in a non-ideal world, consequences emanate from it that are not always under the rational control of the person holding them. It is in the interstices of all these factors, I think, that the tragedy of Ken Saro-Wiwa may be located.

KEN SARO-WIWA AND THE OGONI

Ogoniland is in the Delta area of Nigeria. Its population is estimated at half a million people and its size is approximately 404 square miles with a population density of 1,500 per square mile and spread out over three local government areas. There are six clans which among them hold 111 villages. In *Genocide in Nigeria: The Ogoni Tragedy* Ken Saro-Wiwa turns his mind to the place of the Ogoni in the Nigerian nation-state. More importantly, he interprets the history of Ogoniland as a tragedy. This is significant because even though he is using the term only in its everyday sense, there is an indication that his own personal decision to commit his life to fighting on behalf of his people derived partly from his understanding of their terrible predicament. For him their predicament could only be relieved through the total commitment of his own life. The book itself is clearly an attempt to define the reasons for the Ogoni struggle in the first place, but, in doing this he also delineates an interesting set of contradictions in the formation of the Nigerian nation-state itself which points to a larger problematic of postcolonial identity in general. Saro-Wiwa sets the question of the Ogoni struggle firmly in the context of a larger perceived Nigerian tragedy. Two things are particularly relevant in this respect. The first is his pointer to the different modes by which various tribes were integrated into the colonial project. Because of the swampy terrain of the Niger Delta on which Ogoniland is located, they were a largely self-sufficient people who lived a fairly independent existence from their larger neighbouring ethnic groups. In his words: "Throughout their recorded history, there is no instance of any of their neighbours being able to impose upon them in any manner whatsoever. They were never defeated in war and were not colonized by anyone except the British" (Saro-Wiwa, 1992: 12).

To this fact is added another one of an even more problematic nature. Because they lived an independent existence, and were not colonized except by the British, they entered into the sphere of colonialism very late in their history. If it is recalled that in Yorubaland, serious inter-tribal wars had been raging from about the 1850s (see Johnson, 1921) and that Yorubas themselves were the earliest to gain the benefits of Western education and Westernization, we see then the extent to which, until the second decade of this century, the Ogoni had lived a relatively peaceful existence. The fact that they were integrated into a larger Nigeria along with other ethnic groups that had different paces of historical development is interpreted by Saro-Wiwa as a potential source of tension for the new nation, precisely because the differences in historical experiences of Western contact linked to the different sizes of the ethnic groupings making Nigeria were easily translated into significant political differences as such (Saro-Wiwa, 1992: 19ff).

Flowing out of this earlier point also was the fact that because of the late stage at which Ogoniland was integrated into the rest of Nigeria, they did not feel the potentially unifying experience of an administrative state apparatus until 1914, the very year that Nigeria was formed. It is pertinent to note that among the Ogoni, there was no clear pan-Ogoni sense until the various clans in

Ogoniland thought it necessary to come together to fight on common grounds (see Osaghae, 1995: 327–38). Ogoni do not have a myth of common origin and constitute an ethnic group on the basis of sharing "common language, custom, tradition, farming methods and similar attitudes."[3] Among other things, Benedict Anderson (1983) notes in his analysis of the processes of the formation of 'imagined communities', that the sense of participating in the framework provided by a specific bureaucratic apparatus gradually provides a sense of belonging to the same entity. The interaction with administrative structures and personnel potentially produces not just a sense of common belonging but also an opportunity for definition against such an apparatus. The problematization of the terms provided by a bureaucratic and administrative apparatus in itself feeds into identity-formation as does the quest for political and other resources (see Eboreime, 1992; Bayart, 1993: 55–9). With the Ogoni, however, even after they were subjugated following sporadic British military campaigns from 1903 to 1914 when Ogoniland finally capitulated, there was no serious attempt to integrate Ogoniland into a clear administrative apparatus. Ken Saro-Wiwa (1992) points out that for twenty years after the Ogoni's final capitulation "the area was left to stagnate":

> The British did not establish an administration; the Ogoni nation was administered as part of Opobo Division within Calabar Province. The divisional headquarters was separated from Ogoni by the Imo River and Calabar was about 200 miles away. British rule of the area was "haphazard" (p. 16).

Even more disturbing was the fact that the British seemed to be only interested in collecting taxes. Apart from one or two schools established by churches in the area, there was no clear sense that they benefited from their taxes (1992: 16–7). Because of the slow pace of development of Ogoniland which, to them, was directly linked to their not having a direct local administration, the demands for a separate administrative division in Ogoniland were continually voiced. From the earliest contacts with the British, the central theme of Ogoni demands was for the control of their local administration. These demands increased particularly after independence, when it was clearly perceived that control of resources was tied inextricably to the control of the administrative apparatus.

With the outbreak of the Biafra secessionist bid in 1967, Ogoniland was to be caught in yet another conundrum of the Nigerian state. Because their land bordered the Biafran zone they fell between Federal forces and the Biafran army. According to Saro-Wiwa, the Ibos of Biafra decided to evacuate Ogoniland when a threat from Federal forces was perceived. This forced evacuation, however, led to the Ogoni feeling unnecessarily embattled. For Saro-Wiwa, the terrible mistreatment his people faced at the hands of the Ibos at this time was a clear sign that they wanted them destroyed. It also led to the development of an 'Exodus-syndrome' among Ogoni.[4] In other words, they pined for home and seized on the biblical Israel's bondage in Egypt as a useful historical analogue for understanding their own plight.[5]

By far the worst complication to afflict Ogoniland, of course, was the discovery of oil there in 1958 and the subsequent emergence of Shell-BP and Chevron as key players in the area. The effects on the environment of the drilling of oil in the region have been terrible. A 1995 World Bank Study, *Defining an Environmental Development Strategy for the Niger Delta*, shows that 76 percent of all the natural gas from petroleum production in Nigeria is flared compared to 0.6 percent in USA, 4.3 percent in the UK and 21 percent in Libya. At temperatures of 1300 to 1400 centigrade the multitude of flares in the Delta area heats up everything causing unimaginable emissions of poisonous gases. The flares release 35 million tons of carbon dioxide a year and 12 million tons of methane. According to Claude Ake writing in the Nigerian *Tell Magazine* in January 1996, this means that Nigerian oil fields contribute more to global warming than the rest of the world together. In addition to this, Rivers and Delta States suffer about 300 major oil spills a year which discharge about 2,300 cubic metres of oil.[6] The most disastrous of such oil spills was that which occurred at Dere (Bomu Oil Refinery) in 1972. The damage of the spill was so extensive that, according to Saro-Wiwa, over 20,000 people lost their means of livelihood. Acid rain fell on the area for months following this and both children and adults coughed blood. To add insult to injury, a High Court presided over by a British-born judge awarded damages against Shell to the paltry sum of £168,468, thus pre-empting the imposition of fines of tens of millions of dollars agreed upon by a special governmental committee set up to investigate the matter (Saro-Wiwa, 1992: 44–83).

THE OGONI STRUGGLE AGAINST NIGERIA AND SHELL

Since, as we have already noted, the history of the Ogoni manifested itself to Saro-Wiwa's consciousness as a tragic process, his own choices with respect to his people's plight was always tinctured by the heroic modalities of the tragic paradigm. And it is specifically in his intervention in the history of his people and in the attempt to alter the means by which they as a minority related to the Nigerian state apparatus, that he enters into the realm of tragedy as we have already defined it. For, in doing this, he not only came to represent an ethical position radically opposed to that represented in the Nigerian state, but also triggered processes well beyond his control that in the end came to destroy him. The structural and discursive relations that he sought to redefine lay in respect of four main groupings and organizations: first, there were ordinary Ogoni with whose plight he identified and whose consciousness he sought to arouse; second were the traditional leaders of Ogoniland, with whom he had to work in close alliance; third was the totalitarian bureaucratic apparatus of the Nigerian state; and fourth was Shell, the multinational oil company. The crux of the discursive relations and what ultimately became the key point of contention between the last three of these groupings was the mobilization and control of the popular masses. Until 1990, minority demands all across Nigeria were largely pursued through delegations, petitions and meetings with state and federal authorities. An important turn was to take place in the case of the Ogoni with the formation of the Movement for the Survival of the Ogoni People (MOSOP) in 1990 with Dr. Garrick Leton as President and Ken Saro-Wiwa as spokesperson. This was the organization put together by Ken Saro-Wiwa and other Ogoni elites to mobilize their people in the struggle for better treatment by the oil companies and the government.

The formation of MOSOP could be said to have spelt an important shift in Ogoni identity-formation when they were radically transformed, in the words of E. Osaghae (1995: 329), from an ethnic group-in-itself to an ethnic group-for-itself. In an important sense, the leaders of MOSOP had triggered the processes that Fanon (1993) identifies in 'On National Culture' as critical for the formation of coherent national and cultural identities: "There is no fight for culture which can develop apart from popular struggle." Even though Fanon states this in relation to the formation of national culture in the era just after independence, his thoughts are pertinent for understanding identity-formation in general, especially in the context of minority rights and the creation of a common consciousness of oppression. The first step in prosecuting a common struggle on behalf of the Ogoni for MOSOP was the drawing up of the *Ogoni Bill of Rights* in the later part of 1990. This was presented to the government of Ibrahim Babangida, the UN sub-committee on the Prevention of Discrimination Against Minorities, the African Human Rights Commission, Greenpeace and Rain Forest Action Group among others. Their demands were four-fold: the demand for a right to control their political affairs; the control and use of a fair share of economic resources derived from Ogoniland; the protection, use and development of Ogoni languages; and the demand for the protection of their oil-producing environment from further degradation.

The *Bill of Rights*, then, covered the political, economic, cultural and environmental concerns of the Ogoni. But in raising the question of oil compensation and the environment, the Ogoni were touching a raw nerve in Nigerian politics. For the military junta, dependent so heavily on oil revenues for maintaining its system of patronage, the example being set by the Ogonis was liable to lead to big trouble if it was emulated by other ethnic groups whose lands had oil. Even more disturbing was the faint whiff of secessionism which was implied in MOSOP's strident call for the re-organization of the Nigerian federal arrangements so as to accord minorities greater economic and political rights. In fact, MOSOP argued strongly for the creation of a specific Ogoni State within Nigeria so that they would have oil revenues coming to an administrative framework that they would not have to share with other splintered groupings. And matters took a decidedly alarming turn in the eyes of both the government and Shell when, in December 1992, MOSOP wrote to Shell and other oil companies demanding, among other things, the payment of billions of dollars for environmental degradation as well as for the right to negotiate directly with the oil companies.

The notion of a Bill of Rights, evoking as it does the *American Bill of Rights* as well as the French *Rights of Man* signals something important about the MOSOP leadership's understanding of the struggle into which the people were being led. It was in a sense an attempt to delineate their struggle as an epic one. The epic trope, which had in a way operated at a subterranean level ever since their experiences during the Biafra war, was now being channelled by Saro-Wiwa and MOSOP into a conscious political discursive domain. Ken Saro-Wiwa was at pains to indicate the special nature of his people's plight and regularly referred to them as being the victims of genocidal tendencies in Nigeria. And so, in a newspaper interview in 1993, he pointed out:

> If you take away all the resources of the (Ogoni) people, you take away their land, you pollute their air, you pollute their streams, you make it impossible for them to farm or fish, which is their main source of livelihood, and then what comes out of their soil you take entirely away... if more people in Ogoni are dying than are being born, if Ogoni boys and girls are not going to school... if those who manage to scale through (*sic*) cannot find jobs... then surely you are leading the tribe to extinction (quoted in Osaghae, 330).

The point of this assertion is not whether his people were in fact under a threat of genocide or not. It is that, for the sake of prosecuting the struggle, Saro-Wiwa strategically defined his people within an epic paradigm in which they were the victims of a massive campaign of persecution. This notion of epic scale was joined to the mass mobilization drive in order to give his people a sense of participation in a specifically constructed historical process. More crucially, however, is that by joining this epic trope to the mass mobilization drive, Ken Saro-Wiwa and the leaders of MOSOP were actually suggesting the possibility for the reconfiguration of class arrangements through the mobilized power of ordinary people. It also suggested the possibility of shifting the control of the direction of historical processes away from the governing military-middle class alliance into the hands of ordinary people. And even though this was being suggested only for minorities of the Delta area, it was potentially a problematic signal of the rise of an oppressed class.

Even as an epic trope was being deployed by Ken Saro-Wiwa as a strategic device linked to mass mobilization, it also had the effect of antagonizing other members of MOSOP, as it was interpreted as part of a drive for personal authority. The epic trope could be seen as signalling two contradictory impulses: the impulse to raise his people's consciousness and the impulse to assume the mantle of leadership as irrevocably his. Partly as a consequence of his perceived personal ambitions, the earlier leaders of MOSOP became gradually disenchanted. There was a falling out which was itself due to a complex set of reasons. Most prominent was the fact that, unlike the traditional elders with whom he went on delegations to meet with government authorities, Saro-Wiwa did not trust in the promises made by the government. He favoured a more militant approach. By the early months of 1993, the tension between the two perspectives was beginning to show. Ken Saro-Wiwa spearheaded the formation of the National Youth Council of Ogoni People (NYCOP) along with other organizations for women, teachers, religious leaders and professionals. This move was seen by the rest of the leadership of MOSOP as being Saro-Wiwa's way of creating a corps of dedicated youth on whom he could call and who had allegiance solely to him. Certainly, by April of 1993, NYCOP turned on traditional elders who had written a newspaper advert describing an earlier Ogoni attack on a Shell contractor as the upsurge of 'lawless activities'. NYCOP not only vilified the chiefs, calling them 'vultures' but also set about burning their property and hounding them out of Ogoniland.[7]

Perhaps a good sign of the crucial differences between himself and the rest of the leadership of MOSOP was in their reading of the impact of the 1993 elections on the Ogoni demands. Whereas the traditional authorities along with other members of the MOSOP thought it expedient to bide their time and wait for a civilian administration, Ken Saro-Wiwa interpreted the political campaigning as being coloured by parochial interests that did not take account of minority rights in the first place.[8] He insisted that Ogoni boycott the elections entirely in protest. This led to further friction between him and the others. In the event, he turned out to have been perfectly correct. The results of the elections were annulled and the military stayed in power. The thing to note was that the military junta perceived the election results as threatening to seriously alter the balance of power in the country to their detriment. What Ken Saro-Wiwa clearly saw was that the elections did not promise any meaningful structural changes in the ways in which the federation was run and in how its resources were distributed.

On May 21, 1994 a fateful meeting was called by Ogoni chiefs. Ken Saro-Wiwa was turned away by police as he tried to enter Ogoniland to address a rally. He was asked to return to Port Harcourt. The chiefs' meeting, held at the palace of the Gbenemene Gokana was disrupted by a mob, who, shouting insults, set upon them. Four chiefs, namely Chief Edward Kobani, formerly a commissioner in the Rivers State Government and former deputy president of MOSOP; Chief Samuel N. Orage, another former Rivers State Commissioner; Chief Theophilus B. Orage, formerly Secretary of the Gokana Council of Chiefs; and Mr. Albert Badey, a former Permanent Secretary, Commissioner and Secretary to the Rivers State Government, were brutally murdered. The journalist Chris McGreal, writing under the title 'A Tainted Hero', attempts to reconstruct the Saro-Wiwa story paying attention to the multiple perspectives of his supporters as well as to those of the families whose relatives were killed by the youth mob for which Saro-Wiwa and eight others were eventually hanged. The article attempts to be well-balanced except for the interpretation of moral responsibility that McGreal uses to pin a measure of liability on Ken Saro-Wiwa for what finally befalls the chiefs. McGreal's main contention is that Saro-Wiwa is partly responsible for creating the environment in which the chiefs were vilified and which finally led to their brutal murder. For him, in spite of Saro-Wiwa's absence from the scene of the crime, and despite the lack of reasonable proof that he ordered the murders, Saro-Wiwa is still to be held partly responsible for the murders.

What McGreal fails to take account of, in deploying a largely liberal humanist understanding of 'personal moral responsibility', is the extent to which the environment in which the Ogoni leadership operated was itself heavily overdetermined by the ethos of

Nigerian politics itself. The Babangida years had seen the perfection of a system of political patronage popularly known as 'settlement'. Babangida was generally believed to systematically buy off his opponents by giving them bribes or giving them key political appointments. Even Wole Soyinka, when he accepted the chairmanship of the National Road Safety Corps in the mid-1980s, was accused of having been 'settled' by his critics. Because of this, any one who put themselves up as representatives of their people ran the danger of being accused of being 'settled' if they ever showed signs of compromise. And so when the traditional leaders argued that the aggressive politics of Saro-Wiwa would alienate them from the political authorities and that they should take a more measured stance, it was easy for them to fall under suspicion of having been bought off. It is evident that the chiefs were seen, wrongly or rightly, as 'contaminated' by politics. Attacking them was then seen as partly an attack against the Nigerian state, much as was the case in South Africa during the heyday of apartheid when suspected collaborators with the regime were caught and summarily burned with 'burning necklaces' of tyres. To complicate matters even further, there is evidence to show that a regime of wanton extra-judicial murder had been systematically orchestrated by the government ever since the Ogoni began their protests in 1990.[9] The atmosphere of vilification did not require a Ken Saro-Wiwa as such, particularly as he had vigorously advocated non-violence both in public and in private. McGreal's argument problematically condemns Saro-Wiwa by re-siting moral responsibility away from the governing political ethos and onto the individual.

This takes us back to the point I raised at the beginning of this essay in pointing out the subterranean feeling for violence that subsists in ordinary people under a totalitarian regime. The totalitarian state apparatus in Nigeria has always shown a predilection for violence. Hanging Saro-Wiwa was not so much a sign of disrespect for international opinion but a sign to Nigerians themselves that there was no escape from the State's totalitarian apparatus and that nobody in the whole wide world could save them.[10] Nobody. The entire gamut of the Saro-Wiwa trial, from the fact that the accused persons were tried not under the normal processes of law but under a decree passed by the military itself, the *1987 Civil Disturbances (Spe-*

cial Tribunal) Decree; the fact that defence lawyers were sometimes manhandled and relatives of the accused were refused entry into the courtroom; and the fact that crucial videotaped evidence about the chicanery of certain key witnesses was not allowed in evidence; all these showed that the totalitarian regime was interested in showing their unquestioned power of life and death over its citizens.[11] Such a model of governmentality is far from the 'ludic' and 'convivial' model Mbembe (1992) adduces for the African postcolony. As Saro-Wiwa put it: "To be at the mercy of buffons is the ultimate insult. To find the instruments of state power reducing you to dust is the injury" (*A Month*, 8).

In launching a mass mobilization drive against a multinational oil company and the state of Nigeria, Ken Saro-Wiwa located himself at the vortex of multiple historical processes and interests. At the level of the state, his effect on mobilizing a hitherto quiescent minority around oil and environmental rights was a dangerous signal of a new praxis for other dispossessed minorities both in the oil-producing regions and in Nigeria more generally. At a more local level, he clashed with traditional and more conservative authorities who could not fully grasp the significance of the revolutionary processes that were being unleashed. But, even more problematically, he generated popular forces which were forced to articulate their perception of political action partially from within the ethical framework provided by the system of patronage and violence in place in Nigeria. Obviously, in his absence, the masses deployed the means of understanding politics that was discursively instituted in Nigerian politics itself. To their minds, anyone could be 'settled' and dissension with the militant goals of their struggle was a sign of collusion with the state. Furthermore, violence was the medicine that the State had been using against them ever since their struggle began. In a crucial sense, the anger and violence that was unleashed against their leaders may well have been a turning in on themselves as the State's security apparatus tightened its screws, arrested their more popular leaders and threw them into detention and a carefully orchestrated reign of terror was unleashed upon them. When they called the chiefs 'vultures' and brutally murdered them, they were extending a process of demonization that subtended a combined traditional discourse of morality as well as the dominant discourse of Nigerian politics. It was a singular historic and tragic failure. If Saro-Wiwa exhibited a tragic flaw, it was in misapprehending the extent to which his followers had been subjectivized by the thuggery and violence already delimited by the ethos of Nigerian politics and in not addressing this systematically from the very beginning of the struggle. This subjectivity simultaneously made them both victims of violence as well as prepared to become agents of such violence as an expression of their frustration against the state.

There is one last problematic that needs to be noted before we can properly conclude. And that is: how does the death of the tragic hero in real life affect the lives of others? Can we afford to impose the same forms of closure we impose on literary tragedy on the events of real life? It is here that the literary and the world of real events part ways. For whereas in the literary domain, the tragedy does not call upon us to take a stance or to act, and allows us to go back to our homes with an abstract feeling of having participated in something of a terrible beauty, the events of real life tragedy enjoin a different form of response. Wole Soyinka (1975) speaks of the tragic hero as inspired by Ogun. In the stress of transition Ogun is able to help his people across the abyss of chaos into a new reconstituted domain of significance. And this affects both the imagined community inscribed within the dramatic action as well as the audience itself. None the less, Soyinka's meditations on heroism need a number of qualifications for application in the Ken Saro-Wiwa case. As in Christian conceptions of tragedy, it hints at the redemptive quality of the hero's death. But redemption can breed quiescence and apathy, by suggesting that the action of ordinary mortals is foreclosed by the death of the hero, since the hero is taken as carrying the responsibility for salvation. On the contrary, it is important to hold out the possibility of redemption residing in a continual reappraisal of the life and death of the hero as a means of renewing the resolve to struggle on in the process of challenging the dominant structural and discursive relations began by the tragic hero. And it is also important in the particular case of Ken Saro-Wiwa to understand his ethical position in its truest world-historical significance. The fight for a right to a clean earth, the struggle against a negating totalitarianism, against the predatory privations unleashed by international capital, and the effort at arousing a silent people into an engagement with their history are all values that give his activism a meaning beyond the bounds of Ogoniland.

In this, then, lay Ken Saro-Wiwa's tragic heroism: that he dared to assert an ethical position against a totalitarian state and multinational interests in spite of all the clear processes that threatened to negate this assertion. It is the clarity of his vision joined to the compromising circumstances of an unideal and sullied national history that defines his tragedy. And it is one, I think, that may touch us all whenever we stand up rigorously for what we think is right. Ken Saro-Wiwa is a tragic hero because he committed himself to his people but could not have possibly controlled all the forces he unleashed. In his commitment, and self-sacrifice, in the generosity of his spirit and in his sense of rightness in his struggle, he rose above the ordinary. It is as a tribute to this act of rising above the ordinary that I think his life, activism and death should be discussed with the same emotional and philosophical fervour that we use in discussing our greatest tragedies. And it is in tribute to his memory that the struggle for his people's rights must be supported and continue.

NOTES

*   I want to say a very special thanks to Sarah Irons, Librarian of the Centre for African Studies in Cambridge for her indefatigable support in getting access to the relevant material on the Ogoni for this essay. An earlier version of the essay was published in *Performance Research*, 1.2 (1996).

1   I am thinking here mainly of Nuafrica, an Internet discussion group comprising Africanists from all over the world.

2   See Martin Jay (1992) for a discussion of the aestheticization of politics in Western culture and the perceived dangers and implications for action that have been derived from this by several critics ranging from Walter Benjamin to Terry Eagleton.

3   E. Osaghae, quoting G. N. Loolo, *A History of the Ogoni*, in 'The Ogoni Uprising'. 328.

4   It is interesting to note that during the height of the Ogoni struggle,

at a special vigil on the 13 March called for them to express their sentiments while praying for God's help, one of the songs they sang was 'Go down go down to Abuja [federal capital] and tell government: government, let Ogoni go'. See Osaghae, 337; also Saro-Wiwa, *A Month*. 151–2; 214.

5   Saro-Wiwa returns to the memory of the Biafra War several times in his writings. See, for example *On a Darkling Plain* (1989) and *Songs in a Time of War*. Even *Sozaboy* (1985), his most well-known work, is about the fate of a young recruit who comes back from a civil war to confront the devastation of his village and of his own psyche.

6   See also *The Drilling Fields* (1994) and *Delta Force* (1995), documentaries on the Ogoni environmental crisis put together by the UK's Channel 4 Television in association with Ken Saro-Wiwa; also Greenpeace, 1994.

7   Chris MacGreal, 1996; also Human Rights Watch/Africa (1995: 11ff).

8   For his thoughts on Babangida and the electoral process, see *A Month*, xi, 26, 42, 55, 76.

9   See *Human Rights Watch*, already cited; also Claude Welch, Jnr (1995).

10   I am indebted to Keith Hart of the Centre for African Studies, Cambridge for bringing my attention to this point.

11   See the special edition of *Liberty*, a publication of the Nigerian Civil Liberties Organization, 6.4, for a detailed account of the judicial implications of the mis-trial.

BIBLIOGRAPHY

Anderson, Benedict. *Imagined Communities*. London: Verso, 1983.

Aristotle. *The Poetics. Classical Literary Theory*. Ed. T. S. Dorsch. London: Penguin, 1965.

Bayart, Jean-Francois. *The State in Africa: the Politics of the Belly*. Translated by Mary Harper, Christopher and Elizabeth Harrison. London: Longman, 1993.

Eboreime, Joseph. "Group Identities and the Changing Patterns of Alliances Among the Eppie-Attissa People of Nigeria, 1890–1991." Diss., University of Cambridge, 1992.

Ellis, Glenn. [Director]. "The Drilling Fields." Channel 4, 1994.

———. [Director/Producer]. "Delta Force." Channel 4, 1995.

Fanon, Frantz. "On National Culture." *The Wretched of the Earth*. Trans. Constance Farrington. Penguin: Hamondsworth; repr. in *Colonial*

Discourse and Post-Colonial Theory. Patrick Williams and Laura Chrisman, eds. New York: Harvester Wheathsheaf, 1993.

Georgopolous, N. "Tragic Action." *Tragedy and Philosophy.* Ed. N. Georgopolous. London: Macmillan, 1993.

Greenpeace International. *Shell-Shocked: The Environmental and Social Costs of Living with Shell in Nigeria.* Amsterdam: Greenpeace International, July 1994.

Hegel, W. *Hegel on Tragedy.* Edited with Introduction by Anne and Henry Paolucci. New York: Harper Torchbooks, 1962.

Hutchful, Ebo. "Reconstructing Political Systems: Militarism and Constitutionalism." *An African Debate on Democracy.* Ed. Issa G. Shivji. Harare: Southern Africa Political Economy Series, 1991.

Human Rights Watch/Africa. *The Ogoni Crisis: A Case-Study of Military Repression in Southeastern Nigeria.* New York, July 1995.

Irele, Abiola. "The Tragic Conflict in the Novels of Chinua Achebe." *Critical Perspectives of Chinua Achebe.* Bernth Lindfors and Lynn Innes, eds. London: Heinemann, 1979.

Jaspers, Karl. "The Tragic: Awareness; Basic Characteristics; Fundamental Interpretations." *Tragedy: Modern Essays in Criticism.* Laurence Michel and Richard B. Sewall, eds. Westport, Conn: Greenwood Press, 1963.

Jay, Martin. "'The Aesthetic Ideology' as Ideology; or, What Does It Mean to Aestheticize Politics?" *Cultural Critique.* (Spring 1992): 41–61.

Johnson, Rev. Samuel. *The History of the Yorubas.* Lagos: CSS Bookshops, 1921.

Langer, Susanne K. *Feeling and Form: A Theory of Art Developed.* London: Routledge and Kegan Paul, 1953.

Lonsdale, John. "The State and Social Processes in Africa." *African Studies Review.* 24.2/3 (1981): 139–225.

Mbembe, Achille. "Provisional Notes on the African Postcolony." *Africa.* 62 (1992): 3–37.

McGreal, Chris. "A Tainted Hero." *The Guardian Weekend* (London). 23 March, 1996: 25–8.

Osaghae, E. Eghosa. "The Ogoni Uprising: Oil Politics, Minority Agitation and the Future of the Nigerian State." *African Affairs.* 94.376 (July 1995): 325–44.

Quayson, Ato. "Unthinkable Nigeriana: Crises in the Idea of the African Nation-state." *Redrawing the Map: Two African Journeys.* Gabriel Gbadamosi and Ato Quayson. Cambridge: Prickly Pear Press, 1994.

Samoff, J. "Class, Class Conflict and the State in Africa." *Political Science Quarterly.* 97.1 (1982): 105–27.

Saro-Wiwa, Ken. *A Month and a Day: A Detention Diary.* London: Penguin, 1995.

———. *Songs in a Time of War.* Port Harcourt: Saros International Publishers, 1985.

———. *Sozaboy: A Novel in Rotten English.* Port Harcourt: Saros International Publishers, 1985.

———. *On a Darkling Plain: An Account of the Nigerian Civil War.* London, Lagos: Saros International Publishers, 1989.

———. *Genocide in Nigeria: The Ogoni Tragedy.* London: Saros International Publishers, 1992.

———. Interview in *Tell* (Lagos), 8 February, 1993.

Schatzberg, M. G. "Triple Helix: State, Class and Ethnicity in Africa." *The Dialectic of Oppression in Ziare.* Bloomington: Indiana University Press, 1988.

Shivji, Issa G. *Class Struggle in Tanzania.* London: Heinemann, 1978.

Sklar, Richard. "The Nature of Class Domination in Africa." *Journal of Modern African Studies.* 17.4 (1979): 531–52.

Soyinka, Wole. "The Fourth Stage." *Myth, Literature and the African World.* Cambridge: Cambridge University Press, 1976.

Stark, F. M. "Theories of Contemporary State Formation in Africa." *Journal of Modern African Studies.* 24.2 (1986): 335–50.

Welch, Claude, Jr. "The Ogoni and Self-Determination: Increasing Violence in Nigeria." *Journal of Modern African Studies.* 33.4 (1995): 635–50.

Williams, Raymond. *Modern Tragedy.* Stanford: Stanford University Press, 1966.

———. *Marxism and Literature.* Oxford: Blackwell, 1977.

Poetry

ELEGY FOR NINE WARRIORS
Tanure Ojaide

1

Those I remember in my song
will outlive this ghoulish season,
dawn will outlive the long night.
I hear voices stifled by the hangman,
an old cockroach in the groins of Aso Rock.
Those I remember with these notes
walk back erect from the stake.

The hangman has made his case,
delivered nine heads through the sunpost
and sored his eyes from sleepless nights.
The nine start their "life after death"
as the street carries their standard.

The forest of flowers mock
the thief, commander of roaches;
there are some heads like the hangman's
that will never have a vision of right.
What does a crow know of flowers?

When ghosts sit down the executioner,
let him plead for neither mercy nor pity;

the General will meet the Master Sergeant
and share the naked dance to the dark hole.

I hear voices of the dead assault
the head cultist daubed with blood —
he runs from demons of his high command.
The cockroach will not live through the sun
but those I remember in my song —
nine marchers who died carrying
our destiny on their broad chests —
will surely outlive the blood-laden season.

2

The sun's blinded by a hideous spectacle,
And the boat of the dead drifts mistward.
They will embrace the Keeper of *Urhoro* Gate
even as the soil that covered their bodies
despite guards rises into a transparent temple.
Birds that fly past click their beaks in deference,
the community of stars make space for the newborn;
they will always light the horizon with hope
& those in the wake will raise grieving songs
will look up to the promise of unfettered dawn,
hope against the rope of the barbarian chief.

3

The butcher of Abuja
dances with skulls,
Ogiso's grandchild by incest
digs his macabre steps
In the womb of Aso Rock.
To get to his castle,
you would stumble over skulls,
stumble over jawbones.
With his ordinance of guns,

a trail of mounds; bodies broken
to arrest the inevitable fall.
Flies buzz round him,
throned amidst flukes of courtiers.
Is the prisoner who presides
over cells and cemeteries
not slave of his own slaves?

4

In these days of mourning
some of my fellow singers laugh.
O Muse, reject their claim on you!

These children who laugh at their naked mother
incur the wrath of their creator-goddess.
They forfeit their kinship, these bastards.

Those whose tribal cackles break loose
as the house's torn with grief
draw on themselves the fate of vultures.

They even ride on the dead
with "Tragedy provokes laughter."
Laughter of the flock of vultures!

They smite the upright ones cut down
in full glare of the noon sun.
Earth and Sky dismayed by the apostasy.

From their corners, they laugh
before somber faces reeling from pain
& mourners can only spit at their noses.

In this suffocating gloom
I turn from my own grief
to weep for fellow singers without a heart.

Only a fool fails to reflect his lot
when an age-mate dies,
& I didn't know there were so many in the trade.

Let no accomplices in the murder
of the Muse's favourite son
think they can fool the divine one.

5

The sorcerer to my shame still lives
as I drown in tears over my brother
he sent away at noon from this world.
The cobra to my shame still lives
as I run from home looking for a big
and long enough stick to smash the demon,
or leave it to suffocate itself with bones.
The world sees the sorcerer's harangues
covering himself with a council of diviners
outnodding their heads in complicity.
He has brought down the eagle
and now plucks feathers off the totem bird!
Does he not know of forbidden acts
that he dismembers the nine eaglets?
He forgets he has left Ken's name behind
& the communal chant of the singerbird's name
rising along the dark waters of the Delta
will stir the karmic bonfire
that will consume his blind dominion.
Surely, that name will be the rod which
the cobra will meet its slaughter.
The sorcerer to my shame still lives,
but day will surely break over the long night.

6

We'll surely find a way in the dark
that covers and cuts us from those waiting

to raise the white-and-green flag to the sky.
The eagle nests in the nursery of advancing days.
We'll find a way to reach there
where the chorus rehearses a celebratory chant.
We'll make our way in the dark
but would have lost the fear in our hearts —
the dark will not close eyes
to knowledge of stars, dawn and sun;
nor can it smother the message
of good neighbours, lovers and another country.
No ambush will douse the high spirit
that drives us in the course.
We shall get there
through decades of dark years,
we know we'll have to cross
holes of ambush of hangmen
who do not commit their eyes
to sleep, love and things of beauty.
With the sort of luck we have had
with generals, vultures and presidents,
we'll find a way to reach there in the dark
without government roads and light
but with the rage of being held back
from what we could grasp, stretching ourselves
to the point of exhaustion or death.
None of the survivors will then be
ashamed of being afraid.

THE MAN WHO ASKED TALL QUESTIONS
(a song for Ken)
Niyi Osundare

To the accompaniment of music, part martial, part threnodic.
Heavy drums, occasional flute.

I

The hyena has murdered Thunder's son
An angry fire consumes the land…

A uniformed plague subdues the streets,
Crimson boots, a cartridge of curses;
Viper-belts caress their oily waists
Dreams die in their hands

They launch a thousand guns against the word
Dump innocent songs in voiceless dungeons
Then proclaim to a wondering world:
"As long as we hold the reins

   All commonsense shall be in exile"

And so their hangmen parade the land,
Broken justice between their grins
The nation's head squats on a crooked neck
To every hamlet its gallows

Creaking chains, medieval edicts,
Wounded dreams limp in sleepless terror
A wilderness of thorns erupts,
Seething serpents on every branch

The hyena has murdered Thunder's son
An angry fire consumes the land

II

These, still, are seasons of omens
These, still, are seasons of omens
A cockerel crows out its throat at noon,
Laying seven eggs and seven furies

A goggle-eyed viper hatches the eggs
Into serpent streets and crocodile lakes
The lake wears a robe of fire
The serpent gambols on stolen legs

These, still, are seasons of omens

The sun staggers into the centre
Of the midnight sky
Mountains amble into marketplaces
The sea trades its water for a bowl of blood

The echo is louder than the voice
The mongoose has stolen the monkey's tail
The echo is louder than the voice
Scepter-bearers have seized the crown

These, still, are seasons of omens

A seven-fingered hand reaches for
The throat of our dream
Corpses goose-step in green acres
The wind laughs at its own wound

These, still, are seasons of omens

III

But who are these reptiles from forgotten ages
With sickly scales and rudimentary howls
Flat on their bellies, dim between their ears
Wordless in their wickedness, blind in their greed...?

Alas, dark-eyed reptiles have seized the throne
Crocodile warlords trade swords with salamander monarchs
Our waters are red with grief
Mounted sadnesses gallop down our wound

And just last season
The Tortoise-General smiled, tooth-gapped,
Into the sanctuary of our weakness,
Corralled us all into his bag of tricks

And, one red noon, annulled our sacred dream
Then came the goggled goblin,
Squat-tongued, deaf in one ear,
His eyes behind his head, his toes behind his heels

A basher has truly come to judgment:
Gallows sprout in every street;
The skull-gatherer struts down the road,
Pursued by orphans and wailing widows

Who are these reptiles from forgotten ages?

IV

Crimson screams in Agonyland
Crimson screams in Agonyland
Where the Atlantic empties the Niger
Into gunboats and orphaning treaties

Crimson screams in Agonyland
The Delta fans out a hand of unequal fingers
Knuckles stiff with centuries of accumulated terror
Crimson screams in Agonyland

Fishes fry in the ocean's belly,
Cassava rots in injured earth,
An endless fire roasts the sky
Oily plagues leave a corpse in every home

Shell-shocked,
The Delta is battleground of rigs and rows
The goose which lays the golden egg
Lies sick and spent in viscous perversity

Crimson screams in Agonyland
The moon dabs its face with a tattered shawl
Crimson screams in Agonyland
Dawn's door creaks open to wayward winds...

V

And a short man was seen asking tall questions,
His pen longer than memory
His ink bluer than the sea
His songs stitched our tattered sails

He brewed a tempest in the tyrant's slumber;
Towncriering a tune so terrifically true
Surprising lucrative perfidies with a mirror
Which insists on naked candor

Oh this darkling plain
Dim again with incestuous slaughter!
When the General's hangmen came at last
They noosed a hurricane and a thousand furies

A murdered peace bleeds
A murdered peace bleeds in our frightened land
The mountain counts its tears
Rivers are red with rage

Martyred dreams dangle in our territory of terror
A medieval darkness descends from a martial sky
An urgent lightning holds the candle to this gloom:
Come Thunder: exact your wrath.

   The hyena has murdered Thunder's son
   An angry fire consumes the land

KEN SARO-WIWA
Tayo Olafioye

Your life ended
without completion
Compliment of the uniform
    their rush to judgement
    the boulevard of dubious self righteousness.

Tribal justice spoke
the carnival of gloating
The hot iron, melted
    avenge a pact war.
Some made hefty loot, foreign minders
of our ill health.
The festival of treachery
Congratulations, apogee of Evil.

To the arrogant oligarchy
Little matters any more
But echoes of Saro-Wiwa assail the world.
His spirit forever towards their sleeps
On the bed of ignominy.
He who swallows a pestle
will forever sleep standing up
Whoever eats an onion
will forever be smelly gaggle (gargle)

Nigeria at a loss
Whatever veneer of dignity
Now transparent lowliness
More than silver, we lose;
The cosmetics finally —
to the crudity
No place to hide
The dyke has been broken.
Easy to own a god;
hard to keep its rules —
Rule of the day: remnantly jungle.

REMEMBRANCE OF A CERTAIN DEATH IN NIGERIA
Jonathan Hart

Oil spills are like spilling blood:
Sometimes one leads to the other —
Birds die on beaches, and poets
Languish in prison. The mud

Slides and encrusts the hearts of men
With wives and children. The sun darkens
With the smoke; the stench of sulphur
Is hell. And with a deaf pen

They rig his death even as the others cry
From over the sea and beyond the desert.
There are shells on the beach that fossilize
This people and breach with a lie

The laws of nature. From fossil to fuel
They make him die, and with him some of us,
So we must sing across the land and to the sky
And, united, call out against those so dual.

FAREWELL, KEN SARO-WIWA!
Felix W.J. Mnthali

Some papers here tell us
you and your colleagues
went to your death singing!

Would that Africa as a whole
boasted more men and women with
your courage and your vision.

But we are all caught up in a web of fear
the fear that rules all killers
that web of silence which is the bane of all our
    feelings
the fear of our own shadows
the fear of lizards lurking behind freedom's rays
the fear of being thought weak
the fear of parting with loot and plunder
the fear of losing those peripheral powers
whose only guarantee is the barrel of a gun
cynically backed by the greed of those who have more
guns!

When fifteen years ago I spent a year in your country
I saw with my own eyes
how the fishes and other forms of life
were all slowly dying
in the sluggish brownish and filthy liquid
that had once been water; black gold it seems
demanded its pound of flesh
from everything and everyone around it!

It has now demanded that you too
like the rest of our continent's creme de la creme
pay with your life for this gold this madness;
that the Ogoni like the rest of us
since the days of slavery and brutish colonisation

have been paying with our lives
for treasures that others consume
while our own people go hungry and naked:
it was for reminding it of this simple story
that the sphinx has devoured you
for no sphinx on earth
wants its victims told
how naked and how foolish it looks!

In my own country the sphinx
devoured Dick Matenje and Aaron Gadama
Twaibu Sangala and David Chiwanga
Attati Mpakati and Mkwapatira Mhango
Orton Chirwa and many many others
whose bodies were dumped
into the waters of the Shire
or into the bellies of crocodiles;
many fled into exile which also became an area of
   darkness
when the tentacles of the sphinx would know no bounds
for the kingdoms of darkness
decay and death are all alike:
they thrive best in the midst of silence and despair
our silence and our despair!

If today's death be that of Ken Saro-Wiwa and eight
   others
who have been so brazenly and so blatantly
in the classical fashion of Nazism so openly executed
can the deaths of Moshood Abiola and General Obasanjo
and Ransome Kuti be far off?

Silence, why must heinous acts
be always followed by a deathly silence
oh, OAU,
oh, Africa?

AT KEN'S
Doris Hambuch

It has a man climb up its ear,
preoccupied both seem to be,
one raging, one unwillingly
emptied by those who mastered fear.

Its mouth is torn open as wide
as bones would hold on eagerly,
exposing insides meant to be
a hidden place for him to hide.

He knows not how to open eyes
to those who stare through ignorance.
The space is lost for tolerance
and maybe senses how he tries.

A VILLAGE OWNS THE VOICE OF THE COCK
(for Ken Saro-Wiwa)
Ezenwa-Ohaeto

One house owns a cock
But the village owns its voice.

I will think of your voice
As the question mark
On the question of life;

Some will remember you
As the full stop
To the sentence of disaster,
Or as the bone
In the bone of contention,
Or as the bitter sting
In the tail of the scorpion,
Or as the water
That has flown under the bridge.

But even if the fly
prowls around the smarting sore
You still hit out with care at it.

Many may remember you
But not has the storm
In a teacup of oil,
Not as the barking dog
With more bark than bite.

At death you have grown
beyond the prurience of life,
grown over the self interest
That propels human ego.

They threw death at you
And death set you on fire
But you burned into immortality.

One house owns a cock
A village owns its crowing voice.

I will think of your voice
As the crowing question mark
On the question of the land.

TOM-TOMS
for D.G., K.S.W. & W.S.
Jacqueline Onyejiaka

Who are we
whose voices cry in the night
in the wilderness;
in the papers;
at the bus stops and
in the belly of the children
tugging at the hem of pedestrians.
Like ancestral warriors from ages long ago,
We are those voices shouting
from the rooftops 'freedom now'
We are that flame lighting up
the conscience of yellow-bellied bullets
We are that bitter pill of truth
about ourselves we must face,
to save ourselves

FOR KEN SARO-WIWA
Kofi Mensah

Yet another victim
Of a puny man
Who aspires to equal God
by destroying His finest work
Yet another savage story
of African madness and European greed
From the eternal heart of darkness
For you were an obstruction,
a bottleneck
that had to be severed
So the multinational oil would gush forth
black as death
to further poison your native Ogoniland

Sacrificial victim
Whose blood cleanses your native earth!
Immolated lamb
Whose holy silence
awakens the conscience of an indifferent world!
Already your death quickens a dying nation;
And liberty resurrected
begins to irradiate a whole continent

from Port Harcourt,
your Golgotha

OGONI PEOPLE, THE OIL WELLS OF NIGERIA
Tayo Olafioye

You the trees
on which grows
the Niger gold
You the Ocean
in which flows Texas tea.

Tiny in number
mighty in strength
collossal in image.
Lost a hero
gains in fame
the world
your claim.
Cheated for eons
embraced for life
You the rocks
we your termites
You sons of David
we the gentiles
Without your gold
The Niger flow
a desert remains.
You the grass
We the elephants
What price to pay
your inheritance
to maintain
The world knows
they must avenge.

You the parable:
Goliath the lion
the rich little girl
the mighty heinous giant
Yours the heart of gold

theirs the stench of miens
Only death removes the bitterness
of a blinded people.

OGONI, THE EAGLE BIRDS' AGONY
IN THE DELTA WOODS
Abdul-Rasheed Na'Allah

The sonorous voice of the eagle birds
Overwhelms me like the cloud overwhelms the sky.
The razor cries of the birds in the Delta river,
cut into my skin and tear off its deafening membrane.
Oh, Ogoni, our ears are awakened to your voice,
Our bodies are sensitive to the breeze of the electrified air
That shocked you through the Shell of the death-carrying demon.

Ogoni, your agonies have sent waves across the seas.
They have opened the blinded eyes of the snoring world
To the green snakes breeding under the green grass of our Delta
    ridges.
Your agonies, Ogoni, make a Lazarus of the feet-dragging world,
To the huge fire, consuming a hundred million lives.

Noise.
Will Lazarus return to its grave, and abandon us
To the mercy of the shelling demons?

Eagle birds!
Whether or not Lazarus takes another drinking-prey
And go so early to its grave,
Celebrate,
Warriors in the midst of our coerced lands.
Celebrate, Ogoni!
Your blood, your cries, your wails
Have sank deep into our bodies:
Either we wash clean with the clean water,
Or we remain ridden with dirt for life!

III

Inside-Out

Not an Internal Affair
Niyi Osundare

"You hang people in Nigeria, don't you? Yes, you hang writers and burn their pens!" Those utterances were shot at me by a fellow African a week after Nigeria became chronically famous all over the world for her murder of Ken Saro-Wiwa and other Ogoni activists. "Tell me, what do your dictators do with human corpses: eat their flesh and throw the bones to the palace dogs? Do they read newspapers in your state house? Do they watch CNN? Do they listen to the BBC?" Yet another volley of questions.

But by far the most moving encounter was with a Zambian who held to my arm and asked with agonizing concern:

> Tell me, my brother, why is your country ... Nigeria doing this to us? Why have you brought all this shame on Africa? Look, they called me murderer at my place of work yesterday. They told me there is a new Idi Amin in Nigeria who feeds on human flesh. All of them, white folk so appalled by those terrible hangings in your country. Why has Nigeria done this to Africa?

His grip tightened on my arm, even as tears rolled down his middle-aged face.

Still on the same spot. Still wrapped in the same sanguinary ambiance, a South African with an honest and extremely intense countenance added in almost apocalyptic terms:

> What has come upon Nigeria? Tell me, what? First a fouled up election, now these murders. What gods has Nigeria offended? See,

when Nigeria spoke in the 1970s and 1980s, the world listened. The rest of Africa lined up behind her. Speak for us, they said. See, I am a South African. I know what I am talking about. I have the memory of Sharpeville. I nearly perished in Soweto. I know tyranny when I see it. You see, Nigeria was part of the South African struggle for freedom. Spatial distance notwithstanding, she was regarded as a frontline state. Nigeria took part in the liberation of my country. A very big shame, Nigeria now needs to be liberated from its own black Boers!

The foregoing encounters took place in Britain on my way to a reading engagement. The African brothers who spoke so engagingly had seized the opportunity of my presence to vent their disgust at the foul murders in Nigeria, and even more important, to demonstrate their disappointment at the pitiful plight of a country which everyone sees as the giant of Africa, but whose visionless rulers have reduced to a whimpering dwarf. A country which reminds you of that ill-fated fellow in the tale, whose food is decorated and placed on a royal table, but who ignores the honorable treat and dashes instead for miserable crumbs on their way to the dog. Nigeria, thanks to her dictators and their time-servers, still remains that 'big for nothing' country that Major Chukwuma Nzeogu talked about in that most inaugural of all coup broadcasts.

My encounter with those African brothers brought achingly to mind the yawning gulf between what Nigeria is and what she is capable of being. Or more poignantly, the way others see Nigeria and the way Nigeria is seen by her rulers. For the import of those African brothers' concern is that Nigeria's problem is Africa's problem (and vice versa?); that the evil brush used by Nigerian rulers for tarnishing her image rages up and down the African canvas. In other words, Nigeria is too big, too vociferous a country to remain the Stone Age spot in a world committed to progress. It is now a truism acknowledged and honoured by all civilized nations that judicial murder and allied barbarism can no longer pass as the 'internal affairs' of any country.

The sanctity of human life, the right to basic human freedoms including that to fair trial and civilised judicial processes, have over the years established themselves as inalienable properties of humanity, far beyond the caprices of local despots and their bloody pirates. With old walls falling and icy ideologies thawing and re-arranging, re-formulating into new fluidities and new exigencies, the parameters of humanism are breaking boundaries and tearing through frigid frontiers.

The old, hallowed idea of the nation-state is also undergoing rig-orous interrogation. The welfare of the human being is progres-sively becoming more important than the artificial integrity of a country; the human being is ineffable, sacred, irreplaceable, the na-tion is a political construct perpetually negotiable and subject to constant re-definition. Strictly speaking, it is human beings who make up nations and not vice versa. In other words, it is possible for human beings to exist, even prosper, without a nation, whereas the reverse can never be the case. Which is why intelligent leaders, as distinct from cannibalistic rulers, realise that to build a nation you must first build the person.

For a nation is held together not only by the aggregate of its human and natural resources, but also by a qualitative and progres-sive harnessing of those resources. A genuine nation must therefore have an ethical and philosophical centre which serves as anchor for those moral and material values which glue the crevices and sustain it. At a supra-segmental level, every nation is a nation in its own right by the extent to which it is in touch and in healthy coopera-tion with other nations. The wheel of that cooperation is by shared values and common practices. These are facts made abundantly clear in the information age.

Except by the perverse logic of some antediluvian hell-hole, where state cannibalism is a hallowed practice, there is no way the barbarous hanging of Ken Saro-Wiwa and others can be passed off as the 'internal affair' of any country. How could judicial murder so hastily arranged and so savagely carried out have failed to arouse the disgust and indignation of other nations whose own humanity is so shamelessly desecrated by Nigeria's barbarism? By defending such savagery, our current rulers, the real authors of our national shame, have demonstrated not only the degree of their insensi-tivity but also their alarming ignorance of international politics and the decency which should underpin its processes. I can not resist the question: on whose behalf were those hangings effected? When our rulers say it is Nigeria's 'internal affair', whose Nigeria do they have in mind? Which Nigeria? The gruesome fact is that today Nigerians carry the albatross of an action executed on their behalf by people who rule them without consent. The sanctions and humiliations consequent upon our new pariah status are surely more than the 'internal affair' of a sane and decent country.

Oil Resources, Hegemonic Politics and the Struggle for Re-inventing Post-colonial Nigeria
Wumi Raji

> I am recreating the Ogoni people, first and foremost, to come to the realisation of what they have always been which British colonisation tried to take away from them. So my effort is very intellectual. It is backed by theories, thoughts and ideas which will, in fact, matter to the rest of Africa in the course of time.
>
> (Ken Saro-Wiwa, *The News*, 17 May 1993)

The citation above put in perspective the different dimensions of the protests inspired and led by the former president of the Association of Nigerian Authors (ANA). Indeed, of the different forms of agitations against neglect and environmental degradation put forward, to date, by the different communities of the oil-producing areas, that of the Ogonis remains the most rigorously planned, the most well-articulated and the most sustained.

Since its discovery in commercial quantities in the country in 1956, oil has steadily displaced agriculture as the nation's prime source of foreign exchange earnings. When Shell D'Arcy, the Anglo-Dutch Petroleum Corporation which later transformed to Shell Petroleum Development Company shipped out the first 5,000 barrels in 1958, the price of the mineral resources was only $4.00 US dollars per barrel. By 1981 when almost 15 oil companies jointly produced over 2 million barrels daily from the innumerable oil wells strewn all over the Niger Delta, the price per barrel had risen to 40 dollars. Today, though the production had fallen by about 40 percent and the price to just about $16.00 US dollars, oil accounts for over 95 percent of the nation's yearly expenditure.

Paradoxically, the same resources representing the power-house of national life also serves as a big agency of dislocation and disorientation for the several million people inhabiting the areas where it is produced. Directly, the dislocation and disorientation derive from two complementary and inter-related factors: the first being the devastating impact of the exploration of the resources on the environment, and the second that of the cruel neglect of the people of the area by successive Nigerian administrations.

Claude Ake, the late respected Director of the Centre for Advanced Social Sciences, analysed the first factor in highly scientific and technical terms in his article, "Shelling Nigeria Ablaze," published in the *Tell* magazine edition of January 29, 1996. According to him, Nigeria flares at least 76 percent of the total natural gas derived from petroleum production. At temperatures, in his own words, "of 1,300 to 1,400 degree centigrade, the multitude of flares in the Delta heat up everything causing noise pollution and producing SO_2, VOc, carbon dioxide and NOx and particulates around the clock." Arguing further, Claude Ake contends that with 35 million tons of carbon dioxide and 12 million tons of methane released a year from the flaring "Nigerian oil fields contribute more in global warming than the rest of the world together" (1996: 40). On oil spills, the Nigerian National Merit Award winner reveals that the States of Rivers and Delta as the principal oil producing areas in Nigeria experience about "300 major oil spills a year ... which discharge about 2,300 m³ of oil." As Ake insists, the above analysis fails to take into reckoning the "minor spills which are far more numerous and (which are) invariably under-reported." Ake writes further on effluents, the treatment of which no single oil company in Nigeria has bothered to take interest in:

> According to an European Community study, *Mangroves of Africa and Madagascar*, the waters of the Niger Delta contain at least 8

[parts per million] of petroleum and often up to 60 [parts per million]. An environmental impact study of Shell (*Designer Industries,* 1993) put an average hydrocarbon content of petroleum hydrocarbons in waste water in Oloma creek at 62.7 mg/l. At the Bonny Terminal in Rivers State where Shell does its separation of water from crude oil, the mud at the bottom of the Bonny River has a lethal concentration of 12,000 pm. But Shell lies that the wastewater at Bonny Terminal averages 7.8 mg/l. As the World Bank Report quoted above has noted, the industry is using API separator and TPF basin facilities which are unsuitable for separation of better than 50 mg/l performance. (1996: 40)

To understand the practical import of the above analysis we turn first to a *Newswatch* report of 1985. The report paints a graphic picture of the terrible hazards suffered by the people of Iko, a small community in Ikot Abasi local government area of Cross River State from which Shell has explored oil since 1973. According to *Newswatch*, the white, salty vapour fired into the air in the process of separating gas from oil causes corrosion and perforation on the roofs of the buildings of the villagers. The same vapour, when it settles on the skin turns it into a "charred surface in the form of an unsightly skin disease." An 18 year old boy who fell victim of this disease could not be properly treated because Iko has no single health centre or clinic. In addition, there is also the effect of consistent explosions which cause many of the buildings to shake and the walls to crack. Because of this, many of the villagers have had to abandon their houses, migrating to other villages in search of refuge.

As the same *Newswatch* report shows, the combined effects of oil spills, chemical spills and gas flaring have devastated the lands and polluted the rivers of Mgbede/Ebocha/Omiku of, this time, Ahoada local government area of Rivers State. Indeed, as a result of this pollution, several schools of fish have had to flee and this has made fishing, the traditional occupation of the people, to become sheer indulgence. And the same goes for farming. In fact, a completely burnt down area of about 1.5 km circumference serves to demonstrate the untold disaster that certain chemicals can wreck on plants.

The story is not in any way different in Ogoniland which is located in the north-eastern part of the Delta region. "Ogoni has suffered and continues to suffer the degrading effects of oil exploration and exploitation," says G.B. Leton, founding president of the Movement for the Survival of the Ogoni People (MOSOP). In the statement published as an introduction to *Ogoni Bill Of Rights* issued in 1992, Leton successfully confronts the world with the hazardous consequences of environmental despoilation and contamination. He writes:

> lands, streams and creeks are totally and continually polluted; the atmosphere is forever charged with hydrocarbons, carbon monoxide and carbon dioxide; many villages experience the infernal quaking of the wrath of gas flares which have been burning 24 hours a day for 33 years; acid rain, oil spillages and blow-outs are common. The results of such unchecked environmental pollution and degradation are that: (i) the Ogoni can no longer farm successfully. Once the food basket of the eastern Niger delta, the Ogoni now buy food (when they can afford it) (ii) Fish, once a common source of protein, is now rare. Owing to the constant and continual pollution of our streams and creeks, fish can only be caught in deeper and offshore waters for which the Ogoni are not equipped (iii) All wildlife is dead (iv) The ecology is changing fast. The mangrove tree, the aerial roots of which (*sic*) normally provide a natural and welcome habitat for many a sea food—crabs, periwinkles, mud skippers, cockles, mussels, shrimps and all—is now being gradually replaced by unknown and otherwise useless palms. (v) The health hazards generated by an atmosphere charged with hydrocarbon vapour, carbon monoxide and carbon dioxide are innumerable. (pp. 6–7)

Let us, at this point, return quickly to our earlier argument that the two causative factors of dislocation and disorientation suffered by the people of oil-producing areas are closely inter-connected. Certainly, there is no other way to capture a situation where successive administrations remain unmoved even as these people experience incalculable damages resulting from environmental degradation and abuse if not as criminal neglect. Anyhow, there is a basic sense of the word which refers to circumstances of absolute absence of infrastructural facilities like roads, water, light, health care system and schools. And, as incredible as these may seem, this is the situation with most oil communities in Nigeria.

We take inspiration from Dr. Dappa Biriye, Niger Delta's sole delegate to the constitutional debates in London during the pre-independence era. Biriye suggested in a December 1990 interview with *African Concord* that to fully comprehend the present state of deprivation of oil communities in Nigeria, we adopt Oloibiri, their forerunner as a pattern. The white oil explorers who arrived at Oloibiri in 1956 brought along with them their 'pre-fabricated houses' which served for temporary accommodation while *Shell Oloibiri*, their new quarters were being constructed. On completion, the new city immediately took over as the commercial nerve-centre. Natives also trooped there to take up employment as gardeners, cooks, messengers, cleaners and house-helps. Beside this labour exploitation, Shell staff made sure that there was no other form of contact with the natives. Whatever was needed, but which could not be acquired from the new market, was ferried in from Port Harcourt. The result today is that after oil resources worth several billions of dollars had been exploited from the bowels of Oloibiri, the town now stands in 'limbo'. It has no roads, no electricity, no drinking water, no telephone facilities, no postal agency and no good school or any well-equipped health centre. *African Concord* quotes M.O. Egba, a member of the community's Council of Chiefs as saying that the story of Oloibiri could be likened to that "of a crawling snail picked up by a hunter who (simply) took out the meat inside, and threw the shell carelessly away" (Abimboye 1990: 29).

Oloibiri certainly provides the pattern. Because the story is the same in many other places: in Umuechem, in Oboburu, and in Ogoni — all of Rivers State; in Qua Iboe, Akwa Ibom State; in Obokofia and Obiakpo, Imo State; in Obagi, Akabuka, Oboru, Idu, Erema and Ogborodu, Delta State; and in a hundred other communities of the Niger delta where several barrels of oil are exploited daily.

The same story of stagnation and bare-faced injustice persists everywhere. To cite just one more example, Escravos is an offshore community located in Delta State. For the indigenous people of this area, time has stood still for several decades. The village is completely inaccessible by road. There is drinking water, but no medical facility and no reliable power supply system. Yet, to the other side of this community live 200 staff members of Gulf Oil company. Writes *Newswatch*, December 23, 1985 edition of this residential quarter:

> The housing estate, otherwise called a tank farm, is a Hollywood kind of layout. Well-nurtured lawns, beautiful streets, uninterrupted electricity and ever-flowing pipe-borne water are what the oilmen enjoy. Recreational facilities like lawn tennis courts, bowling alleys, snooker and tennis tables are in abundance. There is a cinema hall that opens at 8 pm every day for the 200 workers that live on the farm. (Indeed), for them life is full of roses after a hard day's job on the oil rigs. (p.17)

It is not as if the people of the different indigenous communities have always remained passive in the face of acute contradictions and oppressive control. In fact, the words of Saro-Wiwa presented as an epigram at the beginning of this essay are located in the context of the minority rights activist's attempt at delineating the point of departure between the struggles of his own people and the one of the mid-1960s prosecuted by Isaac Adaka Boro, arguably the forerunner in the agitations against neglect and environmental despoilation in the Niger delta.

Boro, standing at the head of an ill-equipped but highly determined group of soldiers, had, precisely in 1966, declared the republic of Niger Delta in what G.G. Durah would later describe in *The Guardian on Sunday* of November 19, 1995 as a "12-day revolution." Determined "to demonstrate to the world what and how we feel about oppression" (quoted in *Guardian*, B3), Boro's army had overrun the Ijaw territory, receiving great accolades and ovations from the people of the area. Eventually overpowered by the federal troops, Boro was convicted for treason and consequently condemned to death. He was however a little lucky in the sense that he escaped the hangman's noose via a state pardon he received in August 1966. He was to die a few months later fighting on the federal side during the Nigerian civil war. To Saro-Wiwa, Boro's effort was no more than "a quixotic experiment which bemused his people" (*The News*, 23).

After Boro, oil installation blockades became the major mode of articulated resistance against dislocation. Shell, the leading oil company in Nigeria, experienced at least 22 of such blockades within the first eight months of that particular year (*Newswatch*, October 15, 1990). Also citing from a paper presented by Bola Adewale, a law lecturer at the Institute of Advanced Legal Studies, University of Lagos during a seminar organised for top officers of oil companies, *Newswatch* reveals that 344 of such blockades were officially recorded between 1976 and 1988 and that in over 200 of such cases, real damages were done to the flow-pipes. A typical example of such blockades was prosecuted by the people of Kolo creeks, Brass local government area of Rivers State in July, 1990. Directly, the people of Imiringi, Elebele and Otuesega, three of the communities in the area had invaded the oil installations, took over the control room and locked up the staff on duty. They also took over the helli-pad and successfully prevented Shell's intervention team from landing. Eventually, the company had to seek help from the police and the army but the villagers held on, threatening "to blow-up the installations if any of them sustained any injuries from the police" (*Newswatch*, 33). After a week of the face-off, an agreement was reached which committed Shell to some construction projects in the area.

Palliative measures that hardly scratch the surface, but that agreement is a typical programme of oil-producing companies in their terrains of operations. A few scholarships to some secondary school or university students, provision of drinking water via bore-holes or taps, electricity supply projects, donations to community schools, road construction, reconstruction or rehabilitation, agricultural and fishing projects are representative of some of the community development programmes of oil companies as they struggle to contain the inevitable tensions presented in different areas of the Delta region. The projects are scattered and staggered all over the oil-producing communities and, therefore, are hardly of any impact. Even then, this is when the indigenes are lucky. At other times, the affected company simply drafts in the police once they are faced with any protests. And when such happens, the consequence is often tragic for the indigenous people.

Such is the fate of the people of Umuechem, a small oil town locked north west of Port Harcourt. It was on October 31, 1990 when the people of the community assembled in the town square to peacefully protest against their continual dislocation. Unknown to the villagers, Shell officials, afraid of the possible damages the people might do to their facilities had simply sent for the police as soon as they had sensed trouble. The mobile team arrived to open fire on the unsuspecting people who instinctively decided to fight back. The ensuing clash led to the beheading of a policeman who himself had shot dead one of the villagers. The police consequently withdrew to re-mobilise. The ultimate confrontation led to the death of over 85 people including the traditional chief of the town and two of his grown up sons. In addition, the police set ablaze not only the houses in the town but also its two churches, the only community primary school and the health centre. *African Concord*, December 3, 1990 reports as follows:

> The team forcefully occupied Umuechem for six days; 1 to 6 November. During the week-long siege, the policemen fed on goats, chickens, sheep and pigs. They made a home of the beer parlour in the community, while economic trees such as coconut, and citrus were cut down for food. "It was a revolt against a quiet community, a war in its entirety" commented an eye-witness. (p. 25)

It was against this background that the Ogoni embarked on their own struggles in early 1990. The first thing they did was to draft the Bill of Rights which articulated in intellectual terms the basis of the struggle. Signed by the representatives of the Six Ogoni Kingdoms on 26th August, 1990 and based on Awolowo's proposal in *Thoughts on Nigerian Constitution* that all ethnic groups, no matter the size, be accorded equal treatment in a federation, the *Ogoni Bill of Rights* has far-reaching implications for the Nigerian constitution. The bill demands ethnic autonomy and self-determination for the people of Ogoniland. By ethnic autonomy is meant, and in the words of Ken Saro-Wiwa in a foreword to the bill, "political control of Ogoni affairs by Ogoni people, control and use of Ogoni economic resources for Ogoni development, adequate and direct representation as of right for Ogoni people in all Nigerian national institutions and the right to protect the Ogoni environment and ecology from further degradation" (1992: 2). An added dimension of the declaration was a demand for 20 billion U.S. dollars quoted as royalties and rents "for petroleum mined from our soil for over 33 years" (1992: 13).

The document was officially addressed to General Ibrahim Babangida, then the country's military President, and members of his Armed Forces Ruling Council (AFRC) on October 2, 1990. Having waited for one year without any response whatsoever from the government, an addendum mandates the Movement for the Survival of the Ogoni People (MOSOP) to make representations to relevant international bodies with a view to getting them to prevail on the Nigerian government to respond to the Ogoni demands. This began an intense campaign which took Saro-Wiwa before such international organisations as the Ethnic Minority Rights Organisation of Africa (EMIROAF), the Unrepresented Nations and People's Organisation and the United Nation's Sub-Commission of Human Rights on the Prevention of Discrimination (against), and Protection of the Minorities. Partly to complement the above efforts and partly to keep up the level of awareness, a variety of activities were organised in the home-front. These included rallies, mass protests and demonstrations, award ceremonies, commemorations of important dates, vigils, blockades and media campaigns. So successful were these activities that for the Nigerian neo-fascist regime to have looked on would have meant for it to have sanctioned its own perils. This, exactly is the meaning of Ogoni tragedy.

If we insist that the struggle of the Ogoni people represents the most well-articulated and the best prosecuted of all of the efforts articulated against hegemonic exploitation in the Niger Delta, it is not because of a wholesale approval of the method of, and the vision propelling, the agitations. Saro-Wiwa, arguing that after over thirty years of absolute control of power, the leadership of the majority ethnic groups in Nigeria has shown itself to be inept, corrupt and incompetent proposes a fundamental transformation of the Nigerian structure, which transformation will invest in each ethnic group the control of both as political and economic resources. "I am rallying for ethnic autonomy, resolve and environmental control" says he in *Tell*, February 8, 1993. "The only law to be in Nigeria is: You are free to rule yourself, you're independent now, but you must pay your bills, you will control your resources, you control your environmental, run whatever government you like" (p. 32).

Clearly, Saro-Wiwa's perspective is fraught with profound pitfalls.

For one, it is possible for the leadership of any of the resulting nationalities to be hijacked by opportunists and self-seeking people who, inevitably, will go ahead to foist their own form of hegemonic control on the people and eventually continue the oppression. Saro-Wiwa also perceives the Hausa-Fulani as that ethnic group which dominates the nation's political landscape and which exploits her resources. This, to some extent, may be true, especially if one considers the influential position of the caliphate and the fact that of a total of nearly 37 years of the country's independence, the group alone has produced six out of the country's 10 heads of state and these together have ruled for a total of 24 years (5 ½ years of Tafawa Balewa, 6 months of Murtala Muhammad, 4 years of Shagari and 14 of Buhari-Babangida-Abacha interregnum). However, it is also the case that the common Hausa-Fulani comprehensively in terms of his material condition and available opportunities stands, arguably, among the most hopeless in contemporary Nigeria. The point here, simply, is that this man, the common Hausa-Fulani man that is, may as much be a victim of hegemonic conspiracy as is the Ogoni man.

Lest we be misunderstood, let it be stated categorically that the Nigerian problem has a nationality dimension. Jibril Aminu, as oil minister in 1990 contends that the Niger Delta remains undeveloped because of the "very harsh" terrain. "Transportation is difficult," he says, "because the creeks are difficult" (see Akinrinade 1990: 35). This is after 32 years of oil exploration. Well, we may need to ask Aminu whether the areas, in any way, are more difficult than Lagos. The former capital city of Nigeria, in spite of its many creeks, its marshes and swamps and even the lagoon and the Atlantic Ocean can, guardedly, be described as having a fine network of roads.

But the argument does not stop here. Because, while successive governments in the same Lagos expend several billions of naira to contain ocean surge in Victoria Island on a yearly basis, the slums of Ajegunle and the ghettoes of Mushin remain neglected. If, indeed, the Niger Delta terrain is so difficult, how come Gulf Oil is able to erect a tank farm in Escravos? A comprehensive analysis of Nigerian problem will have to take into consideration the nature of the relations of production and the system of distribution. It will also have to contend with the strong alliance existing between the ruling class (military as well as civilian) and the several multinational corporations. It is this alliance which in the specific case of oil producing areas, makes it possible for the oil companies to simply call on the police (and the army in some instances) as soon as they perceive any security problem. Claude Ake (1996: 40), in the same article of his referred to earlier in this paper has raised an alarm over what he describes as "the privatisation of the state" by Shell. By privatisation of the state, Ake refers to the presence of armed troops and policemen in the residential quarters as well as the offices and operational bases of the company. He writes further:

It is indicative of Shell's privatisation of the state and its prerogatives that it buys substantial quantities of firearms through open tender for its own use. *This Day* of Friday, December 22, 1995, reports a case before a Lagos High Court in which an arms dealer, Humanities Nigeria Limited, sued Shell Nigeria for 30 million [Naira] for a breach of contract which Shell awarded in 1993. In a 17-paragraph affidavit sworn by the chief executive of the company, Gabriel Akinluyi, the company says that Shell was making the purchase to update the firearms of its security across the country. (1996: 40)

Ake calls for an inquiry into the purchase and use of firearms by Shell but I think he misses the point. The way that Shell has carried on so far, including its vehement rejection of any blame in the Ogoni tragedy can only be indicative of one thing: that it enjoys the full cooperation of the state. The only thing to do for now is to take solace in the words of Ken Saro-Wiwa. "There is no doubt in my mind," he says in 'Before I am Hanged', the statement he presented before the Justice Ibrahim Auta panel on 31st October 1995, "that the ecological war the company has waged in the Delta will be called to question sooner than later" (*ANA Review*, 22). We all stand at the door-post of history.

REFERENCES
Abimboye, Demola. "Massacre at Dawn" in *African Concord*. 3rd December 1990: 23–31.

Ake, Claude. "Shelling Nigeria Ablaze" in *Tell*. 29 January 1996. 40.

Akinrinade, Soji. "Killing the Geese" in *Newswatch*. 15 October 1990: 32–6.

Akinrinade, Soji. "Paradox of Oil Areas" in *Newswatch*. 23 December 1985.

Darah, G.G. "Dying for the Niger Delta" in *The Guardian on Sunday*. 19 November 1995: B1–3.

Ogoni Bill of Rights. Port Harcourt: Saros International Publishers. 1992.

Omonubi, Rolake. "Oil, Oil, Where Is Naira" in *Newswatch*. 5 December 1987: 55–6.

Saro-Wiwa, Ken. "Before I Am Hanged" in *ANA Review*. November 1995: 23.

———. "They Are Killing My People". Interview. *The News*. 17 May 1993: 22–7.

———. "We Will Defend Our Oil With Our Blood". Interview. *Tell*. 8 February 1993: 28–33.

Death and the King's Henchmen: Ken Saro-Wiwa and the Political Ecology of Citizenship in Nigeria

For Ken Saro-Wiwa, 1941–1995.

In memoriam.

Andrew Apter

O n November 10, 1995, Nigeria's military strongman General Sani Abacha shocked the world by ordering the hanging of Ken Saro-Wiwa and eight fellow Ogoni activists on trumped up charges of inciting violence and murder. The trial was a sham, taking place in a military tribunal that played by its own rules, denying the defendants legal counsel, visits from family members, and after the fact, any kind of public burial. The corpses were purportedly disfigured with acid, literally defaced to prevent their resurrection into martyrdom as fearless critics of the venal military regime. The United Nations condemned the act, countless ambassadors were called home, Nigeria was suspended from the Association of Commonwealth Nations, the United States denied visas to Nigerian military officers, but the only truly effective response — a U.S. led embargo against Nigeria oil — was never pursued. Oil, Nigeria's black gold turned toxic waste, against which Ken Saro-Wiwa struggled in defense of his land and his people, won the day. After the harsh talk and half-measures taken against Abacha's disreputable regime, the ambassadors trickled back to Lagos and Royal Dutch Shell brazenly signed on to a $4 billion natural gas liquification project.

Saro-Wiwa's fight against Shell was largely environmental, highlighting the ecological devastation of riverine ecosystems in the Niger Delta area, where Nigeria's oil is pumped from the ground. In the global media, the struggle came to represent the rapacious appetite of oil-capitalism and the ruthless abandon of military dictatorship, as oil spills, burnoffs and blowouts destroyed the creeks and farms of the Ogoni people with no compensation provided in return. From the outside, Saro-Wiwa's death was a heroic tragedy of one man against a Leviathan, a hybrid beast of corporate profiteering and military domination violating human rights and destroying nature. Within Nigeria, however, Saro-Wiwa's struggle was tied to ethnic politics, championing the cause of the Ogoni minority against the Hausa-Fulani, Yoruba, and Ibo power blocs which stole from the state and gave only to their own. If Ken Saro-Wiwa was a respected writer, producer and critic in Nigeria, many saw him as a troublesome gadfly who resented his people's lack of patronage opportunities. In the vast Nigerian nation of nearly 100 million people, few really cared about the Ogoni, who, in the popular press, were sometimes likened to pygmies of a lower evolutionary order. What most outsiders forget, or never realized, is that although Saro-Wiwa's demand for oil revenues and reparations began in the 1960s and gained momentum during the oil boom of the seventies and early eighties, his cry was hardly heard. The majority of Nigerians did not really care about the relatively isolated, tiny 'tribe' of a mere half million people who were considered scarcely human, happy to be fishing their mangrove creeks and planting their gardens, cut off from the modern world. Given this general contempt for the Ogoni, why did Ken Saro-Wiwa's struggle erupt into a Nigerian *cause celebre*?

To answer this question, we will examine how the plight of the Ogoni people came to represent the contradictions of oil-capitalism in Nigeria at large. We will see how the pollution of natural ecosystems and environments provided the language for opposing historically specific forms of economic alienation and political dispossession throughout the nation, as rentier-capitalism and prebendal politics privatized the state and undermined the public sphere. Only then can we appreciate how Ken Saro-Wiwa's demand for Ogoni autonomy escalated into a struggle for universal citizenship in Nigeria, and why, as the world waited to see what would happen, he was hanged.

THE STATE OF NATURE

Of the many novels, poems, short stories, plays, critical studies and essays that Ken Saro-Wiwa published in his life-time, his last two books, *Genocide in Nigeria: The Ogoni Tragedy* (1992) and *A Month and a Day: A Detention Diary* (published posthumously in 1995), chronicle his cause most fully. Reviewing this struggle as he presented it serves two initial purposes: first, it illustrates the main actors and events in the history of Ogoni persecution, leading to the founding of the Movement for the Survival of the Ogoni People (MOSOP); and second, it illuminates the 'organic' idiom in which this struggle was framed, and which developed into a *political ecology* of citizenship for all Nigerians.

The main actors in the Ogoni Tragedy are the multinational Shell Petroleum Development Corporation with its British and Dutch subsidiaries; the Ethnic Majority, referring directly to the Hausa-Fulani in the north who have dominated Nigerian politics since the days of the British Protectorate, but also relativised into the Yoruba and Ibo, who reign as majorities over the Ogoni and other ethnic minorities; the Military Dictatorship, which — through seven different regimes that assumed power through coups — has ruled by decree and plundered the country in all but nine of Nigeria's thirty-five years of independence; the Ogoni, the paradigmatic ethnic minority who live on the oil-fields, and whose society and habitat have been destroyed by pollution; and finally, the American, European and Japanese markets for Nigerian oil, those impersonal consumers who drive the global oil economy but remain largely in the background. If I recount the Ogoni tragedy as a drama or morality play, it is to highlight some of its mythic themes and to prefigure those allegorical dimensions linking Ogoniland to the Nigerian nation. For Saro-Wiwa, however, *Genocide in Nigeria* is a work of empirical documentation.

The book opens with an account of precolonial Ogoniland as an Edenic paradise or primitive commune, where production was for use, and where social, economic, ecological and religious orders were integrated into 'natural' rhythms and routines:

> To the Ogoni, the land on which they lived and the rivers which surrounded them were very important. They not only provided sustenance in abundance, they were also a spiritual inheritance. The land is a god and is worshipped as such. The fruit of the land, particularly yams, are honoured in festivals and, indeed, the Annual Festival of the Ogoni is held at the yam harvest. The planting season is not a mere period of agricultural activity: it is a spiritual, religious and social occasion. 'Tradition' in Ogoni means in the local tongue (*doonu kuneke*) the honoring of the land (earth, soil, water).... To the Ogoni, rivers and streams do not only provide water for life — for bathing, drinking, etc.; they do not only provide fish for food, they are also sacred and are bound up intricately with the life of the community, of the entire Ogoni nation. (Saro-Wiwa 1992: 12–13)

In political terms, this foundational account of an "original affluent society" (Sahlins 1972: 1–39) serves as a charter for Ogoni ownership of the land, a resource framed as a cultural and spiritual heritage which was later spoiled by oil and stolen by the state. According to the correspondences established in this vision, the devastation of land and water is tantamount to the destruction of tradition itself, one which sustained a harmonious balance between a natural ecology, economy and community. The predations of the military-petroleum complex upon this pristine 'state' of nature — organized into six ancient kingdoms of Babbe, Eleme, Gokana, Nyo-Khana, Ken-Khana and Tai (what anthropologists would call clans) — are thereby framed as crimes against culture and humanity, violating the sacred foundation of human community. Hence Saro-Wiwa's use of the term 'genocide' to describe the destruction of Ogoniland, although military 'scorch and burn' campaigns against Ogoni protestors would follow.

As we shall see, the mythic model of Ogoniland served a specific agenda which Saro-Wiwa pursued with total conviction. Although he demanded reparations from Shell and the Nigerian government for the ravages of oil pollution, he also sought a much greater share of reallocated revenues for the Ogoni people, arguing that the oil from their land belonged to them. Small wonder that most Nigerians were uninvolved with this cause. Saro-Wiwa was pleading special circumstances for his people, with that persecution complex that came to be associated with Ogoni 'cannibal rage' and ethnic chauvinism. For Saro-Wiwa, trouble was always associated with outside intervention. In 1914, the British subjugated the Ogoni by force, denying their autonomy by incorporating them into Opobo Division within Calabar Province, thereby subjecting them to a remote administrative center that demanded taxes and ruled through courts. Saro-Wiwa recounts with pride how the Ogoni participated in the 1929 Women's Tax Riots, otherwise known as the Igbo Women's War, in which several Ogoni women were killed. Their deaths attest to the Ogoni tradition of mobilization and resistance against external domination. Under the British, it was not until 1947 that the Ogoni Native Authority was established, framing Ogoni ethnic identity in the administrative terms of indirect rule, and securing representation in the Eastern House of Assembly in 1952. Politically, however, the Ogoni were overwhelmed, swallowed by the dominating Ibo interests of the Eastern Region, to which they were unwillingly consigned by the 1951 Constitution. In an attempt to join with other delta minorities to found an autonomous Rivers State, the Ogoni broke from Azikiwe's NCNC party and voted for Awolowo's Yoruba Action Group Party. Zik's party won, and the Igbos took reprisals against the Ogoni, denying them scholarships and social amenities (Saro-Wiwa 1992: 23) and splitting the Ogoni Native Authority into three local government units. In a move echoing the divide and conquer tactics of the British, the Ogoni were thus subjected to a form of internal colonialism by the Ibo majority of the Eastern Region, who were to prove even more brutal as overlords during the dark days of the Biafran War.

The federal structure of the Nigerian state in the early years of independence was fragile at best, comprised of three semi-autonomous regions competing with each other for power at the center. The three dominant parties of the First Republic had in fact developed largely from cultural organizations and platforms that capitalized on ethnic affiliation — such as the Yoruba Omo Egbe Oduduwa, the Ibo State Union, and the Hausa Jamahiyyar Mutanen Arewa in the north — consolidating regional identities in terms of ethnicity and political party, and through regional market-ing boards.[1] The balance broke down with the first coup after inde-pendence, led by General Ironsi in 1966, in which as Saro-Wiwa (1992: 26) reminds us, "the Federal Prime Minister, Sir Abubakar Tafewa Balewa was killed along with two other Regional Premiers of the Yoruba and Hausa-Fulani ethnic majorities." Ironsi's regime attempted to replace Nigeria's weak federalism with a stronger unitary state, but the effort was cut short. The Hausa-Fulani retaliat-ed in the north, massacring thousands of Igbos, killing General Ironsi in Gowon's counter-coup, and unleashing the tide of vio-lence that swept into the Western Region, where Igbos had to close down their shops, leave their government jobs, and flee for their lives. Ken Saro-Wiwa's *On A Darkling Plain: An Account of the Nigerian Civil War* (1989) reveals another side of the bloody struggle for secession led by Col. Ojukwu and his aspiring Biafran nation. The Ibo's valiant struggle for Biafra, and their remarkable military and technological ingenuity has earned them the respect even of their critics. Less appreciated and understood, however, was their treatment of the Ogoni and other delta minorities who were cor-ralled into Biafra against their will. When federal troops swept through Ogoni Division and on to take Port Harcourt, the Ogoni were scapegoated as saboteurs, and were evacuated to concentra-tion camps and refugee centers where many starved to death. Others were sent to the Training Depots en route to the front, where they were used as canon fodder and from which they never returned. From May to August of 1968, 4,000 Ogonis died from forced relocation and Ibo 'reprisals'. Bombed and shelled by federal troops, the Ogoni were then persecuted by Biafrans. According to Saro-Wiwa's calculations, an estimated thirty thousand Ogonis, over ten percent of the ethnic population, died in the war. Whether the figures are biased or exact hardly matters, for it is clear that in the ethnic politics of Nigerian federalism, the Ogoni were universal-ly despised and had nowhere to turn.

After the Biafran defeat in 1970, Nigeria's three regions were replaced by twelve states in a plan to stabilize the federal govenment, and the Ogoni joined the newly formed Rivers State with other delta minorities. By this time, however, the Ogoni were fighting another battle for survival — this time against oil. Although Shell-BP first struck Ogoniland oil in 1958, in the village of Dere, production was curtailed by the Biafran War, and began in earnest toward the close of violence. By the war's end, the Ogoni had come to realize that the oil company's promises of development and economic prosperity were empty lies, as the new industry brought no benefits and only hardships to the area. Virtually no new jobs were created for the Ogoni, and profits were siphoned away without any returns to the villagers. Company projects such as the Ogoni Rural Community Project existed in name only, with diverted funds counting as tax deductions. What Shell brought to Ogoniland was not profit but pollution, contaminating the mangrove swamps and farmland with seepage and spills while fouling the air with black smoke and lethal gases from flare-offs that burned day and night. Growing discontent erupted in July 1970, when a blow-out in one of Shell's oil fields wreaked havoc on the surrounding villages. An entire village ecosystem was destroyed, prompting petitions to the military governor and protests against Shell-BP's unwillingness to help. One such letter from an Ogoni school teacher likens the horrors of the blow-out to the violence of the Biafran War:

> We in Dere today are facing a situation which can only be compared with our experiences during the civil war ... an ocean of crude oil has emerged, moving swiftly like a great river in flood, successfully swallowing up anything that comes on its way. These include cassava farms, yams, palms, streams, animals etc. etc. for miles on end. There is no pipeborne water and yet the streams, the only source of drinking water is coated with oil. You cannot collect a bucket of rain water for the roofs, trees and grass are all covered with oil. Anything spread outside in the neighbourhood is soaked with oil as the wind carries the oil miles away from the scene of the incident.... Thrice during the Civil war the flow station was bombed setting the whole place on fire.... Now a worse fire is blazing not quite a quarter of a mile from the village ... men and women forced by hunger 'steal' occasionally into the 'ocean' [of oil], some have to dive deep in oil to uproot already rotten yams and cassava. I am not a scientist to analyze what effects the

> breathing of dangerous gases the crude oil contains would have on
> the people, but suffice it to say that the air is polluted and smells
> only of crude oil. We are thus faced with a situation where we have
> no food to eat, no water to drink, no homes to live and worst of it
> all, no air to breathe. We now live in what Hobbes may describe as
> a STATE OF NATURE — a state where peace or security does not
> exist '...and the life of man is solitary, poor, nasty, brutish and
> short'. (Reprinted in Saro-Wiwa 1992: 58–9)

Oil, fast becoming the life-blood of the new Nigeria as the oil boom
took off, was for the Ogoni the scourge of development, transform-
ing the putative precolonial 'natural' economy — considered to be
the food basket of the Eastern Niger Delta — into a postcolonial
state of Hobbesian 'warre'. Prefiguring the hidden costs of an 'un-
natural' enclave economy which would burn hot and then out, the
plight of the Ogoni would come to stand for the plight of all
Nigerians subjected to the losing combination of oil-capitalism and
political kleptocracy. In the 1970s, however, Saro-Wiwa's struggle
still seemed ethnically motivated, in that from his perspective, the
ethnic majorities and the nation at large gained at the Ogoni's expense.

At issue was the method of revenue allocation by an increasingly
unitary and autonomous state. As Watts (1992: 35–6) has observed,
the oil-economy transformed the regional structure of the First
Republic into a "centralized, bureaucratic petrostate" that consolidated control over oil rents and revenues and embarked on a
program of states creation — twelve states out of four regions in
1966, nineteen states in 1976, up to thirty states in the early 1990s
and thirty six states in 1996 — which increased direct fiscal depend-
ency on the center. During the oil crisis of the early 1970s among
the industrial powers, Nigeria joined OPEC and became extremely
wealthy, with a robust currency backed by petro-dollars that
financed an expanding public sector fueled by national development schemes. Taking control over multinational capital through
two indigenization decrees (Biersteker 1987), the state became the
broker of virtually all productive ventures financed by oil, establishing a pattern of patronage in business and politics that allocated
licenses and revenues in exchange for kickbacks and loyalty. As

administrative units, each state depended upon federal disburse-
ments, with ethnic blocks consolidating around economic as well
as political resources and opportunities. I will examine the rather
complex structural consequences of this incorporative and distribu-
tive modality in the next section. For now, we can focus on the view
from Ogoniland, which was quite simple. For as far as the Ogoni
were concerned, the federal government and its expanding circle of
'lootocrats' were stealing from the poor and giving to the rich. Sitting on the wealth of the nation — the black gold that was mined
from their land and appropriated by the center — the Ogoni were
screwed over twice. First, by the federal government, which successively swindled the local areas out of any share in their oil by revis-
ing the revenue allocation formula to benefit the ethnic majorities.
Thus the share of mineral rents for the minorities in the oil producing areas fell from twenty percent down to two percent and again to
1.5 percent, which in any case was never paid. By 1979, the constitution of the imminent Second Republic vested all mineral rights in
the federal government, adding a land-use decree that appropriated
all lands as well. Secondly, the Ogoni were further oppressed within
Rivers State, which diverted federal revenues to its own Ijaw ethnic
majority at the expense of the most basic amenities and utilities in
Ogoniland. Sitting on the nation's wealth, the Ogoni lacked adequate funds for water, roads, even primary education. As the
nation's program for universal health care and primary education
built more hospitals and schools in the arid north and populous
west, the local government areas of Ogoniland could not pay their
doctors and teachers.

The situation intensified as the number of states in Nigeria
increased, giving the ethnic majorities more states, and hence a
greater proportion of reallocated revenues while consigning the
Ogoni and other oil producing minorities to virtual if not literal extinction. With characteristic clarity, Saro-Wiwa summed up the sys-
temic obliteration of his people in the language of ethnic domination. At the federal level: "Under the military dictatorships which
have ruled the country from 1967 to the present (1992), the determination has been to subvert the federal culture of the country,
establish a unitary state, corner the oil resources of the nation at the
centre and then have these resources transferred by the Big Man

who has come to power either by electoral fraud or military coup to the ethnic majority areas" (Saro-Wiwa 1992: 89). And within Rivers State, the same siphoning underwent a secondary elaboration:

> In Rivers State, the majority Ijaws are more interested in their own welfare than in establishing a fair and just state. The constituent ethnic groups spend more time fighting for crumbs which fall from Nigeria's federal table at which the ethnic majorities preside, than in creating social and economic progress. In short, Rivers State is but a microcosm of Nigeria in which the majority ethnic groups triumph while the minorities gnash their teeth in agony. But it is even worse because the multi-ethnic Rivers State is run as a unitary state without the nod which is made at the centre towards federalism. In such a situation, such ethnic minorities as the Ogoni are condemned to slavery and extinction. Thus, political structuring and revenue allocation have been used to completely marginalize the Ogoni, grossly abusing their rights and veritably consigning them to extinction. (ibid.)

The Ogoni thus suffered a double indemnity under state sector oil-capitalism, and a double alienation from their resources and rights. Added to such formal dispossession was the prebendalism of public office and the privatization of the state, in the form of kickbacks and embezzlement that again could follow ethnic lines.[2] As we shall see, Saro-Wiwa's nearly exclusive focus on ethnic politics and clientism was one-sided, overlooking the development of class fractions and what Bayart (1993: 150–179) calls "the reciprocal assimilation of elites" on trans-ethnic grounds. But the ethnic factor was obvious and striking enough to provoke an ethnically framed reaction.

Called the Autonomy Option by the Movement for the Survival of the Ogoni People (MOSOP), the Ogoni response to oil pollution, government kleptocracy, ethnic cronyism and the resultant cultural 'genocide' was a demand for political autonomy that fell short of a full-fledged secessionist movement but invoked the language of independence in its 'Ogoni Bill of Rights'. Presented to President Babangida (who turned a deaf ear) and the military governor of Rivers State in October 1990, the manifesto called for greater political autonomy for the Ogoni as a distinct "ethnic nationality" with greater participation in the affairs of the federal republic. The pamphlet highlights seven specific guarantees which define the unit of autonomy and its sphere of operations in formal and substantive terms. These are: a) political control of Ogoni affairs by Ogoni people, b) the right to the control and use of a fair proportion of Ogoni economic resources for Ogoni development, c) adequate and direct representation as of right in all Nigerian institutions, d) the use and development of Ogoni languages in Ogoni territory, e) the full development of Ogoni culture, f) the right to religious freedom, and g) the right to protect the Ogoni environment and ecology from further degradation (Leton et al 1990: 4). As we will see, the steps toward a political ecology of citizenship formulated for a specific ethnic nation would become paradigmatic of Nigeria at large, as the meaning of political autonomy widened to embrace an embattled public sphere. But in 1990, Saro-Wiwa's Ogoni platform was defiantly parochial, and the benefits that would accrue to Ogoniland were both tangible and enormous.

Although never explicitly defined, the distinct and separate unit of autonomy would presumably be a state, just like the many other new states carved from selected ethnic communities in Nigeria under Babangida's administration.[3] The economic implications of such an arrangement within the national federation involved huge sums of money, based on the assumption that Ogoniland would receive 'a fair proportion' of oil revenues — in Saro-Wiwa's judgment a whopping fifty percent, following the *regional* allocation formula established before independence, although presumably this proportion was negotiable. Depending upon calculated exchange rates, net oil revenues, and estimated damages to the land and people, government reparations to the Ogoni totalled about $20 billion. The figure was not exactly realistic, and it is not clear whether Saro-Wiwa sought these damages in literal monetary terms, or more figuratively, as a monetary value placed on environment, cultural heritage and minority rights. Added to the economic guarantees would be instant appointments to 'quota' positions in education and the civil service, based on minority representation within the federation. The remaining demands in the *Ogoni Bill of Rights* identify language (Gokana and Khana), territory, Ogoni culture, religious freedom, the environment and ecology as guaranteed parameters of an autonomous entity; one which, located between the state and civil society, would become the kernel of a national public sphere. For Saro-Wiwa, however, the Ogoni struggle would remain that of persecuted minorities against the so-called ethnic majority, the lootocratic regime, and the profiteering oil companies. Oil-capitalism destroyed the Ogoni state of nature by devastating the environment and draining, through its oil pipes, "the very life-blood of the Ogoni people" (Saro-Wiwa 1992: 82). Saro-Wiwa concluded his *Genocide in Nigeria* with an image of a 'vampire-like' Nigeria, sitting over the Ogoni and expropriating their oil to finance a corrupt and wasteful regime. He may not have appreciated how well this model applied to the nation as a whole.

THE VAMPIRE STATE
How did the most robust national economy in black Africa, fueled by an oil bonanza that inaugurated an era of unprecedented prosperity, give rise to the cannibalistic vampire state described so vividly by Ken Saro-Wiwa? How did the engine of development and progress that burned so brightly in the seventies and early eighties — bringing contracts, commodities and new opportunities to virtually all sectors of the Nigerian economy — degenerate so thoroughly by the 1990s into a self-consuming predatory regime? Many Nigerians today bewail the wasted opportunities of the oil boom, blaming unscrupulous leaders and self-serving ministers who were unprepared for the enormous windfalls of oil rents and revenues and became intoxicated by the power of the petro-dollar. Indeed, the oil economy reconfigured an interethnic elite whose inner circle straddled old family and nouveau riche, developing a notorious culture of conspicuous consumption with shopping sprees in Europe, mansions in America, fleets of Mercedes Benzs, designer clothes and expensive imported lace, lavish parties with lobster thermidore and Don Perignon, and for the really successful, private jets. During the boom years, of course, such visions of excess were largely perceived as the icing on the national cake, with more than enough to go around for everybody. As academics received car loans, school teachers bought stereos and televisions, and all manner of commodities flooded the markets from the sprawling cities

of Lagos and Ibadan throughout the rural hinterlands, Nigerians put the recent trauma of the Biafran War (1966–70) behind them, and celebrated the blessings of good times. "Our problem is not money," an overconfident Head of State General Gowon once boasted, "but how to spend it."

General Gowon was soon ousted in a military coup that prefigured the cycle of military governments and aborted civilian regimes that would characterize the literal and figurative corruption of the Nigerian petrostate that followed. Underwritten by access to high grade crude oil, the state was simultaneously strengthened and destablized; centralized as a mechanism of accumulation and distribution, funding national development schemes and dispersing patronage, it became increasingly vulnerable to internal competition for control of the commanding heights. To understand how and why things fell apart in Nigeria so soon after they appeared to be taking off, we need to look past the limits of ethnic politics and poor leadership per se, to grasp the underlying contradictions of oil-capitalism in Nigeria's enclave economy, what Watts (1994: 418) has called "the paradoxes of prosperity" that consumed the state from without and within. From this more inclusive perspective, Saro-Wiwa's struggle against the majority ethnic oil barons and power brokers took place within more general transformations entailed by the development of Nigeria's oil economy. As described by Watts (1992: 35–6), these occurred on three distinguishable levels that were intimately linked to the global restructuring of capital and commodity flows signalled by the oil crisis of late 1973, when the world price of crude suddenly quadrupled. First, the oil boom *internationalized* the Nigerian state as an emergent player in global energy markets, extending its influence throughout Africa and the Third World, to the industrial nations then in crisis. Second, Nigeria's oil economy *centralized* the state, giving rise to a 'bureaucratic petrostate' of unprecedented autonomy and fiscal control which expanded the civil service and "embarked upon a massive program of infrastructural and industrial investment" (Watts 1992: 36). These two processes were of course inversely linked to the international export of Nigerian crude and the domestic accumulation of oil revenues. At the same time, however, the state was effectively *privatized* through a complex network of payoffs, kickbacks, and negotiated prebends. As we shall see, this privatization of the public sphere — occurring behind the scenes and signs of national development and prosperity — undermined the petrostate from within, giving specificity to the general form of what Chatterjee (1993: 43–49), following Gramsci (1971), has called the "passive revolution" of the postcolony at large. To grasp this collapse clearly, we return to the boom years before the self-appointed giant of black Africa was brought to its knees.

On the international arena, Nigeria's importance and popularity grew with demand for its oil and the rise of its value. In the 1970s, as the world price of crude climbed from \$2.50 to \$40.00 per barrel, Nigeria strengthened its political and economic ties with Britain and the United States, while gaining new European and Asian trading partners. During the oil crisis, Jimmy Carter visited Nigeria to become the first American incumbent president to set foot in Africa, with Nigeria's Head of State Olusegun Obasanjo reciprocating in Washington. Nigeria's rising prominence in world affairs was marked by its membership and even leadership of OPEC, which not only inflated the world price of oil but changed the very mechanisms of its determination, tying the market price to a fixed level of rent rather than the other way around (Coronil 1987: 29; Watts 1994: 412 n. 5). The results of this reversal of the transnational terms of trade in oil were manifold, generating new anxieties in the industrial nations matched by an exhilarating sense of new powers and possibilities among OPEC nations and their Third World allies. Nigeria's growing leadership in international political and economic affairs took many forms: assuming the helm of the Organization of African Unity (OAU) to fight against apartheid in South Africa and develop the continent; taking charge of the Economic Community of West Africa States (ECOWAS) to integrate the regional markets of Anglophone and Francophone west Africa; and championing the formation of a New International Economic Order though the United Nations, in order to redefine the terms of trade between the (so-called) North and South in more equitable terms.[4] In a more spectacular idiom, Nigeria's emergence on the world scene was signalled by FESTAC '77, the extravagant world festival of African arts and culture which Nigeria hosted and financed with oil, bringing cultural groups and heads of state from the expansive reaches of the black and African world to celebrate its Pan-African heritage and imminent emancipation from neo-colonial domination (Apter 1996). That Nigeria placed itself at the center of this black global imperium gave cultural expression to the nation's privileged position — primus inter pares — in the expanding global economy, framing the internationalization of the petroleum state in Pan-African terms. As I have argued elsewhere (ibid.), FESTAC reduced ethnic and national differences to the cultural patrimony of all black nations, associating racial unity with commodity value through the general equivalent of the money form. Oil, the life-blood of the Nigerian nation, not only internationalized the petrostate but also revitalized the black and African world.

As Nigerian oil coursed through the body politic and beyond, into the major arteries of the global economy, petro-dollars flowed into the nation, underwriting an expanding state and its development projects. During the 1970s the Udoji Reform nearly doubled the salaries of all civil servants, while new highways, hospitals, schools and universities transformed the national landscape into a modernist vision of economic take-off. As Watts (1994: 421) explains, "the oil revenues flowed directly to the state via the Nigerian National Petroleum Company (NNPC), which both centralized and expanded federal power," with revenues growing at 26 percent per annum, creating what Joseph (1987: 83–7) has called an "entrepot state" mediating domestic relations with foreign capital. The political consequences of this oil bonanza were profound and complex, but the immediate impact was unprecedented state centralization as the government created new states, overwhelmed the regional marketing boards, and rationalized the administration of the public sector from the top down.[5] Under Lt-General Obasanjo, for example, the state championed universal primary education, established local government areas, conducted a national census, standardized academic salaries, and built state councils of art and culture under an umbrella national organization in Lagos, all of which were funded by oil revenues disbursed from the center. Even electricity was rationalized by the National Electric Power Authority (NEPA), a federal grid which distributed light to masses through an impressive if often ineffective armature of generators, towers, wires and transformers.[6] Whatever political and practical impediments militated against such modernist measures of rationalization and standardization — and there were many — the result was an appearance of a new state colossus, rising with new national monuments, highways, bridges, and banks, reflected by fleets of shiny official luxury cars, and imprinted on the insignia of the mushrooming parastatal industries.

As Coronil (1987: 5) argues from the Venezuelan case, the economic autonomy of the oil-based rentier state vis-a-vis society's productive capacity produces an effect whereby "the state appears to stand above society, and is represented as the locus of extraordinary power." Or as recapitulated by Watts (1994: 418), "the state appears suspended above society — it is represented as *the* source of power since oil is power…." This historically specific modality of what Mitchell (1988) has called the "state-effect" — referring to the reification of the state standing apart from civil society — can be understood in Nigeria as a type of state fetishism, in the double sense of the commodity fetish and, following Taussig's "maleficium" model, the state's "aura of might" (Taussig 1993: 218). Unlike Mitchell's discussion of colonial Egypt, however, this separation was effected not by disciplinary practices of learning, policing and military training — which had already occurred in colonial Nigeria — but by the accumulation and redistribution of oil revenues, in the form of taxes and rents. The distinction is significant because oil-capitalism in a rentier state entails a specific phenomenology of power and value, one in which Saro-Wiwa's political ecology must be located to understand his vision of the vampire state. This phenomenology embraces several value forms, spheres of exchange, and domains of objectification not usually associated with each other.

As the oil boom peaked, the Nigerian state appeared formidable but friendly, presiding over the nation's dramatic renewal as master of ceremonies. During the dizzy days of FESTAC '77, Nigeria's Head of State was literally designated the Grand Patron of the international festival, a fitting title for the centralized source of subsidies and gifts including money, houses, land, cars and import licenses. Although the state disbursed oil revenues to reward friends and loyal clients, the General emerged as patron of the people, pumping money into public works for the benefit and enjoyment of all. If the deal seemed one-sided, with the state providing and the citizens receiving, the new prosperity was real enough. The naira, Nigeria's national currency, was valued at $1.60 in 1976, affording an unprecedented influx of imported commodities and accelerated market activity. Linked so directly to money and commodities, oil was seen in the popular imagination as 'the life-blood' of the nation, circulating through the body politic to revitalize the nation. Invoking the magic of money fetishism, popular expressions like 'the goose that laid the golden egg' described Nigeria's good fortune to be sitting on oil. Indeed, oil money had magical properties, in that its extraordinary value seemed to come out of the ground, accruing to the state and returning to the nation, creating wealthy contractors and millionaires overnight, with no ostensible relation to investment or hard work (Barber 1982). And in the complex formulae which economists use to analyze petroleum rent, either in the neoclassical tradition of 'pure economic rent' as a windfall surplus on normal profit (Kemp 1987) or in the Marxian tradition distinguishing absolute from differential rent to identify the social power and political costs of landed property on capitalist competition (Coronil 1987: 23–4 *et passim*), the government ownership of the oil fields produced a seemingly unlimited source of dollars. With costs and risks assumed by multinational oil corporations like Shell, Chevron, Elf and Agip, government could sit back and literally count its blessings all the way to the National Bank.

Following this model of magical money as pure profit emanating from the ground, mediated as it was through OPEC's control over global distribution and market price, and subsequently channeled through the Nigerian state, the fetishism of oil wealth and state power developed dialectically, achieving a synthesis through the objectification of national culture. To be sure, oil as the life blood of the nation was literally pumped from the ground, siphoned off by the state in the form of royalties and rents, and reallocated to the people. But to whom, and in what ways? Here is where Saro-Wiwa's trenchant criticisms challenged the official story. In principle, the oil boom was "for everybody."[7] In the popular dramaturgy of FESTAC '77, when Nigeria refashioned its national culture in the image of the commodity form, the wealth of black nations was a cultural patrimony underwritten by oil, and abstracted from ethnic differences and regional opposition to transcend sectionalism and celebrate common nationhood. If oil was identified as the life-blood of the revitalized nation in the popular imagination, a subtler association further developed between oil as the substance of commodity value rendered commensurable — like culture — by the money form, and what Balibar (1991: 86) calls the "invariant substance" of the modern nation form, resonating as it has with mystical notions of racial purity and collective destiny. Indeed, the racial dimensions of Nigerian national unity became more pronounced in FESTAC's collective representations of its common past and imminent emancipation (Apter 1996: 454). In this sense, the black gold administered by the state infused the black culture of the Nigerian nation as a common substance of intrinsic value. As Nigeria's national and natural resources converged, the nation was grounded in the soil and naturalized in one body — the self-proclaimed 'giant of black Africa'.

It was within this national phantasm (Ivy 1995: 13) of collective self-fashioning, in which "representative value becomes a mobile sign, detachable from locale but dependent on perpetually invoking it," that the value of oil as an economic resource flowed into the national body as the blood of one people. I am not suggesting that this was consciously recognized by the emerging citizenry preparing for a return to civilian rule, but that it motivated the remodelling of the nation currently taking place. According to the bureaucratic semiology of a rapidly changing oil nation, the cultural traditions of Nigeria's so-called 'tribes' or ethnic groups — judiciously documented in *Nigeria Magazine*, choreographed by the national dance troupe, and exhibited in the national Museum — became tokens of a type; namely, a singular national culture on the road to a brighter future. Culture was not only produced and objectified in exhibitions and staged performances, separated off from the state as an autonomous domain of one nation and people, but also served to link Nigeria's 'traditional' past with its postcolonial future.

And it is against this vision of national-utopian development that the vampiric consequences of Nigeria's prosperity can be contrasted, not only in terms of the ethnic clientism which Saro-Wiwa so desperately opposed, but in relation to the privatization of the state itself, and the 'passive revolution' which ensued. To be sure, the ethnic particularism putatively transcended by the new Nigerian nation was in many ways reinforced by the oil boom, in that ethnicity could be deployed strategically to gain access to centralized resources. The failure of the Second Republic (1979–1983) was in many ways due to the intensification of ethnopolitical competition, represented by the strong association between the three dominant political parties (NPN, UPN, NPP) and the ethnically framed regional blocs of the Hausa-Fulani, Yoruba and Ibo majorities. Many southerners today blame Nigeria's failure on northern hegemony and the unwillingness of the Kaduna Mafia (itself an alliance between old aristocracy and the rising commercial-military elite) to relinquish power, and in a sense they are right. But the situation was complicated by the logic of prebendalism, what Joseph (1987: 86–7) describes as the privatization of public wealth through the allocation of state offices and contracts to the political brokers and clients of the inner circle. Top ministerial and civil service positions, ranging from the directorship of the NNPC and its subsidiary parastatal industries to permanent secretaries, rural development directorates, educational commissioners, state governorships and even local government areas funded from the center were prizes rewarded to clients for personal aggrandizement and enrichment. To be sure, the system had its own redistributive imperatives, since the price of effective big manship is the satisfaction of followers. But such redistribution of the national cake was not, in economic terms, particularly productive, and undermined the grand schemes of national development from the very start. As summarized by Joseph (ibid.):

> The high proportion of the development budgets which was committed to construction projects (which in turn, favored the issuance of contracts), the political manipulation of the classification of eligible contractors, the increasing shift to negotiated contracts from open bidding practices ... the process of channeling projects to particular areas and the indigenes thereof, these and many other practices came to serve as effective instruments for privatizing public wealth more than they contributed to achieving balanced socio-economic development.

The system was complicated by a system of kickbacks and mobiliza-tion fees to get projects started, all of which inflated contracts and rerouted resources back to the brokers and into their private coffers. In his penetrating and prescient *Time, Naira, Politics*, Nigerian writer and critic 'Jibs Akinkoye (1983: 21) describes the moral econ-omy of the inflated contract system during the bonanza days of easy wealth:

> The tithes demanded or expected of course rose steeply from the proverbial 10% of the 1960s to the unlimited portions of the 1980s. It reached a point where the kickforwards and kickbacks a contrac-tor had to pay to chairmen and members of tenders boards in the hope of landing a contract, and later to clerks, accountants and chief executives of ministries, institutions and parastatals in order to get his vouchers processed, his cheque written and signed, and the signed cheques released to him — all began to represent more than half of the total contract sum. It reached a point where a con-tractor would find himself labelled 'greedy' and 'selfish' because he had collected a government cheque for a large amount and gave a small amount as 'dash' or 'tip' to those who believed that without them he never could have got the contract (which might have been true) and that they were entitled to as much of the total proceeds as they wanted....

Unfinished highways, abandoned building projects, idle tractors and embarrassing white elephants like the Ajaokuta Steel works were among the most tangible signs of such growth without devel-opment, while diatribes against corruption fell upon deaf ears. But as we say in the language of political economy, the problem was not moral but structural. The entire system of state managed oil capital-ism rested on a system of payoffs and kickbacks that could remain in place as long as there was enough oil-money to go around. Access, moreover, was not limited to ethnic majority favoritism, but followed a complex tapestry of factions and coalitions within and between ethnic groups. From the perspective of Ogoniland, one can appreciate how the state's appropriation and squandering of petroleum resources was seen in ethnic terms, but the contradic-tions of the oil economy were more pervasive if less obvious. As the state absorbed whole sectors of the economy together with their internal class divisions and tensions, it internalized the entire process of class formation (Berry 1985: 13–4), drawing "*within itself* the actual struggle for financial resources which normally obtains within civil society" (Joseph 1987: 87, his emphasis). It was therefore in more unilateral terms that the Nigerian state expanded at its own expense, ostensibly pumping oil-money into the nation while secretly sucking it back into private fiefdoms and bank accounts. And it was here, I would argue, behind the dramatic facades of "fast capitalism" (Watts 1992) and national development, that the vampire state was born.

To appreciate how state vampirism made sense in the popular imaginations of a vast and variegated Nigeria, we must return to the magical qualities of royalties and ground rents in relation to transethnic idioms of money-making medicine. In brief, the mysterious sources of oil profits emanating from the ground and accruing to the state may have generated a collective jubilation of manifest opportunity, but they also produced a national anxiety based on pervasive notions of 'bad' wealth and 'hot' money gained not through hard work but by nefarious means. Such anxieties have been documented in the popular theater of the oil boom era (Barber 1982), drawing on popular literatures in English and Nigerian vernaculars (Fagunwa 1950; 1961; Emecheta 1982; Oyegoke 1981) detailing the money-making medicines of kidnappers who sacrifice humans for money. The accounts of such practices vary — some focus on dismembered body parts and other on buckets of blood — but together they comprise a moral genre of illicit gain at the cost of human life. One typical story I collected in the Yoruba town of Ayede-Ekiti in 1984 related how a rich man kidnapped children by stunning them with juju medicines and leading them to his house, where he had a large calabash which he would fill with their blood and bring to a room with no windows. After uttering certain incantations, the blood would turn into crisp new bills, which the man spent whenever he needed. Another story that broke out in the town, during the 1983 Oroyeye festival ostracizing social malefactors, concerned one Oladiran who kidnapped and killed his paternal half-brother for *lukudi* money making medicine.[8] This notion of effortless gain at the expense or even 'consumption' of others is echoed in various witchcraft beliefs as well, but the underlying template which motivates this genre is the transmutation of human blood into money—bad money, to be sure, curiously 'infertile' in its capacity to be spent frivolously, without reciprocal advantage or gain. As Watts (1994: 427) explains in his insightful review of money magic idioms during the oil boom, "money magic, whatever the empirical status of its liturgy of body parts and juju narratives, captured perfectly in this respect the magical and fetishistic (and violent) qualities of the petro-naira," representing what Barber (1995: 219) identifies as "the convertibility of people into money ... in the petro-naira narratives of money-magic." Thus if rooted in local socioeconomic fields and cultural forms, money magic, like the money it invoked, was iconic of the nation and symptomatic of its unproductive wealth. Whether articulated through Hausa distinctions between fertile (*uwa mai anfi*) vs. ominous (*jarin tsaya*) money (Watts 1994: 425), Ibo stories of body parts in suitcases (Bastian 1991), Yoruba notions of blood-draining profit, or the many minority perspectives—including those of the Ogoni—between and beyond, the discourse of evil surrounding the negative values of money fetishism acquired national focus and circulation. Writing from a Yoruba perspective, Matory (1994: 124) contrasts local reports of money magic with its larger relevance to the nation-state: "*Lukudi* and the similar *eda* moneymaking magic occupy a nightmarish space in the national imagination far out of proportion to their actual incidence. They not only tap an extant and widespread symbolism but vividly symbolize the sense that acquisitive strategies in the mercantile capitalist state cannibalize normal forms of collective and personal life."

Following this development of money magic into an allegory of the national economy, we can map its life-consuming and even blood-draining logic more precisely onto the accumulation and distribution of oil royalties and rents, not only in terms of the enormous wealth that was mysteriously conjured and publicly invested, but more specifically in terms of the hidden costs exacted by the concurrent privatization of the public sphere—the kickbacks, prebends and wholesale diversion of public funds into private accounts and personal fiefdoms. If, as we have seen, oil represented the lifeblood of the nation, the petrostate paradoxically expanded by consuming this life-blood of the people—sucking back the money that it pumped into circulation while absorbing the process of sectorial competition and even class formation within its hypertrophic belly. The oil-economy may have energized domestic markets through the intensified circulation of money and commodities, but it enervated and undermined the real productive base of Nigeria, those agricultural resources which not even a state-sponsored green revolution could revive. But during the halcyon days of the oil boom and its spectacle of national development, these contradictions were nowhere to be seen. Not even Ken Saro-Wiwa understood the generalized condition of state-vampirism gestating within. Perched as federal administrator for the oil port of Bonny in Rivers State from 1968–1973, where he witnessed the beginning of the boom, Saro-Wiwa well understood the siphoning off of oil from Ogoniland to the so-called ethnic majorities, but he remained less concerned about the logic of *étatization* writ large. If his struggle, like his vision, appeared parochial on this issue, it would not remain so, for after the demise of the Second Republic in the 1980s and the failure of the farcical 1993 elections, when the world price of oil plummeted and the growing demands on Nigeria's oil revenues far outstripped their value, the vampire state boldly emerged to suck the life-blood of the nation in full daylight. Thus consumed, oil as black gold turned to "devil's excrement" (Watts 1994) and toxic waste. In the next section, we will see how the anemic anatomy of a dying nation took an ecological turn, invoking the state of nature and the sanctity of the land to restore the 'natural' conditions of civil society and effective citizenship from the ravages of oil.

THE UNCIVIL SOCIETY

"Why are you people doing this to me? What sort of a nation is this?" (Soyinka 1996: 149). Ken Saro-Wiwa's last words were uttered during the fifth and final attempt to operate the gallows that left him hanging and dead. Softly uttered, his words echoed throughout Nigeria and the international press as the global community waited in disbelief. With respect and dismay, Nigerians shook their heads over the tragic irony maintained by Saro-Wiwa's trenchant wit to the end. His final double entendre implicated not only the killers of Abacha's ruling band of thugs, and the excuse of a nation which they pretended to represent, but the tattered country that could do nothing right — not even kill a man on the gallows. Unused and imported, not even this dreaded technology of execution was correctly operated by the state.

But Ken Saro-Wiwa did die, and his death represents not just a dramaturgy of arbitrary power, following Mbembe's model of the postcolonial *commandement* and its farcical mimesis of judicial process and authority (Mbembe 1992), but the ultimate collapse of that elusive distinction between the Nigerian state and civil society, and the demise of effective citizenship. We can follow this drama in a linear narrative of linked events, as a convergence of local and national struggles in the global context of oil-capitalism, to achieve an instrumental understanding of Saro-Wiwa's death and transfiguration into a spokesperson for all Nigeria. From this perspective, two series of events converged on the annulled national elections of June 12, 1993 and the aborted delivery of Nigeria's Third Republic. From below, Saro-Wiwa's leadership of MOSOP to defend the Ogoni against the military-petroleum complex developed greatest momentum as an ecological struggle for the natural environment, not surprisingly related to Greenpeace's estimates that "between 1982 and 1992, 37 percent of Shell's spills worldwide — amounting to 1.6 million gallons — took place in the Delta" where the Ogoni (and other minorities) reside (Hammer 1996: 62). Organizing an Ogoni youth wing that sabotaged oil pipes and installations, Saro-Wiwa's activism caused Shell to pull out of the region by January of 1993, costing the company and the government 28,000 barrels of crude oil a day (ibid.). The struggle had been violent since 1990, when paramilitary police called 'Kill and Go' massacred about fifty neighboring Umuechem residents demanding reparations from Shell, and proceeded to foment machine gun and grenade attacks — thinly disguised as 'tribal' animosity — between Ogoni and Adoni peoples. The 'slow genocide' of Ogoni by oil pollution was now supplemented by the 'scorched earth' campaigns of military kill squads amounting to over 2,000 Ogoni deaths, lending eerie credence to Saro-Wiwa's prophetic accusations. Thus it was that when members of MOSOP's radicalized youth wing attacked the conservative chiefs and Ogoni 'turncoats', resulting in the death of four elders, the government seized Saro-Wiwa and eight Ogoni associates on charges of incitement to murder, although Saro-Wiwa had been far away from the scene.[9] From the military perspective, Saro-Wiwa and his Ogoni activists, like the Jews of Nazi Germany, were the saboteurs of the economy. Eliminate the Ogoni problem, and oil could flow freely again. On a more tactical level, Abacha's rush to the gallows followed the internal colonial logic of divide and rule. If the Ogoni were not alone in opposing the alliance of Shell and the military junta, neither could they be joined by the other indigenous peoples such as the Okrika and the Andoni in a Delta revolt when government violence masqueraded as inter-ethnic conflict. According to Soyinka, the immediate execution of Saro-Wiwa was to remove the pivotal figure of opposition around which a united Delta front could emerge. The 'trial' was thus a sham:

> Ken Saro-Wiwa's fate had long been sealed. The decision to execute him and his eight companions was reached before the special tribunal was ordered to reconvene and pronounce a verdict that had been decided outside the charade of judicial proceeding. The meeting of the Provisional Ruling Council to consider the verdict was a macabre pretence, a prolongation of the cynicism that marked the trial proceedings from the outset (Soyinka 1996: 152).

But as I shall argue, Saro-Wiwa's struggle also transcended riverine politics to capture the frustrations of a nation — in the now understated words of Chinua Achebe — no longer at ease. The identification was not of course uniform, resonating more immediately with the south's resistance to Hausa-Fulani hegemony and political repression than among northern constituencies.[10] To see how this second series of national events converged with Saro-Wiwa's struggle, we can return to the collapse of the oil economy and the era of IBB.

Briefly stated, Ibrahim Badamosi Babangida (IBB) came to power in a bloodless coup (1985) that seemed intent on liberalizing the flagging economy by privatizing parastatals, stimulating domestic production through import substitution, and by floating the naira on a two-tier foreign exchange market to encourage greater foreign investment. The new regime started off in good faith, and the benevolent leader — soon to turn dictator — held public debates on domestic policy (such as the viability of IMF loan conditions) as well as a constitutional conference to bring back civilian rule. By 1986, when the world price of crude plummeted, the value of the naira plunged, setting off a spiral of inflation and devaluation that virtually wiped out the Nigerian middle class which had accumulated savings during the oil boom. At this stage, IBB initiated his much vaunted Structural Adjustment Program which appeared to push the domestic economy over the brink — civil servants received their old salaries with scant provision for the rising cost of living; the price of petrol climbed as the national subsidies were cut, increasing distribution costs and the price of staples in urban markets; clothes became threadbare as used clothing markets sprang up; private banks offered pyramid schemes masquerading as high interest accounts; books and papers became scarce at the universities, and the luxury cars of Lagos and Ibadan, once the glittering symbols of petro-development, fell increasingly into disrepair, running on patched-up tires and improvised spare parts. By the early 1990s the national infrastructure began to seriously collapse — banks closed wholesale, universities remained on permanent strike, businesses were squeezed by higher kickbacks and lower profit margins, while the police, military and law courts basically survived on bribes. Emblematic of this state of decline was the rise of armed robbery at night and in open daylight, the fraudulent schemes known as '419' in which Nigerian and foreigners were indiscriminately duped, the rise of Nigerian drug trafficking through private couriers and diplomatic channels, the lack of medicine in the hospitals, and a growing despair that no end was in sight. As those with anything left to steal barricaded themselves into their homes, locking gates and even electrifying doors and window-bars to keep out thieves, entire neighborhoods would close off access by locking gates at dusk so that nobody could pass in or out. This informal 'enclosure act' represents a larger trend in the national economy — the parcelling up of public space and the privatization of civil society itself. As if following oil's lead, which was increasingly bunkered by industry insiders and sold on the black market, or used to underwrite Babangida's political payoffs from an invisible 'development' account within the National Bank, the public good was converted wholesale into private gain. The state was still powerful, suspended above the people as an obstruction to personal movements and capital flows, and yet its representative forms held no institutional content and little governmental function. Directives and decrees were issued from Aso Rock, Babangida's fortress-retreat in Abuja, in an arbitrary and meandering fashion that earned the self-appointed president the nickname of Maradona (after the Argentine soccer player who dribbled back and forth across the playing field), but politics was reduced to farce as the entire national assembly was repeatedly dissolved and reconstituted at IBB's whim.

As a result, the state became personalized and privatized through personal connections and prebendal spoils. Career paths, business opportunities, and coveted access to foreign exchange were protected not by rights and duties obtaining in the public sphere, but were enabled by the cultivation of personal ties with the gatekeepers in charge. Ethnicity remained viable as a cultural resource for establishing connections, but as competition intensified for the shrinking national cake, stratification and division were as marked within as between ethnic blocs, generating labile configurations of sudden opportunity rather than entrenched positions of power and advantage. As the naira continued to drop, a crisis of value and representation produced a general condition of instability, a phenomenology of value forms stripped of 'substance', of social appearances without fixed referents. Like the sapeur of Kinshasa or Brazzaville, the shrewd Nigerian survived with many guises, simulating and dissimulating access and expertise, pushing the boundary between professional elegance and social death to find his or her daily bread. And it was in this climate of hunger and indeterminacy that the ill-fated 1993 elections were held. Or so it appeared. In fact, the elections, like Nigeria's development during the oil boom, never really took place.

I have examined the 1993 elections elsewhere in some detail (Apter 1995b) as a grand '419' and a politics of illusion, not because they were rigged or manipulated, but because the entire charade hovered above civil society, a simulated process dislocated from any political constituency or social base. IBB repeatedly postponed elections, disqualified contestants, revised conditions of eligibility, reversed balloting procedures, and then eventually dissolved all parties, only to write the platforms of the Social Democratic Party (SDP) which was 'a little to the left' and the National Republic Convention (NRC) dubbed 'a little to the right', in a putative effort to avoid ethnic triangulation between Yoruba, Igbo and Hausa-Fulani blocs. On 12 June 1993, when national elections were finally held between the northern unknown Bashir Tofa and the Yoruba business tycoon Moshood Abiola, the wrong man took the lead. As Chief Abiola began to sweep the polls, IBB simply turned off the lights, annulling the elections with a decree that violated the immunity of the High Court (which opposed the annulment) and reversed a prior decree against just such interference. By this time, Nigerians of all ethnic stripes and religious persuasions took to the streets in a series of demonstrations, riots and even general strikes that would have brought the country to its knees if it had not already collapsed into such sorry disrepair. In a last gasp of civilian energy, the unions allied with the various associations for democratic rule, only to be smashed by the armed forces who replaced the union leadership with drones. It was at this moment, in Soyinka's words (1996: 9), that Nigeria was *robbed of its nationhood*.

I would emphasize, however, that the crisis of Nigerian nationhood fundamentally represented a crisis of citizenship. IBB was finally ousted in a series of manoeuvres by disaffected rulers and military factions who convinced him to 'step aside' for a transitional figure (Ernest Shonekan) who was soon toppled by Abacha in a pro forma coup. The final nail was now driven into the national coffin, for unlike IBB who bought off his enemies, Abacha was known as a ruthless hatchet man who — as events would soon prove — incarcerated and killed his opponents. The total crackdown on Nigeria's formerly open press; the life-time prison terms of such political luminaries as Shehu Yar'adua and former Head of State Olusegun Obasanjo, together with other alleged coup-plotters whose death sentences were so benevolently commuted to life terms for crimes cooked up by Abacha's paranoid imagination; the interminable incarceration of president-elect Moshood Abiola, whose wife was gunned down by unknown assailants whom everyone knows were government thugs; and of course the cold-blooded execution of Ken Saro-Wiwa and his eight Ogoni associates — these are only among the more blatant symptoms of the death of a nation and the demise of its citizenry, reduced not only to subjects of the northern political oligarchy, but to veritable inmates, as the government seizure of passports belonging to critics and intellectuals continues. There is no sphere of *res publica* in Nigeria; no effective system of interest articulation, legal process, public education, press coverage or publicity, nor is the most basic protection of life and liberty even recognized by the state. In one of his later editorials, Saro-Wiwa (1991: 131) maintained faith in the nation as he appealed to Babangida to convene a national conference and initiate real dialogue with the people:

> ...the down turn (to put it politely) in the economy of the nation is exacerbating every possible source of tension and creating new ones ... it takes a lot to maintain a belief in Nigeria. In these moments of doubt, there is need for self-examination and re-examination, a need to dip into reserves of energy at individual level to find that faith that fuels belief. And at national level, there has to be considerable soul-searching to clean the springs of political co-operation and self-restraint, to identify the homogeneous fundamental interests upon which reliance and voluntary collaboration must be based and to seek that common consent without which federation is meaningless.

Under Abacha, Saro-Wiwa died for these ideas, for they resonated beyond the disaffected minorities to all victims of a ruinous oil economy now held hostage to a kleptocratic regime. To grasp the underlying dialectic of Nigeria's particular form of immiseration, linking the plight of the Ogoni to the collapse of civil society, we can return to the forms of fetishized value under oil-capitalism and the naturalized idioms of land and nation which were so enriched and then polluted by an oil boom gone bust.

In terms of the model of the vampire state sketched in the previous section, in which the production of false value equals the consumption of human blood, the riverine model of rentier capitalism effects a shift from blood to soil and water. It is historically appropriate that the Niger Delta area where the Ogoni reside is part of an historic complex of chiefdoms and trading networks known in the nineteenth century as the Oil Rivers, based on the extensive trade of palm oil that gradually supplanted the slave trade. Palm oil was sold domestically as a vitamin rich source of cooking oil (rich in ritual properties as well), but also for export to overseas markets, primarily British, where it lubricated the growing cosmetics industry and the heavy machinery of the industrial revolution. So basic was palm oil as a measure and standard of social and economic value in the Delta that it actually served as a trading currency, in the form of containers or "puncheons of oil" (Jones 1970: 91). It was this type of exchange that has misled some scholars to characterize this trade as a barter system, in which a dominant commodity assumed a money form, but whatever the technical economic description best applies, the palm oil economy may well correspond to that period of greater abundance in the past when, as Batom Mitee, brother to one of the condemned Ogoni activists would say, "in the old days ... you could fish, farm, and survive without money" (quoted in Hammer 1996: 61). As a moral economy recalled, the palm oil trade and the forms of 'natural value' which it invokes — found in nature, and sold together with such commodities as timber, ivory and beeswax (Dike 1956: 57) — establish a profound contrast with the immoral economy of petroleum which pumps bad money from beneath the ground only to pollute and destroy the productive base of the ecosystem.[11]

It is here, within this idiom of natural goods and value forms, that the *unproductive* relations of oil-capitalism are ecologically expressed. As Harvey (1982), rereading Marx, explains, ground rent produces specific forms of fetishized value, in which land is perceived as the source of value itself (a perspective refined in economic terms by the physiocrats). As Nigeria's oil boom took off and the good times rolled, the nation was naturalized as one blood and territory, blessed by God, heritage and natural resources in the heady words of FESTAC. Was it not in 1976 that Shell-BP, in partnership with the Nigerian Oil Corporation, published a large glossy book on *Nigerian Heritage*, representing within one singular category Nigeria's land and people, arts and culture, trade and industry, power and mineral resources, as if to ground the wealth of nationhood itself beneath the very soil? Did not the Head of State, Lt-Gen. Olusegun Obasanjo personally launch the book, amid much media fanfare? Whether or not the book received much popular attention is not the point; rather it was the underlying logic motivating its publication and launching that so accurately captures how the indigenization of foreign capital — oil rents to be specific — underwrote the naturalization of the nation. Nigeria, after oil and FESTAC, was no longer a colonial or neocolonial entity, but could boast a long and valuable singular heritage extending deep beneath the ground and back into the precolonial past.

It followed from this ideological formula and baseline that as the contradictions of oil-capitalism developed and as the nation, with its currency, declined, the soil and waters of the oil producing regions were sullied. These contradictions, we have seen, follow an 'alienated' form of false value and bad wealth, conjured by the state through nefarious means to promote growth without development and erode the very foundations of citizenship and civil society. As the oil economy imploded and collapsed, the signs of wealth and development became increasingly estranged from their referents, infusing the value forms of everyday exchange with ghostly simulacra — food that does not satisfy, clothes and uniforms that disguise, financial instruments that have no legitimacy, banks that have no capital, hospitals without medicine, and finally a democracy that has no *demos*. As the condition of the Niger Delta waterways converged with the collapse of the nation, the Ogoni autonomy option became a movement for the survival of all Nigerians.

CONCLUSION

If the plight of the Ogoni and all Nigerians under the current petromilitary regime raises political issues of considerable urgency which must be pursued with unflagging vigilance, it also points to broader conceptual issues in the anthropology of what Appadurai (1996) has dubbed "the global cultural economy." Oil-Capitalism after OPEC has produced specific economies of meaning and power as well as specific modalities of hyperexpansion and underdevelopment (like the so-called Dutch disease) that acquire a distinctively ecological salience, not only in terms of contamination and deforestation but also in struggles over citizenship and civil society. To be sure, oil in Nigeria has undermined riverine ecosystems, and weakened the nation's agricultural base when imported staples and the lure of easy money drew Nigerians away from the land and into the urban undertow of the petronaira. But it also had less material effects which belong to an economy of representation and value forms, and it is here that Saro-Wiwa's struggle conveys lessons he may not have anticipated.

As we have seen, the transnational capital of the global economy into which the Nigerian state was so suddenly injected in no way weakened national boundaries, but had the opposite effect. Although Nigeria was ideologically universalized as the preeminent Pan-African nation, it was also strengthened domestically as a nation-state whose centralized administrative apparatus rose up, as it were, above the people, who were represented as one blood and territory. As the oil boom peaked and the economy accelerated, the internal distinction between a vertical state (top-down in its military command structure) and a horizontal nation became progressively objectified as an external boundary, by performances of art and culture which portrayed ethnic traditions on an even stage and also by a dirigiste state that sought to standardize the nation through universal education, health care, local government, and infrastructural development. But it was according to the commodity form, and its universal measure of value, the money form, that the Nigerian nation form came most clearly into focus, emphasizing the commensurability of ethnic difference through the invariant substance of one heritage and blood. Backed by pounds sterling and US dollars, the naira entered the circuits of global capital, representing the wealth of a nation not only reborn, but also one to be reckoned with.

As with the nation, also with the citizenry who came to embody the normative framework of self-government and self-determination, whatever practical barriers still remained to be overcome. The concept of citizenship in Nigeria (as in the rest of the world) is multifaceted and ambiguous, resting to some extent on its contrast with the prior category of colonial subjecthood, from which it struggled to emerge. Following the logic of the commodity form — its prescriptive equivalence, commensurability and convertibility of value forms — citizenship provided the clothing or armor protecting the national body, securing its borders, safeguarding its rights and duties, while defending a principle of political representation along horizontal lines of universal inclusion. Never mind that the Fulani still saw themselves as God's chosen rulers over the south (an attitude that was bolstered by British indirect rule), that the rich regarded the poor with ontological disdain, and that entire ethnic minorities and class fractions were differentially incorporated into the public domain. In the blinding light of the oil boom, the new citizens of the new Nigeria were to occupy, in principle, an emergent space of association and commerce in which the flow of money and commodities was visible and tangible. As the state rose up to cultivate the nation within, a new civil society built on 'natural' resources and universal citizenship came to occupy the space in-between. It was in this climate of imminent political and economic reconstruction that General Obasanjo prepared his country for a return to civilian government after more than a decade of military rule.

As the contradictions of Nigerian oil-capitalism intensified, expanding the public sector while privatizing the state, the conditions of civil society eroded, precipitating failed elections, more military coups, and the generalized phenomenology of the '419'. If the false wealth of oil ruined the nation, consuming the blood of the people while polluting their land and waterways, eco-politics took on particular salience as a critique of a mode of rentier oil-capitalism that violated the natural foundations of real wealth and legitimate commerce. Compared with the 'natural' economy of the Ogoni, the money and wealth of the national economy was unrelated to productive labor, intensifying circulation while actually undermining the nation's productive base. As the 'natural' relation between wealth and hard work became more obscure, the pollution of the land and waterways became more apparent. And Nigerians rallied to Saro-Wiwa's cause. Thus Soyinka (1996: 110) writes: "The Ogoni predicament has provoked, sometimes in the most unexpected quarters ... open debates that increasingly posit the assumptions of nation being—be it as an ideal, a notional bonding, a provider, a haven of security and order, or an enterprise of productive co-existence — against the direct experience of the actual human composition within the nation." I would extend this national identification with the Ogoni struggle to the erosion of citizenship and civil society, not only in terms of unrealized ideals to be achieved or minimal standards to be maintained—the language of the activists today—but to shed light on the character of the breakdown itself as the oil economy burned itself out.

In an immediate sense, MOSOP's reclamation of Ogoni land and waterways represents an appeal to the very ground of civil society itself, as adumbrated by the autonomy option which the organization pursued. The state, we recall, had quite literally taken possession of all mineral-rich land, extending its sovereignty into the earth according to the 1979 Land Use Decree and appropriating its oil according to the mysterious mathematics of derivation, by which oil revenues were nationally 'chopped' and redistributed. And what the state seized, the oil companies destroyed, polluting the farmland and fishing creeks with spills and runoffs while filling the very air with noxious gas and acid rain. As MOSOP invoked the language and iconography of secession, boycotting the 1993 elections and rallying around an Ogoni national anthem and flag (Welch 1995: 643), it set the stage for a more inclusive 'war of position' against the vampire state and transnational capital. From this perspective, Ogoni activism suddenly resonated with the general struggle for a civil society by a country robbed—in Soyinka's words—of its nationhood. Stripped of its social base and its representative mechanisms, Nigerian democracy proved to be a politics of illusion, depriving civil society of its president-elect and any effective participation or collective voice in national affairs. After June 12, as citizens took to the streets in defense of their citizenship, the Ogoni struggle joined hands with a larger national cause. Thus the ecological destruction of creeks and waterways in the remote areas of the Niger Delta emblematized the pollution of the public sphere by an invasive and extractive petro-state.

But what is this sphere of civil society that functions rhetorically in the language of liberal political economy as the 'natural' ground of effective democracy through a free market of interests and preferences? In a larger sense, the extended crisis in Nigeria today sheds light on the location of civil society in postcolonial Africa, where, following Kunz (1995: 181–2), two dominant perspectives compete. The one, more Lockean position, "posits [civil] society as a self-regulating realm, the ultimate repository of individual rights and liberties, and a body that must be protected against incursions of the state" (ibid.). This vision concurs with the American constitutional separation of powers and protection of civil rights and liberties, such as free speech, assembly, et cetera that are ultimately grounded in a market mechanism with its own assumptions of natural law. It also presupposes norms of sincerity, trust and accountability in the representation of individual and collective interests. A second, more 'Hegelian' understanding of civil society presents "an integrationist or holistic picture of civil society and the state" (ibid. 182) where the former functions more as a sphere of communication and interaction within the nation-state as a whole. There is no question that as African states have liberalized in the late 1980s and early nineties, pursuing uneven paths of structural adjustment and democratization, the liberal model has re-established itself in Africanist scholarship, particularly among political scientists focusing on 'weak states' and predatory regimes. The Ogoni situation and the Nigerian crisis appears to support this perspective, in that natural eco-systems have provided the moral framework of a civil society besieged by the state. As a strategic essentialism of political activism, moreover, such an organic idiom of civil society makes instrumental sense.

The dialectics of Nigerian rentier-capitalism, however, and the forms of commodification which it has entailed, suggest a more Hegelian or even Marxian approach to civil society in Africa, not as a natural and autonomous domain to be protected and reclaimed, but as a fetishized *sphere of circulation within the national economy*. We have seen how notions of citizenship and national culture were animated by the logic of the commodity form in idioms of reciprocal equivalence and commensurate value. As oil boosted the national economy, accelerating the circulation of money and commodities through what were primarily political relations of distribution, the nation was naturalized as one blood and soil beneath a benevolent state rising above. But as the oil economy burned out and the dollar dropped out of the Nigerian naira, the illusory basis of the country's wealth became apparent, draining the very blood of the nation and its citizens. Within the sphere of circulation, the arteries of the nation were blocked by irrational shortages until even oil disappeared from the petrol stations. As inflation soared, arbitrary exchange values destabilized the very phenomenology of exchange itself, giving rise to the era of the '419' — of fraud, con artistry, deception and desperate survival. From this perspective, the breakdown of civil society and the norms of intersubjectivity governing accountable interaction and political representation in Nigeria can be attributed not only to the rapacious appetites of predatory rulers and multinational companies, but to the collapse of a sphere of circulation whose previously obscure relation to "the hidden abode of production" (Marx 1976: 279 quoted in Postone 1993: 272) has almost literally disappeared.

NOTES

1 For a masterful synthesis of this political and social history, see Coleman (1958).

2 For a sophisticated discussion of prebendalism in the Second Republic, see Joseph (1987).

3 Nigeria reorganized its regions into twelve states in 1967, expanding to nineteen states in 1976, twenty-one in 1987, and thirty in 1991 (Gundu 1991: 9). The proliferation of states involves complex agendas which include a more 'equitable' distribution of federal resources, the breaking up of entrenched political 'mafias', and the buying off of disaffected factions by expanding the spread of administrative spoils.

4 That the initiative largely failed, largely due to Arab reluctance to subsidize African states, in no way undermines the significance of the attempt, which illustrates Nigeria's sense of politico-economic possibility using OPEC and the OAU.

5 Regional marketing boards in the colonial economy established monopsonies on cash crops like cocoa and cotton that were designed to protect producers from fluctuations on the world market but actually appropriated profits for investment in British securities to finance general development projects. See Helleiner (1962: 162), who estimates that 39 percent of 'potential producer profit' was thus siphoned off by the marketing boards. The point here is that the siphoning off of economic surplus by the state began under colonial rule.

6 The frequency of blackouts and power failures has made NEPA something of a national joke, renamed 'Never Expect Power Again' — a

fitting allegory for the failure of the state.

7 Thus a popular FESTAC theme song by King Sunny Ade shifted refrains from "FESTAC for black people" to "FESTAC for everybody."

8 This story is recounted and analyzed in Apter (1995a).

9 Soyinka (1996: 151–2) argues convincingly that the Ogoni elders were murdered by Abacha's hired hands.

10 Watts (1996) argues convincingly that the dislocations of oil-capitalism in the north provoked reactions that were framed within dissident Islamic movements, such as Maitatsine.

11 It is interesting how the European trade for Delta oil was based on a credit system called 'trust', whereby English goods were trusted to Delta middlemen for periods from six months up to two years (Dike 1956: 102–4) in exchange for palm oil, establishing a normative contrast with the violation of trust endemic to the petroleum economy. On a more abstract and theoretical note, Pietz (1993: 146), following Marx, reminds us that "When a given type of useful thing comes to function as a general-equivalent exchange object in trade activities, it comes to be recognized as embodying a new quality: that of a general form, the very medium of exchange (money)." It is possible that palm oil as a general equivalent of exchange came to signify a general form of trust and value associated with that exchange, almost as the moral substance of good economic faith.

REFERENCES

Akinkoye, 'Jibs. *Time, Naira, Politics: An Imaginative Socio-Economic Analysis of a New Nation-State*. Ibadan: B. I. O. Educational Services Ltd., 1983.

Appadurai, Arjun. *Modernity at Large: Cultural Dimensions of Globalization*. Minneapolis and London: University of Minnesota Press, 1996.

Apter, Andrew. "Discourse and its Disclosures: Yoruba Women and the Sanctity of Abuse." Paper presented at the Department of Anthropology, Manchester University, 6 March, 1995a.

———. "IBB=419: Nigerian Democracy and the Politics of Illusion." Paper presented at SOAS, University of London, 9 March, 1995b.

———. "The Pan-African Nation: Oil-Money and the Spectacle of Culture in Nigeria," *Public Culture* 8.3 (1996): 441–66.

Balibar, Etienne. "The Nation Form: History and Ideology." Eds. Balibar and Wallerstein. *Race, Nation, Class: Ambiguous Identities*. London and New York: Verso, 1991: 86–106.

Barber, Karin. "Money, Self-Realization, and the Person in Yoruba Texts." Ed. J. Guyer. *Money Matters: Instability, Values and Social Payments in the Modern History of West African Communities*. Portsmouth, NH: Heinemann, 1995: 205–24.

———. "Popular Reactions to the Petro-Naira." *Journal of Modern African Studies* 20.3 (1982): 431–50.

Bastian, Misty. "My Head Was Too Strong: Body Parts and Money Magic in Nigerian Popular Discourse." Paper presented at a conference on "Meaning Currencies and Monetary Imaginations: Money: Commodities and Symbolic Process in Africa," University of Chicago, 1991.

Bayart, Jean-Francois. *The State in Africa: The Politics of the Belly*. Trans. Mary Harper. London and New York: Longman, 1993.

Berry, Sara. "Oil and the Disappearing Peasantry: Accumulation, Differentiation, and Underdevelopment in Western Nigeria." Working Papers no. 66, African Studies Center, Boston University, 1982.

Biersteker, Thomas J. *Multinationals, the State, and Control of the Nigerian Economy*. Princeton: Princeton University Press, 1987.

Chatterjee, Partha. *Nationalist Thought and the Colonial World: A Derivative Discourse*. Minneapolis: University of Minnesota Press, 1986.

Coleman, James S. *Nigeria: Background to Nationalism*. Berkeley and Los Angeles: University of California Press, 1958.

Coronil, Fernando. "The Black El Dorado: Money Fetishism, Democracy and Capitalism in Venezuela." Ph.D dissertation, University of Chicago, 1987.

Dike, K. Onwuka. *Trade and Politics in the Niger Delta*. Oxford: Oxford University Press, 1956.

Emecheta, Buchi. *Naira Power*. London: Macmillan, 1982.

Fagunwa, D. O. *Ogboju Ode Ninu Igbo Irunmale*. Lagos: Nelson, 1950.

———. *Aditu Olodumare*. Lagos: Nelson, 1961.

Gramsci, Antonio. *Selections from the Prison Notebooks*. Trans. Q. Hoare and G. Nowell Smith. New York: International Publishers, 1971.

Gundu, M. "Federalism and State Creation in Nigeria." *The Nigerian Interpreter* 5.5 (1991): 8–11.

Hammer, Joshua. "Nigeria Crude: A Hanged Man and an Oil-Fouled Landscape." *Harper's Magazine*, June, 1996: 58–68.

Harvey, David. *The Limits to Capital*. Chicago: University of Chicago Press, 1982.

Helleiner, G. *Peasant Agriculture, Government, and Economic Growth in Nigeria.* Homewood, IL: Richard D. Irwin, 1966.

Ivy, Marilyn. *Discourses of the Vanishing: Modernity, Phantasm, Japan.* Chicago and London: University of Chicago Press, 1995.

Jones, G. I. *The Trading States of the Oil Rivers: A Study of Political Development in Eastern Nigeria.* London: Oxford University Press for the International African Institute, 1963.

Joseph, Richard. *Democracy and Prebendal Politics in Nigeria: The Rise and Fall of the Second Republic.* Cambridge: Cambridge University Press, 1987.

Kemp, Alexander. *Petroleum Rent Collection Around the World.* Halifax: The Institute for Research on Public Policy, 1987.

Kunz, Frank. "Civil Society in Africa." *Journal of Modern African Studies* 33.1 (1995): 181–7.

Leton, G.B. et al. "Ogoni Bill of Rights: Presented to the Government and People of Nigeria." 1990. (printed pamphlet)

Marx, Karl. *Capital*, vol. 1. Trans. Ben Fowkes. London, 1971.

Matory, J. Lorand. *Sex and the Empire that is No More: Gender and the Politics of Metaphor in Oyo Yoruba Religion.* Minneapolis: University of Minnesota Press, 1994.

Mbembe, Achille. "The Banality of Power and the Aesthetics of Vulgarity in the Postcolony." *Public Culture* 4.2 (1992): 1–30.

Mitchell, Timothy. *Colonising Egypt.* Cambridge: Cambridge University Press, 1988.

Oyegoke, Lekan. *Cowrie Tears.* London: Heinemann, 1981.

Pietz, William. "Fetishism and Materialism: The Limits of Theory in Marx." Eds. E. Apter and W. Pietz. *Fetishism as Cultural Discourse.* Ithaca and London: Cornell University Press., 1993: 119–51.

Postone, Moishe. *Time, Labor, and Social Domination: A Reinterpretation of Marx's Critical Theory.* Cambridge and New York: Cambridge University Press, 1993.

Sahlins, Marshall. *Stone Age Economics.* Chicago: Aldine Publishing Co., 1972.

Saro-Wiwa, Ken. *On a Darkling Plain: An Account of the Nigerian Civil War.* London, Lagos and Port Harcourt: Saros International Publishers, 1989.

———. *Similia: Essays on Anomic Nigeria.* London, Lagos and Port Harcourt: Saros International Publishers, 1991.

———. *Genocide in Nigeria: The Ogoni Tragedy.* London, Lagos and Port Harcourt: Saros International Publishers, 1992.

———. *A Month and a Day: A Detention Diary.* New York: Penguin Books, 1995.

Soyinka, Wole. *The Open Sore of a Continent: A Personal Narrative of the Nigerian Crisis.* New York and Oxford: Oxford University Press, 1996.

Taussig, Michael. "Maleficium: State Fetishism." Eds. E. Apter and W. Pietz. *Fetishism as Cultural Discourse.* Ithaca and London: Cornell University Press, 1993: 217–47.

Watts, Michael. The Shock of Modernity: Petroleum, Protest, and Fast Capitalism in an Industrializing Society." Pred, A. and M. Watts. *Reworking Modernity: Capitalisms and Symbolic Discontent.* New Brunswick: Rutgers University Press, 1992: 21–63.

———. "Oil as Money: The Devil's Excrement and the Spectacle of Black Gold." In S. Corbridge, R. Martin, and N. Thrift (eds.), *Money, Power and Space.* Oxford: Basil Blackwell, 1994: 406–45.

———. "Islamic Modernities? Citizenship, Civil Society and Islamism in a Nigerian City." *Public Culture* 8.2 (1996): 251–89.

Welch Jr., Claude. "The Ogoni and Self-Determination: Increasing Violence in Nigeria." *Journal of Modern African Studies* 33.4 (1995): 635–49.

Poetry

KEN'S BLUES
Jacqueline Onyejiaka

From a distance
You wear a foul expression
i recall our childhood
our bond was based on your immortality
but now you are dead.
disillusioned by false promises,
Your congealed form
lies there
An eyesore.
The obnoxious reminder
of our infamous neglect.

DELTA BLUES
Tanure Ojaide

This share of paradise, the delta of my birth,
reels from an immeasurable wound
bored through roots of the heart.
Barrels of alchemical draughts flow
from this hurt to the unquestioning world
that lights up its life in a blind trust.
The inheritance I sat on for centuries
now crushes my body and soul.

The rivers are dark-veined,
a course of perennial draughts.
This home of salt and fish
stilted in mangroves, market of barter,
always welcomes others
& hosts and guests flourished
on exchange of palm oil, yams and garri.
This home of plants and birds,
birthmarks of the sky,
least expected a stampede;
there's no refuge east or west,
north or south of this paradise.

Did others not envy my evergreen,
which no reason or season could steal
but only brighten with desire?
Did others not envy the waters
that covered me from sunstroke,
scourge of others the year round?

My nativity gives immortal pain
masked in barrels of oil —
I stew in the womb of fortune.
I live in the deathbed
prepared by a cabal of brokers
breaking the peace of centuries

& tainting not only a thousand rivers,
my lifeblood from the beginning,
but scorching the air and soil.
How many aborigines have been killed
as their sacred soil was debauched
by prospectors, money-mongers?

My birds take flight to the sea,
the animals grope in the burning bush;
head blindly to the hinterland
where the cow's enthroned.
The sky singes my evergreen leaves
and baldness robs me of youthful years.
These are the constitutional rewards
of plenitude, a small fish in the Niger!

Now we are called to banquets
of baron robbers where space's belatedly
created for us to pray over bounties,
the time to say goodbye to our birth
right, now a boon cake for others.

With what eyes will *Olokun*
look at her beneficiaries,
dead or still living in the rack
of uniformed dogs barking
and biting protesters
brandishing green leaves?
The standard-bearer's betrayed
in the house by thieves, relatives,
& the reapers of the delta crop
could care less for minority rights!

And I am assaulted by visions of
the hangman on a hot Friday noon,
the cries in the garden streets of the port
and the silence in homes that speak loud
in grief that deluged the land's memory.

Those nine mounds woke
into another world, ghostly kings
scornful of their murderers.

Nobody can go further than those mounds
in the fight to right chronic habits
of greed and every wrong of power.
The inheritance I have been blessed with
now crushes my body and soul.

UPON RECEIVING AN INVITATION
TO A MEMORIAL FOR KEN SARO-WIWA
Marcielle Brandler

Was there one more letter
which could have been sent
to save the life of an author
whose words imprisoned him?

I cannot say I had too many
errands or miles to go before
defending my colleague's right
to live. How guilty am I

of negligence? When I heard
his government had recaptured
him, I had intended to act, No
guilt can write his essays

or birth the children,
grandchildren he might
have had. For the memory
of Ken, whom I had never

met nor read, for writers
who should have the right
to express any ideas they
choose, my action will be

immediate and swift. I
shall never again hesitate
to use my collective
power to defend you.

THUNDER FROM THE MOUNTAINS
Haba G. Musengezi

On that day the Nigerian generals will quiver
They will try to flee
But their feet will fail them.

The chorus will get louder
Like thunder from the mountains.
Men and women, patriots
Crying out loud:
        Give us liberty or give us death.

And the iron gates shall be opened
        to set free
Those languishing in the dark
With no one to nurse their wounds
Those who are famished
With no one to give them water
                or a morsel of bread.
Those who are weak in body
With no one to prop them up
And the weak in spirit
Who have no one to assure them that
                        one day soon
There will be thunder from the mountains
Of patriots crying out loud and clear
Give us liberty or give us death.

THE LIE
Jonathan Hart

Bones bleach on the great shore
Drums, long silent and afar, implore
Atavistic masks that cry
When the world gives the lie.

Where black gold pours from the land
Seeps through the dead hand
Prisoners in the margins sigh
While accounts give the world the lie.

Once gold and God burned in glass
Together first and last, God soon buried
In the blast, now yellow dust
Lies like blood on a white plate.

WHY?
Oluwatoyin A. Asojo

waves dyed black
beg to be freed
of their burden
striking rocks
in vain...

pebbles refuse
to skip...
fishes belly up
adorned and drowned
in black gold...

semi-senile babes
squint hardly seeing
rarely caring...
[distended bellies...]
across the hill a mansion...

gold poisons
her veins...
gold blinds him...
gold... black gold...
feeding dogs
while babes starve...

DAGA NI SAI KAI[1]
Abdul-Rasheed Na'Allah

(traditionally followed by heavy drumbeats, but in this occasion,
needs mellowed *Kalangu* — Hausa talking — drum rhythms)

Lead: Daga ni sai kai
Chorus: Rui!
Lead: Kunun zaki
Chorus: Rui!
All: Kunun zaki
           Rui!!
           Daga ni sai kai
           Rui!!

For you, araa mi
           naked I remain;
before your ghostself
           my heart (I offer).

Chorus: Daga ni sai kai,
           Rui!
           Kunun zaki
           Rui!

Your skeleton
booms ornamental perfume
of a decaying beauty.
My habeebah, before your corrugated hole,
           my heavy eyes.

Chorus: Daga ni sai kai,
           Rui!
           Kunun zaki,
           Rui!

Your mindin-mindin[2]
those flies extracted from

Your bonemarrows:
Oliver Twists!
Stampeded
For another round.

Chorus: Daga ni sai kai
   Rui!
   Kunun zaƙi
   Rui!

Ferocious Flies:
tasted from the honey pots
drowned, lost in the ecstasy
   of greed.

   Daga ni sai kai
   Rui!
   Kunun zaƙi
   Rui!

Wonder, my love!
Your limestone
Yet,
Maintains its lime
in its stone.
Oh, those sqeezemania-crushers!

   Daga ni sai kai
   Rui!
   Kunun zaƙi
   Rui!

Alarm,
Our eyeswater,
now in million buckets,
Freezes under
this inept temperature of our strange day.
Love, I'm losing my eyes to this coldness!

Daga ni sai kai
Rui!
Kunun zaƙi
Rui!

Oh, acquaint me!
Our bold eyeballs
see only darkness.
Our blistering sun
unable to melt ice.
Our molars
incapable of grinding banana.
Acquaint me, love,
What a grotesque is't?

Daga ni sai kai
Rui!
Kunun zaƙi
Rui!

Pray, Ferocious Flies,
What has the Minaret
and the Cross undo in thou?
Or, how much
undoing hath thou maketh of thyselves!

Daga ni sai kai
Rui!
Kunun zaƙi
Rui!

The Parrot knows
When the music gets bitter
He knoweth when yeh hath
Turneth the verses blank!

> Daga ni sai kai
> Rui!
> Kunun zaƙi
> Rui!

Except they can tell the rout through which water enters a coconut,
How lines get unto the palm of their hands,
They never can dim the colors I see in your eyes,
Whatever dust the Flies fern into them.

> Daga ni sai kai
> Rui!
> Kunun zaƙi
> Rui!

Darling,
Your singing voice shall boom again.
Your children
Shall demand for justice
On the death that killed their father!

> Daga ni sai kai
> Rui!
> Kunun zaƙi
> Rui!

Mtun
It's you and I
Kai,
A delicious pap,
Rui!!

> Daga ni sai kai
> Rui!
> Kunun zaƙi
> Rui!

NOTES
1   Hausa popular song among traders and popular freelance drummers
    (especially in Sokoto areas), usually a love song meaning 'darling,
    it's you and I forever', or 'alone in our den')
2   A word in Ilorin Yoruba describing sweet food substance, especially
    in the brand of 'goody-goody', etc.

I WILL KEEP YOU IN MY HEART
Lisa Mahoney

Although we never met,
I knew you in my heart.
And the way they stole your life from you,
Has torn my faith apart.

I fought, I prayed, I wept for you,
But to no avail.
For now your pen lies silent…
It won't write another tale.

I could not save your life,
I accept that now.
But I will try to save your voice,
Keep it alive, somehow.

I will pick up your pen,
And hold it in my hand.
And together we shall tell your tale,
So others understand.

I hope someday we will meet,
In a place that's just and fair.
But until then, you are in my heart,
And I will keep you there.

GOOD MORNING NIGERIA
Abdul-Rasheed Na'Allah

Good morning, Nigeria.
(Kin tashi lafiya?),
Did you wake up well?
Or still crumbling on your knees?
Staggering?
Tell me, Nigeria,
Are you still in bed,
When the world has already taken a leap.

Good morning!
Yes, so we want,
Your morning to be good.
We want you to fly in the plane of your desires.
We all here want your day to be great,
So that at night, you'll look back
And smile that you're already high
beyond the sky.

But,
Do your corridor-wolves make your morning good?
Do the ants at your hills wish your morning good?
Do the worms in your intestines pray your morning well?
Their dagger-teeth dig deep into your flesh:
They suck your blood to the marrow,
And drink your wells to finish.

Nigeria,
If your morning must enjoy the soothing sun,
Those parasites
Must be drained of strength.
Your gold house, guard,
Mount your proud presence!
If your wall does not crack
No lizard can enter it!

IV

Lament, Struggle

The Ken Saro-Wiwa Echo
Tayo Olafioye

The recent festival of insanity in Nigeria sacrificed Ken Saro-Wiwa and others in the bonfire of naked power and ignominy that echoed the world. It was only in Nigeria that some were laughing, blinded by their crude arrogance while the rest of the world mourned. Ken Saro-Wiwa, thus, has joined the ranks of glorious eternities that outlast the new Neros of Africa.

Writers are most often the light that penetrates the darkness of power. Hence the pen shall forever murder their sleep and pull the rug of complacency off their feet. Both exile — the castration of the soul — and death, have been the prices that writers pay for justice and truth to make existence manageable for humanity. The enemies of the power of the mind and truth will not succeed.

They inundate the world with ignoble excuses for the barbaric sacrifice of Saro-Wiwa because their conscience, decency and perception of reality have turned into stones. Their rush to irrationality had been guided by ethnocentrism, greed, selfishness, myopia, insensitivity and Godlessness. They never listened to the world when it pleaded for Saro-Wiwa's life. Why should the world listen to their religion of falsehood with which they proselytize the globe? They are maggots swimming erratically in their own stench. They forget history. They will not escape. They row backwards in the boat of progress. Not only that, they have eaten the head of an owl and so owe the devil a debt. They have farmed pythons in the honey pots of incredulity. They have finally travelled in the stormy seas of perversions. Their redemption is no longer achievable.

Oh Spirits of the Deep, hear our pains today and help. The present is too difficult to live. Your land is now occupied by demons who eat falsehood for dinner. Our noon is the night of sorrow. Nigeria is now a dead fish. It rots from the head.

Having lamented in concert with the chorus of outrage from the rest of the world, the passing of Ken Saro-Wiwa, what exactly was the perception and mood of the authority that annihilated him? The government faked consternation at the reaction of the world against a seemingly innocuous event which the extermination of the nine 'agitators and conspirators' represented in their fuzzy thinking. David Atta, the Press Secretary to General Abacha, the Head of State of Nigeria, in an interview with the BBC, London, published in *West Africa* of the week of 27 November to December 1995, said:

> Everything we do in Nigeria in the jaundiced eyes of the world will be seen as a travesty of justice. There is an organized conspiracy against our country. Under General Abacha, definite steps have been taken so that Nigeria can become a responsible member of global democratization. Some people were tried for attempting to overthrow the government violently. Our Head of State yielded to international pressure, commuted the sentences, but this is not sufficient to placate a hostile international community against our country. (p. 18)

One should offer a million kudos to Mr. Atta and his government for this brilliant gaseous effusion and linguistic confusion based on disconcerting illogic. The world must truly be sick to collectively drub Nigeria an evil, without a transparent cause to precipitate the speedy, tornado-like judicial process that lacked substantive distancing between judicial activities to allow the jaundiced world to sufficiently appreciate the government's case. What was the haste intended to achieve that expended Saro-Wiwa and company? The fury behind the giddy justice was vengeance from allied forces against the voices that alerted and exposed a system that lurched on to undue privileges and denials. It was common knowledge that Saro-Wiwa resisted Ibo oppression of his Ogoni people when they were under the rule of the Ibos in the regional political arrangement of the First Republic. The Nigerian civil war liberated his minority ethnic group. The liberation denied the Ibos their hold on the economic and social life-line of the Ogoni people whose habitat harbors the oil wealth of Nigeria till today. Some members of the Ibo leadership cadre must extract their own pound of flesh when the illogic of Nigerian politics permits it. The northern oligarchy, on the other hand, could not be expected to embrace a radical group that sought fair redistribution of the economic wealth that lubricated the north's political stranglehold on the rest of the country.

It is ironic that the Nigerian government and its spokesmen honed on a global conspiracy against them. Hard to believe. What exactly would the world gain to unjustly besmear Nigeria? How could the leadership read diabolics into or twist what were was obvious entities against which the might of Nigerian government was set? If Nigeria's propaganda machinery could not change or affect the perception of the world, shouldn't they rethink their behavior? Or how could the whole world be so silly and petty to pick on almighty Nigeria? Didn't Mandela feel betrayed? Perhaps Mandela was part of the conspiracy too! Nigeria should remember that those who matter in the world have direct access to authentic facts of events in Nigeria other than what the government spins. Perhaps the credit for this poor disingenuity should go to its engineers of misinformation as I have stated in this poem:

"Missions Abroad"
Consulates of stench;
Their masters' voices;
Consummate defenders of hell;
sounding cymbals of ignominy;
Agents of Nero;
Egregious maggots of state;
Eclipse of the African genius;
Incubus at large;
Sons and daughters of January;
Farmers of the crops of deceit;
Engineers of misinformation;
Architects of retrogression;

Doctors of lunacy;
Professors of vacancy;
Editors of misology;
Christians without Christ;
Muslims without Mohammed;
Ambassadors of bashing;
Soyinka, their victim;
Others, their minced meat;
Lawyers ignoble;
Flocks without a shepherd;
A nation without Caesar.

In another poem titled 'Mandela Berates Nigeria', from a collection called *The Anthology of Agonies,* the poet observed:

The uniforms thought
everyone a sergeant-major
in their boot-camps.
Poison of the rum
in the gumption
hemlock of their air-headedness.
Hence, Mandela, the man who —
tamed wilder howlings.
An older woman not old
When it's the dance she knows.
Then Mandela told the world court:
their crudities
and prodigalities.
Not fit in the committee
of nations, civilized
beyond reproach.
That which an old man sees
sitting down,
the young cannot
standing up.

These wild howlings and behaviors, repugnated the world over, were the indices of Nigerian government democratization and the heroic exploits of the affectionately heralded General! The Nigerian government appreciated its own horror when it looked at its own image in the mirror. Hence, they could not understand the insensitivity of the world to their own position. Chief Tom Ikimi, the Foreign Minister, was quoted to have said in Auckland, New Zealand, during the last Commonwealth meeting, that the Ken Saro-Wiwa issue had been, "Over politicized and dramatized." The members of the global democratization had no reason to squawk at all. In a show of the myth of action, therefore, the government recalled some of its envoys abroad. The world was too blinded to appreciate Nigeria's self-righteousness. Someone must be playing games.

The flame of the government's spurious indignations continued in its citations of a so-called 'Harare Declaration'. The Commonwealth, it claimed, had violated Nigeria's human rights. It feared this would subvert its sovereignty as a member state and shake up the existence of the Commonwealth itself. Did anyone with judicious critical analysis embrace Nigeria's claim to human rights — a case of the pot calling the kettle black? How eminent is Nigeria's importance to the Commonwealth that its unratified violent governance would destabilize the Commonwealth? Who needs who? Satan would cite the Bible or Koran to best suit his need.

In 'Elegy for Nine Warriors', Tanure Ojaide, a past winner of the Commonwealth Prize for poetry, celebrates in his *Delta Blues*, the hubristic activities assailing Nigeria and its citizenry:

> Those I remember in my song
> will outlive this ghoulish season,
> dawn will outlive the long night.
> I hear voices stifled by the hangmen,
> an old cockroach in the groins of Aso Rock.
> Those I remember with these notes
> walk back erect from the stake.
> The hangman has made his case,
> delivered nine heads through the sunpost
> and soared his eyes from sleepless nights.
> The nine start their "life after death"
> as the street carries their standard.

Nigeria has behaved the hangman in a ghoulish fashion. It is the hanged ones who have a place in glorious history because they confronted the cyclonic fury of evil, with the ultimate they had. To remind the uniforms as the commanders of roaches, the artist painted their image in unflattering terms, if at all, they were sensitive to infamy and indecency:

> The forest of flowers mock
> the thief, commander of roaches;
> there are some heads like the hangman's
> that will never have the vision of right
> What does a crow know of flowers?
> When ghosts sit down the executioner
> let him plead for neither mercy nor pity;
> the General will meet the Master Sergeant
> and share the naked dance to the dark hole.

That some compatriots alert the conscience of the global democracy, is an act of eternal vigilance. It is the summons to collective global condemnation. It is a reminder of the judgments of history on perverse rulers that danced the naked dance to the dark hole. They may not believe it now or expect it, but internal convulsions, native to distress and discomfort, will gain sway as they have in many classic conditions of degeneration and abuse. Global consciences will see fit to participate in more substantive terms. And of course, they are doing so already. What with the recent United Nations Commission of enquiry sent to Nigeria to collect on the spot, facts of the Nigerian condition. That cannot have been a good report card for the 'giant of Africa', that claimed a faked sense of democratic responsibility. If one finger is sick, the rest of the hand would feel the pain.

The Ogoni people for whom the nine heroes died are equally heralded. Tayo Olafioye paints them in 'Ogoni People: Oilwells of Nigeria', as:

> … the tree
> on which grows
> the Niger gold.
> … the ocean
> in which flows

the Texas tea.
Cheated for eons
but now-embraced for life.
Theirs: the stench of miens
Only death removes the bitterness
of a blinded people.

The world cannot remain silent when this evil scourge invades a people, not even the smallest spot on the globe. The world must respond to agonies from any of its praxis.

The democratic world was not the one to hold culpable for the Nigerian conspiracy. Rather, it was the Anglo-Dutch Shell Petroleum Company, that conspired with Nigerian officials against the world. They denied culpability for the Nigerian sacrifice of the famous nine. Yet, it was within their influence in their financial dealings with the Nigerian government, to stop the execution. All they needed to do was to threaten withdrawal and exposition to force the oligarchy to behave in a civilized manner. But the lure of billions of dollars in oil revenue was too strong to resist. After all, the Ogoni people and their welfare were too insignificant to wretch the conscience of oil magnates. The oil company needed only to cushion the pockets of power to gain compliance in eliminating the enemies — the crooked woods that destabilize the hearth of raging specks of fire. MOSOP (the Movement for the Survival of the Ogoni People) once declared in a sardonic tonality:

Oil exploration has turned Ogoni into a wasteland. Lands, streams and creeks are totally and continuously polluted. Acid rain, oil spillages and oil-blow-outs have devastated Ogoni territory. (*West Africa*, 18)

But the oil company claimed that one of their significant roles in Nigeria was and is to create wealth for the people. Hogwash!! Even the blind can see the transparent poverty of ordinary Nigerians today. The Ogoni landscape was devastated and so were the people, sent into penury. They lost the land as well as the financial returns due them to build a prosperous society. The termites, who have nothing of their own, demolished the economic possibilities of the

Ogoni people. The Shell company had made up to thirty billion dollars in oil revenue since 1958, when they started exploring and exploiting oil in Nigeria. Not a trickle of remuneration dropped on Ogoni land as compensation due them. On top of it all, the evil hands dealt them, killed their leadership core for demanding the rights of Ogoni people. Is Nigeria a 'responsible democratization' or the most inconsiderate and infinite maldistributor of wealth amongst its people so malnourished?

In an example of dyslexic leadership that reads the mood of the country upside down, the eminent Minister of Information in Nigeria, Dr. Walter Ofonagoro, claimed ludicrously, in a recent BBC program on Lagos shown in London, that the only people his government needed to impress are Nigerians, not the outside world, which the like of the BBC represented. The man in charge of the polish of the image of the country seemed to need polish himself. It simply means that the political culture of Nigeria is used to insensitivity and untruth as the way of life. So gullible are they that they built a religion in which they expect the rest of the world to believe. This is a long way into the night. Saro-Wiwa's death will forever remain the echo of pain in the ears of Nigerian Neros that have brought the country to its knees. It is a very bleak afternoon in the morning of Nigeria. Ask the ordinary citizens of Nigeria about it. They would tell you how truly impressed they are.

BIBLIOGRAPHY

BBC: London — Interviews. 1995–1996.

Ojaide, Tenure. "Delta Blues." Charlotte North Carolina, 1996. (An unpublished collection written in the wake of Ken Saro-Wiwa's death.)

Olafioye, Tayo. "An Anthology of Agonies." 1996. (An unpublished collection, newly written, to celebrate Saro-Wiwa.)

West Africa. November–December 1995.

The Writer and the Junta
Taiwo Oloruntoba-Oju

'The Odd, the Odious and Our Very Odia' is the title of an article by Ken Saro-Wiwa (1989). At the time he coined this title, nearly ten years ago, he was not to know that he would one day become eternal victim of a heinous oddity, perhaps one of the most that civilized existence has been forced to witness — the despatch, by hanging, of a relatively temperate writer by a desperate junta — more odious by innumerable quantums than the phenomenon in question when he wrote. At that time, Saro-Wiwa was locked in a critical and somewhat bantersome exchange with fellow writer and critic, Odia Ofeimun. For, whatever else Ken was, he was first of all a writer, with a writer's sensitivity, a keen perception and, inevitably, a critical mien. That he picked up the gauntlet thrown by the despotic and genocidal ravaging of oil-rich Ogoniland was indeed a reflection of this mien. At the time he wrote, Saro-Wiwa was not to know that he would become President of the Association of Nigerian Authors some day soon, and that Odia Ofeimun would actually succeed him in that position. Now bodily transited, he would not know that, in a rare combination of the odd and the odious, our Odia was also recently arrested by the same Nigerian authorities, only about four months after they despatched himself, Odia's predecessor, to those wobbly Nigerian gallows, replica of the nation's political and judicial system.

It is fairly odd that the operatives who carried out this latest act of aggression against writers could not see it as a further smear on the ugly visage of the current regime. Surely they could with their mind's ear perceive a resounding OH NO, NOT AGAIN from the civilized world when it gets about that the new President of the Association of Nigerian Writers, after Saro-Wiwa, has also been arrested. Except that it is the special orientation of soldiery, especially soldiery of the unsupervised *immediate effect and automatic alacrity* variety such as ours, to rate precipitate action and superficial accomplishment above reasoned analysis or long-term consideration.

Even with such 'rationale' it is alarming that the Nigerian authorities would think nothing of hounding Nigeria and Africa's first intellectual citizen (by virtue of the Nobel and other, long-standing attainment) all over the world, hanging the immediate past President of the Association of Nigerian Authors, arresting the current one, and adorning their jails with the incarceration of several other writers.

Odd as it may appear, the anti-writer, anti-intellectual stance of the Nigerian military is a mere strain of a grand anti-logic. The greatest oddity, reminiscent of classic dog wagging tail absurdity, is that the soldier should rule over the writer in the first place. If a choice were to be made, freely, the writer is arguably more suited to the leadership of a nation. When in hubristic agony a General Babangida (immediate past Nigerian military dictator) cries out: "We are in power and with power," the writer, amongst other profound elements of society, responds with a knowing smile — broader still when the man fell from power soon after the utterance — that power and the holding of it is all too transient. The writer is in knowledge and with knowledge, the lasting legacy.

The profound writer, almost invariably a thinker or philosopher, ruled rather by elevated ideals than by the instinct of self and of immediate survival, not oriented towards the use of force or the substitution of same for reasoned argument, etc., is by this additional attribute also more suited to the leadership of a nation. The latter trait is no doubt possessed by all animals in common, but it is specially cultivated by the soldiery in the human society, given their peculiar function. It is to be employed, however, only under the strict guidance of, and directive from, civil authority. Is anti-intellectualism on the part of the military manifestation of a deep-seated complex?

It is certainly odd that, in any body's scale of values, the intellectuals and writers of a nation should be considered fair game — in *anybody's* scale of values, let alone in the scale of values of supposed leaders of the nation in question. What, after all, is any nation without its cream of intellectuals and writers? True, the writer had often been regarded as fair game by dictators whose constant fear is that the pen might indeed be mightier than their tanks. Especially for rulers who wield power without glory, whose authority is founded on illegality and is therefore sustained by stratagem, the writer as bearer and barer of the truth must be wiped off the face of the earth, a bane to their very existence. Even so, one would have thought that today, at the dawn of the 21st century, civilized existence does show sufficient models of pacification, of sanity, and of qualitative valuation.

What we are confronted with here in Nigeria, therefore, is a faulty valuation model or, better still, a faulty valuer model. The writer, yes, is repository of the collective wisdom and noble aspirations of the society. The writer, yes again, functions as 'the record of the mores and experience of his society and as the voice of vision in his own time' ... etc., etc. But then, it takes an equally visionary leadership to perceive all this. Niyi Osundare did put it nicely, as always, when he said that if our leaders ever read books, held books and similar matter in their hands everyday, they would be a lot more appreciative of the writer's role in society, and a lot less eager to send writers into their detention holes — a faulty valuer model.

We insist that this oddity must derive from a faulty perception, by the Nigerian military, of the writer's significance in the social scheme of things. Yet, a critical comparison of the relative input of Nigerian writers and the Nigerian military to the nation's image, growth and well-being does not justify any negative or inferior assessment of the former. Indeed, it is true that Nigerian writers have done a lot more for the nation than the Nigerian military — it is about time the truth of this were loudly established.

Let us square up to the comparison in terms of actual attainment. To start with the history books do not record a whimper from the Nigerian soldiery when our writers and nationalists (among them intellectuals and writers too) risked jail terms, etc., in quest for the nation's independence. The bravado and messianism that the military now displays in confronting the ordinary citizenry were not quick to manifest in those days in the face of the colonial machinery, within which, rather, black military elements quietly acquiesced. To repeat, the anti-colonial struggle had to draw from the class of intellectuals and writers rather than from military elements.

Since independence, too, the Nigerian military machine has brought little glory to the nation, being untested in independent external warfare, or in warding off any serious threat to the security of the nation. Only infamy, as Nigerian armoured tanks are adept at mowing down defenseless Nigerian citizens and at capturing the seat of civil authority, thus disrupting the natural process of political education and emancipation, acquiring, for the military, a reputation for usurpation, and additionally slapping a reputation for insipid reticence on the unsuspecting populace. The anachronism of warlords acquiring kingdoms through the force of arms never seems to occur to our military. At least those warlords of old proved so to the very core of the word; mostly assembling their own armies and fighting expansionist wars with the stakes high and the risks enormous — not sneak into reckoning through an easy and treacherous subversion of state security apparatus ready-made and placed in their care. Such latter had a name different from 'warriors'.... Oh, we know that the Nigerian military often chest-beats about fighting an internal war to procure unity for the country. This was a war provoked by the military itself, mind you, not to mention expending an eternity on a frequently muddled up programme to subdue a rag-tag, hurriedly assembled, ill-equipped liberation force.

By contrast to such infamy, Nigerian writers have constantly functioned as the voice of vision in their society. The input that brought the nation to independence was mostly intellectual and, in the specific case of Nigeria, non-military. Apart from writers' contribution to Nigerian independence, and their input in the educational and cultural sectors, Nigerian writers have, through sheer intellectual prowess, constantly brought fame and glory, including enduring international honours, to the nation. According to what scale of values therefore, should the clan of writers in Nigeria be 'exterminated' or persecuted just to keep the military in authority!

II

Of course the Nigerian military do not rule over *just* writers, but over the entire community of academics, intellectuals, professionals with academic orientation (lawyers, journalists, engineers, etc.) artisans, politicians, traditional 'rulers', etc., some 80 million or so otherwise eminent souls turned into virtual sods by their unfaithful servants and their own fitful resolve to the contrary. The guilt of this absurdity of soldiers ruling over the nation is a collective one.

Following from this grand anomaly, several 'minor' others. Observe the manner in which logic has been long stood on its head, begetting related aberrations — the catalogue is long and it is gory. First consider the progeny theory of military rule ('child of necessity', etc., etc.), the philosophical plank on which the odium is based. It is spawned by apologists of military rule — principally, needless to say, the military themselves. The acceptance of this theory by some otherwise revered individuals, manifests a collective failure of cognition. What manner of cognition after all conceives of a phenomenon as a necessity and at the same time as an aberration, or vice-versa. I have often suspected the phrase 'necessary evil' to be only superficially tenable, a dubious coalescence of incompatible paradigms. What is deemed necessary within positive, humane, competent and comprehensive valuation cannot be evil anymore relative to the engendering moral and philosophical imperative. Even Satan (to employ a well-know paradigm) cannot be evil within any moral/philosophical framework that designates him (?) a necessity. Hence it is the paradigm, 'necessity', that should be focused upon and be rigorously appraised beyond a fleeting, orchestrated apparentness.

To proceed, then, since when it has been deemed 'necessary' for civilians without requisite training or orientation to run a battalion simply because there is feuding or mutiny inside a military formation — even if the ensuing damage could actually be catastrophic? By a simple vice-versariness, the bogey of the 'necessity' of military rule is damaged beyond logical retrieval.

A disciplined, well-trained and *disinterested* soldiery may be called upon to contain rioting within the populace, to separate feuding parties and even, if necessary, employ force to maintain a peaceful atmosphere for necessary dialogue within its area of operation, all this without necessarily getting involved in overall governance. Trouble starts only when, whatever the nature of the feud, the soldiers themselves become interested parties, not at the service of the superintending civil leadership but at their own service, with their own 'felo Naijeriens' agenda to prosecute. Then they become the evil, *not* the necessity.

When the military say they are a child of necessity, all they mean apparently is that it was necessary for some of them to realise their personal ambitions opportunistically through the force of arms placed at their disposal by, ironically, the civil populace. The fact that they invariably install themselves in positions of governance belies any claim to altruism in their intervention in the political destiny of the nation. In their foray into governance the military compromise their professionalism and therefore the security of the nation, among sundry other anomalies. Indeed there are certain children that should never be born.

Since this faulty genetic manipulation called 'child of necessity', the polity has known little sanity. Consider how justice, a necessary condition for sanity, has itself been stood on its head, most especially in recent times. All the honest people are in jail or detention. A law is put out prescribing jail terms for would-be derailers of yet another 'trans-sit-on' programme put in place by the military, etc., etc. The laugh is that this law itself is put out by the actual annulers of our emerging nationhood, via the annulment of an earlier protracted transition which culminated in the June 12, 1993 presidential elections, after which the absurdist drama has continued unabated.

We have witnessed more absurdity, as otherwise respectable sectors of the society repeatedly acquiesce to the anomaly. Again and again we witness with drooping jaws the absurdity of traditional 'rulers' turned vassals, flying with flowing robes and other paraphernalia of feigned dignity to pay dues of obeisance to Abuja, returning to their respective 'domains' with the sceptre or other insignia of this modern conqueror held aloft, but with little cheer for their hungry, maimed, detained and otherwise abused 'subjects', who sometimes include their own chieftains. Hardly in the character of their forebears who invariably equated life with honour.

We have witnessed others, mostly politicians but also the occasional academic stray, even the occasional 'writer' (no pretension to classificatory absolutism here), who equally betray principle to prop up the anomaly of military rule. Frequently they cite 'realism' and, sometimes, 'expediency' (these are convertible currencies, mind you) as rationale for their unworthy action. One does recoil at the prospect of such people eventually attaining leadership of the nation — at what manner of national ethos such elevation would automatically foster. For their fee (there is a fee alright), these people also pay the price of ignominy that constantly dogs their steps. Every so often they are made to confront the reminder that, however huge your haul as a whore, everyone still knows that your clients hurl you down on your back, and that you rake in just as much muck in the dark.

In this long, unending and gory catalogue occurs the latest smokescreen of 'transition' (to civil rule), tagged the 'zero party' election, with the smattering vestiges of credibility zeroed out (or is it screened out?) of the exercise, leaving mostly the unemployed, opportunist, etc., centre stage. In a number of places the election was won by students, while in some, people who never even contested also 'won' and were sworn in. Some of the candidates thrown up by this bizarre exercise were so minuscule in reckoning that area boys, children of the times (of necessity?), lined them up and whipped them up at the polling station on polls day, to explosive applause by pollsters! Nigeria is about the only country in the world — and countries with competing credentials are welcome to contest this claim — where you can become anything from a local government chairman to a head of state without the benefit of a good reputation — or even any reputation for that matter. Indeed, it is Nigeria's grand tragedy that most of the country's heads of state since independence have been previously unknown entities (unknown to the civil populace) who take the country over at night (and sometimes in daylight) when Nigerian citizens are, as usual, asnore.

The writer, constantly calling for renewed consciousness, clashes inevitably with the junta. This, precisely, is the story of Saro-Wiwa.

The persecution of the writer by the junta is indeed one item in a long string of odious oddities. Principally, it is a fallout from that huge anti-logic that has been our affliction in this country for three decades on — the military in governance. It is the constant obligation of the Nigerian writer to — what else — continue to write them off the corridors of governance.

194 · Ogoni's Agonies

REFERENCES

Saro-Wiwa, Ken. "The Odd, The Odious and Our Very Odia." *Guardian*, 5 January 1989. 10.

Ken Saro-Wiwa — in Short, a Giant[1]
Bernth Lindfors

For some time Saro-Wiwa spearheaded a move to safeguard the rights of the Ogoni, a small ethnic group in an oil-rich area of South-central Nigeria that has been impoverished by exploitation of its lands by the Nigerian government and various Western oil companies. Ogoni rivers have become polluted, destroying the livelihood of fishermen, and natural gas burnoffs have polluted the air, endangering the health of everyone in the region. When the Ogoni attempted to protest their plight a few years ago, federal troops marched, burnt hundreds of homes, and killed scores of protestors. In response, Saro-Wiwa formed a Movement for the Survival of the Ogoni People (MOSOP), drafted an *Ogoni Bill of Rights*, wrote numerous articles for Nigerian media on maltreatment of his people, and tried to bring the situation to the attention of the United Nations. He also made a documentary film detailing the suffering and repression of the Ogoni. For these efforts he was imprisoned for treason by the Babangida government in June of 1993; he was released by a new Nigerian government a few months later, but it was feared that he might still face trial or other political repercussions for his outspoken activism.

Such threat did not immediately silence him. In January 1994 he testified before a commission of enquiry investigating recent ethnic clashes in which over 400 Ogoni were killed. He continued to speak up fearlessly for his people and for others who have been denied basic human rights in Nigeria until he was finally hanged along with eight others by the Abacha regime on the 10 of November

1995. In his Presidential Address at the 1992 conference of the Association of Nigerian Authors he said:

> Human rights is the only guarantee of peaceful co-existence of peoples, the insurance of justice for individuals and groups. Denied, it creates conditions of social and political unrest and often leads to violence and conflict — I therefore consider it a worthy service to humanity and a patriotic duty to protest the denial of rights to individuals and communities.

Saro-Wiwa lived by this creed. But he was not a fulltime political activist. He also distinguished himself as a Commissioner of the Rivers State, a successful businessman, a television producer, a newspaper columnist, a publisher, and an author of more than two dozen books. He may be best known in Nigeria for his popular television comedy series, *Basi and Company*, which ran for six years (1985–1990),[2] and is estimated to have attracted a viewing audience of more than thirty million every Wednesday night. In addition to producing this show, he recruited and trained its actors and actresses, and penned its more than 150 episodes himself. To keep even busier, he wrote widely for the press too, eventually starting his own column, 'Similia', in the Lagos *Sunday Times*, which he filled with salty commentary on current Nigerian political, economic and cultural events. During this same hyperactive period his star was rising in the literary world, largely due to the success of his first novel, *Sozaboy* (1985),[3] which had been written in an amusing experimental idiom he called 'rotten English'. And in his spare time he published volume after volume of his own poetry, short stories, plays, essays, folktales, children's literature, analyses of the Nigerian civil war, and narrative and dramatic spin-offs of his *Basi and Company* scripts. On one day in 1991, his fiftieth birthday, his own publishing house, Saros International Publishers, launched eight new titles by him. In this manner he managed in less than a decade to establish himself as a veritable literary dynamo.

Despite the popular nature of much of his writing, Saro-Wiwa won the respect of literary critics and commentators who appreciate his colloquial directness and vibrant humor but also commend his craft and underlying seriousness of purpose. Abiola Irele has called him "a major new figure in our national literature," an opinion borne out by the fact that more has been written about him in recent years than about any other Nigerian writers except such canonical colossi as Wole Soyinka and Chinua Achebe. Some of the press reports on Saro-Wiwa jokingly refer to him as a 'short giant' or a vertically challenged giant, but it is clear that he was already looming high enough to cast a long shadow and that his energy and vitality had raised him far above many of his peers.

In his writing, in his politics, in his impulses, Saro-Wiwa was truly a man of the people. But unlike Chief Nanga, he was also, first and foremost, a man *for* the people. He wrote to move people — to make them laugh, think, protest, act. And in his political work he moved to help people, defending them from injustice by pleading their case in the most conspicuous public arenas. In word and deed he excelled as a champion of the little man and as an advocate of human rights for all people, regardless of size and stature.

NOTES
1   This paper was originally written by Lindfors as a tribute to Saro-Wiwa on behalf of the selection jury of the 1994 Fonlon-Nichols Prize.
2   He later published some of these plays as *Basi and Company: Four Television Plays*. Port Harcourt: Saros International, 1989.
3   *Sozaboy: A Novel in Rotten English*. Port Harcourt: Ewell: Saros International, 1985.

Poetry

WAILS
(after *udje* dance songs)
Tanure Ojaide

Another ANA meeting will be called
and singers will gather.
I will look all over
and see a space
that can take more than a hundred —
the elephant never hides.
I ask the god of songs
whether all the singers will come,
but that silent space
that can take more than a hundred
stares at me with nostalgia
and gives me a bad cold.
I won't find one singer
when another ANA meeting will be called.

Aridon, give me the voice
to raise this wail
beyond high walls.
In one year I have seen
my forest of friends cut down,
now dust taunts my memory.

If I don't open my mouth,
I will be a dumb-and-deaf
who's unable to forewarn
after a bad dream.
The world needs to hear this —
there's one absent in the assembly,
the singers will never be complete
without the elephant in their midst.

I must raise the loud wail
so that each will reflect his fate.
Take care of your people,
they are your proud assets.
The boa thoughtlessly devours
its own offspring, Nigeria's
a boa-constrictor in the world map.

Streets echo with wails.
A terrible event has befallen the land,
everyone is covered with shame or sorrow —
this death exceeds other deaths.
They have murdered a favourite son,
this news cannot be a hoax;
for the love of terror,
they have hanged a favourite son
and eight other bearers of truth.
Nobody fools others about these deaths.

The god of songs sobs for a favourite son
and threatens the murderers with repercussions.
None of them will escape the fallout of this travesty
of justice in the name of law and order.
Their heads will be sought everywhere
for the mortal blow they deserve.

Death's such a savage ogre —
show me the road of Death
so that I can fake another course.

That's the song of childhood and fear.
Now I will not choose another course
just to avoid death in the right path.

Who will make me laugh,
who will bring *Basi & Company* to life?
Who will speak to me rotten English,
the lingua franca of the coastline?
Who will tell the forest of flowers?
Who will traverse the darkling plain of the delta?
Who will stand in front as the *iroko* shield
to regain the stolen birthright?
It's for his immeasurable services
that the giant's remembered.
There will be no end to this wail.

"If we had known it would come
to this,…" but he's gone—
let no one defile his memory
with regrets and devious wishes.
Death's so impenetrable he hears not.
Nigeria has lost her true diviner
but let no one regret his course.

The Delta breeds giants only to lose them,
but after each warrior-chief's fall,
somebody else carries the standard—
Boro left for Saro-Wiwa to take over,
the stump will grow into another *iroko*.
The hardwood shield is broken,
the people are exposed to enemy missiles;
the diviner's spell is broken
& everybody's left in the open.
But the diviner's words are never halted
by death—Ominigbo is my witness.

There's a terrible death in our midst.
The death of a king, president, or general

will not raise a tenth of this wail.
This wail's for the diviner and his eight acolytes,
he glistens in and out.
Capitals carry his pictures
to the clamour of marchers for justice,
the world rebounds with tearful wails.

There's devilry of soldiers
in this death that exceeds other deaths.
The singers will never be complete
without the elephant in their midst.
Aridon, give me the insuppressable voice
to raise this wail to the world's end.

ON SEEING A DEAD BODY AT OSHODI
Wumi Raji

She has been lying there for days
in her own pool of blood:

flies feast on her flesh,
nobody cares;

dogs tear at her parts,
nobody cares;

vultures peck at her heart,
nobody cares;

women hawking their wares,
children munching their bread,
conductors shouting their routes,
touts collecting their tolls,
nobody cares.

When I cry:
they ask if she was my mother
or my aunt,
or my sister,
of any relation of mine.

I mourn
not her death
but my own.

THE SCORCHING SUN
Abdul-Rasheed Na'Allah

For the subarid sands of Maiduguri
For the thick forest of Edo-Benin
For the roaring crowd of Eko-Ilumota
For them, emerged the sun today, scorching,
Yet singing for the sobbing masses to chorus:
Èéh, óó mà sèéé!

Refrain: Èéh, óó mà sèéé

(Óse, óse, óse oo!)
For Okrika, Ibibio and Efik
For Fulfulde, Ijaw, Igbo
For Yoruba, Ebira and Nupe,
For them emerged the sun today, scorching,
Yet singing for the sobbing masses to chorus:
Èéh, óó mà sèéé!

Refrain: Èéh, óó mà sèéé

(Óse, óse, ó mà se!)
For Hausa, Angas and Kanuri
For Tiv, Baruba and Jukun
For Ogoni, Kalabari and Urhobo,
For them emerged the sun today, scorching,
Yet singing for the sobbing masses to chorus:
Èéh, óó mà sèéé!

Èéh, óó mà sèéé

Today, the sun's rolling tears are inquiries from you:
With the fertility of your fadama soil,
With the flowing rivers across Benue, Niger and Rima,
With the fleshy gold flowing in Delta, Warri and Port Harcourt
With your hairs of 'timber and caliber',
Nigeria, this odor is sneaky!

Èéh, óó mà sèéé

You'd offered your rams, your sweats in sacrifice for your growth
Yet today, you're crippled in the ocean of healthy fishes.
Today, you cast in the garbage your Kano-pyramid, your Benin-
    palmnuts, your Ondo-cocoa
You murder your brains, Murtala, Saro Wiwa, who? you? mother?
Today, Nigeria you rear vultures in your farms.

Èéh, óó mà sèéé

The tears today,
For the Ogoni, for all the tattered in Oyo, Sokoto and Umuahia,
Are tears of kin from Cape to Cairo
Tears for Nigerians, from Canada to Korea:
These sweats, these sacrifices mustn't be in vain!

DELTA
Jacqueline Onyejiaka

You were beautiful — once
Majestic even
Your white sands stretched
For miles and miles
Loose and clean
A virgin
Saturated with catfish
While your waters
Playfully kissed the sandy banks.

Now, a green monstrosity
molests you, and
your stench defiles the air
Raw sewage, rotting fish,
and blood-thirsty vultures
are now your close and constant companions
Living witnesses to progress.

SLICK SHELLS
Andre Karl

Beings are burning North, South & Central.
Petrol is burning North, South & Central.

Northern garages, cozy with comfort.
Affluent mowers, warm & abundant.

Central thermostats control natural gas.

On is off
Off is on … Don't be confused
Corporate truth behind
             faces burning
Monetary gain
Multinationals hold

Fists wave peaceful leaves underneath our world
Humanity suspends life ethylene high.
Trees live choked green.
Manipulated ripe.
Fruit twists in roots
Tightly contrived.
Traditional rhythm protests contorted lies.
Shackles drip clinching exposed pipelines.
Oily fire seals buried seed.

Global disregard fosters a martyr military
                      military martyr

Ken Saro-Wiwa
wanted: Dead

Defeated earth remains burnt

Light a candle
Join a vigil
March for the Ogoni People.

HEAVY CURTAINS...
Ikhide R. Ikheloa

For you Ken Saro-Wiwa, hunch back that cannot be put down.
What are they going to do to you now? The myrmidons of darkness, the maplots of Hades have found a white fowl but when they
find the four corners to nowhere the white fowl will be gone. Don't
worry about it; it is not you, it is them. This is not for nothing...
Everything is as it should be, you'll see. And our people raise their
manacled fists to your courage...

Dusk dusts the earth
Chilly winds chill the earth's bones
Darkness darkness darkness...
Winds furious flapping furious
At a scared land...

Darkness drapes sad heart
Tired earth wipes tired brow
Mother exhausted
Leaning against this shame
And now...
You will lay down
On this reed-mat.

Perhaps...
Phoenix...
You will wake up
Again...
To fight
Again...

Jaundiced eyes...
Roam sad shores
Chasing jaundiced eyes
And hard hearts
Huddle together
For solace...
Solace that eludes naked gods

Some kind of country...
We have the matchetes
What happened to the farm?

And the calabash
The calabash
Goes round and round
Round and round
Chasing our palmwine tapper
Gone scared...

And...
When the fog cleared some
We saw...
We had inherited a country
Some kind of country

And now...
What are we going to do?
What are you going to do?
This is your country too

BUT THE DREAM WAS STOLEN…
Ronke Luke Boone

Dawn had broken thirty years ago,
Freedom rang out high and low.
Along the length, across the breadth,
A continent stirred, raised its head.

Reclaiming its land that'd been taken before.
It selected its own,
Replacing rulers from afar.

At that dawn there was hope,
There was faith, there was joy.
The birth of new nations
The continent was sure.
The wealth in the earth,
The resolve of her people,
Would meld together
And build prosperous nations.

But the dream was stolen before it was won.
The earth's riches plundered before true wealth was known.
The laws corrupted before the ink seals were dry.
The people deceived before they'd known the whole truth.
The nations destroyed before their true greatness was known.
The continent ruined by those who did rule.

A violent dusk now slowly descends,
Thirty years after that hopeful dawn light first broke.
Wracked and weary, she now lays down her head,
Mourning a dream that slipped away.

Will her true glory be known, the continent's greatness achieved?
Will her wealth be unleashed for the good of her soul?
Will a new generation rise up, redeem her spirit from the ashes?
Will her people know truth from those who will rule?
Will the dream remain a vision of what could have been?

The fate of her people, her destiny unknown,
The answer she awaits...
But for now she bows down her head.

TYRANTS
Jonathan Hart

Once they thought there was truth
In torture, which never could have been,
Now they torture without truth,
And hang him in a political wind.

Tyrants come but never go
Away entirely: they leave their scars
On bodies, buildings, cemetaries,
Play with children in rooms without bars.

They bathe but never wash quite,
Sins in the marrow, rage in the hollow,
But leave traces like snails that never were
Or almost: they die in the shallow.

In time a quiet descends
And the scaffolds and slaughter fields
Dissolve, an unreal pastoral
Remains as if innocent ghosts could yield.

SIEGE
(for the martyrs of Umuechem and the Ogoni people)
Pius Adesanmi

Deep down in the bowels of our land
The land of our ancestors
Wealth immeasurable abound
Wealth after the heart of men
Wealth after the heart of nations

In this land
Birds sang melodious tunes
Proud rainbow lizards tail-lashed one another
Over the provocative females,
Butterflies sought after nectar,
Squirrels partook of nature's bounty
And the drums would penetrate the heart of the moon
Setting the rhythm right for the luscious waists
Of ripe virgins on the playing square.

Then they came.
White strangers with strange ways
Who smelt our buried wealth beyond the seas
'Crude oil!' they shouted.

The birds choked over their songs
The lizards scurried into the crevices of mud walls,
The butterflies felt nervous,
The squirrels trembled
And the moon went to sleep

Our guests promptly took possession of our land
And the buried wealth thereof
As we peeped fearfully
From the fringe of extinction

They fed us on promises.
Our light, the White man's light

Shall replace your hurricane lamps;
We shall plant iron rods in your streets
To urinate water into your drinking pots
In place of your frog-infested creeks

Grandpa died,
Grandma passed on
Hoping that we the children
Would reap the sweet words
Of the white man's tongue
But we didn't.

At last our guests took their leave
And our brothers replaced them
Brothers of the black skin
Who re-echoed the promises
Of their predecessors.

For years they milked our wealth,
We waited,
But time did not.
Frustrated, we all trooped out
Men
    Women
      Young
        Old
Unarmed, headed for their enclave
Our dues we must have.

Our wealth-licking brothers
Called the black-skinned hawks
Of the black uniform.

They came,
    saw,
        crushed.
Corpses littered the land
Blood-curdling cries of

Pregnant women haunted
Our huts.

And the look in the eyes of this child
Made me tremble
As he watched his mother's belly ripped open
His father's head crushed
By our brother's bullets

Then their parrots crooned:
"In pursuance of
efforts to maintain law and order,
the villagers laying siege on the
oil company have finally been rounded up."

But this child will grow
He will grow up someday
And he will ask questions.

NOT FOR LONG
Jacqueline Onyejiaka

Today the people sit
and eat the dust of promises broken;
Today they are held down by brutality
while the streets drown
in the blood of the youth;
Today they are helpless to stop
Corruption's kleptomanic hands
from ravishing the land of their fathers;
Today they are muzzled by poverty
while the eyes of their children
recede further and further
into their skulls
like two elusive jewels
being sucked in by the
omnipotent hands of
a quicksand

But not for long.
Soon,
They will gather from East to West
Like an angry sea during a storm
Disgorging the filth, the decay,
and the bullshit
that has for so long been
a pimple on the face of a nation

LIBERATION IN OUR TIME
Felix W. J. Mnthali

No, this was no Rip van Winkle sleep:
our thirty years of fitful dreams
and never-ending nightmares;
we had already hollered at a dying dispensation:
"Enough is enough, let our people go!"

Forgotten skeletons rattled their way
out of the house of bondage
speaking in tongues
only their damned lot would understand:
they mumbled something about detention orders
and prison warders and head prisoners
and falling in and falling out and looking sharp
and looking dead as if they had been to war.

They had been there, they said,
because someone had spoken to someone
who had known someone who was
a sister, a brother, a cousin, a friend, a wife
a concubine, (did it really matter?), who had
known, heard, seen, imagined, (did it really matter?),
someone who had been near or there or somewhere there
when a drunken wag had abused, mocked, admired,
worshipped, spoofed or adored (did it really matter?)
our one and only hero, his friends, his mistress, his
ministers, his women, his clowns, his stooges or his old pioneers!

Did it ever really matter, anyhow?

We saw and we heard evanescent silhouttes
of all our beginnings and endings gliding past us
like hopes's smouldering embers of yesterday
smarting from our fires of detention and the muffled
hammers, pistols and silencers of our state assassins
fulfilling their prophecies and their midnight missions

on roads and by-ways and river banks
next to the heart of darkness!

You may well wonder now how
after the season of rogues who have been found out
and after all those winters of our incarceration and
the unsung summers of all our releases
you may well wonder how it feels to be free
and to guard against the return
of the ever watchful rogues of yesterday!

What we have gained we have gained
from the anguish and the drama which all our winters
brought and all our summers may yet destroy.

TOWARDS THE LIGHT
Olu Obafemi

Fight, hungry friend, fight.

Do you take heed of the promise
In the angry whirlwind
Forcing its war
Through the dryness of the evening;
The yet unfulfilled promises
Of the expected rain?
Do you hear?

Can you hear the leaves
Rustling with force
Through the thick
Of tonight's forest of pain?
Do you hear?

The murmur of the deprived;
Yesterday's plenty
Yielding today's hunger
And tomorrow's anger?
Do you hear?

Do you listen
To the rumbling
Of protesting intestines
In a season of drought?
Do you hear?
Do you hear?
The harrowed whistling
Of the wind
Breaking
Into the bedroom
Of mass want?
Do you hear?

Can't you hear
The clattering of the cold teeth
In the hot furnace of the noon;
As Alsatian dogs
Bark us away
From the palace of abundance?
Don't you hear?

ZANI FADA — I SHALL FIGHT!
Abdul-Rasheed Na'Allah

(To be accompanied by flute rhythm or music from simple imple-
ments like calabash, etc., or just hand clappings! Performers could
also just throw struggle fists.)

Zani faɗa[1],
Wallahi zani faɗa da la'ananne
Sun ƙi 'yan uwa na
Duk aka samu su ƙaɗai
Sun bar Nijeriya ramemme
Sun bar talaka shanyeyye
Asusun gwamnati sun buɗo
Ko sisin kwabo basu bar ba
Ko cin anci ai sai su
Maƙiyin Allah, duk sai su
Ba za ni gyale su ruɗe ƙasa,
Na ƙi in barsu kwancecce
Rui, naƙi naƙi!
Rui, naƙi naƙi!

You may call me *Jakin kano*, Kano's donkey
or even continue to say I'm *Raƙumin Sakkwato,*
          Sakkwato's camel.
Or is't your *áláàru* at *Oja gbooro*[2]
Or *Omolanke* — Push Truck for Lagos!

Refrain: Rui, naƙi naƙi!
              Rui, naƙi naƙi!

Keep singing your song that I'm nothing,
Laugh it off that my complaints are *maganan banza,*
          rabbish talk!
Keep telling me that until I pick from the gabbage,
Despite that I farmed my farm from morning till night,
I say, keep saying that until I cry to finish,
Before you recognize my misery.

222 · Ogoni's Agonies

Barayin gwamnati — government thieves, today
      I shalln't leave you to sleep.

Refrain: Rui, naƙi naƙi!
               Rui, naƙi naƙi!

Every stone thrown at the sky
Descends to the ground.
Akawu, you've taken yourself to the weightless air above
You'll descend to the ground with the ferocious force
      outside your grip.
At your fall, even *Jakin Kano* will worth more than you!
Chief *Jaguda*-armed robbers of Nigeria,
The Commanders of harlots at Lagos bitches
Grand-Directors of smugglers at Port Harcourt oil-wells,
The Oba-Kings of *gbajue*-419 Fraud at Ibadan money market,
Babban akawu — the general lismo of marauders at
      gidajen gwamnati, govenment houses,
You have denied your mothers any sleep,
Yourselves would know no sleep!

Refrain: Rui, naƙi naƙi!
               Rui, naƙi naƙi!

Nigeria, ours too!
Because our mouths're mute for long,
Taken us you have for *gawa*-dead bodies.
Because the cat went on a journey,
The house soon became the abode of rats.
You *Jaguda* of our oil,
Yes, I won't let you go.

Rui, naƙi naƙi!
Rui, naƙi naƙi!

This country was really fat,
I mean rea-ea-lly fat.
Look, today,

You've sucked it to its bones.
You'll rather your swiss bank swells
Than sweeten the hearts of *talaka* — poor at home.
You'll rather your Country's crippled dies
Than you cut your swelling accounts in Switzerland.
Jaguda,
You'll rather brutalize the Ogoni
Than your Britain boozes be threatened.
You'll rather Nigeria dies,
Than end your suffocation of our souls.
Never, I'll rather I die than your rots to prosper!

Rui, naƙi naƙi!
Rui, naƙi naƙi!

Get up you Farmers!
Market women,
Malamai — Teachers, Traders,
Agbegilodo — truck drivers,
My country people, men and women
Oya — Here, it's our song for freedom:
Rui, naƙi naƙi!

Rui, naƙi naƙi!
Rui, naƙi naƙi!

Our response to those rogues is
From now: "No More!"
No more "suffering, smiling!"
No more "monkey de work, baboon de chop"
No more "*Olorun yo mu* — God go catch am."
No more "*mu barsu da halinsu* — leave them to their characters,"
Their smoky attitudes have suffocated many to their graves.
Never, naƙi naƙi!

Rui, naƙi naƙi!
Rui, naƙi naƙi!

As soon as our songs enter their ears,
They will catch cold in the sunny day,
Thay will get wet at the buttocks of their pants.
No, their *Babalawo* — Witch doctors died just yesterday!
Their escape rout have since been blocked.
Nigeria today is our freedom,
Our songs will walk us off
from their ropes,
Rui, naƙi naƙi!

Rui, naƙi naƙi!
Rui, naƙi naƙi!

Faɗa — Fight, I shall fight!
I swear I'll fight those accursed — cheats:
They hate my people
Our resources, they monopolized and
Left our poor starved.
Even the treasury,
Not a kobo left-over.
God's admonitions?
Blunt.
Their God, their pockets.
No, I shalln't let them dazzle our land,
I won't leave them to sleep.
No, I refuse, I refuse!
No, I refuse, I refuse!

Rui, naƙi naƙi!
Rui, naƙi naƙi!

NOTES

1   This stanza, written in Hausa, is translated into English in the last
    but one stanza of this poem.

2   *áláàrù*, is a Yoruba word for a dog's body who gets paid very little for
    carrying people's loads and luggage from one spot to the other. *Oja
    gbooro* is a name of a traditional market in Ilorin, Nigeria.

FISTS THAT CAN MOVE THE UNIVERSE
(in memory of Ken Saro-Wiwa)
Sonia Atwal

How insignificant is an individual
Who stands poised with dignity
On the ancestors' land,
Fists defiantly battling the sky
Full of circling purple-stained carrion
And the occasional graceful dance
Of a butterfly?

How insignificant are words
Cried out in the moment of death
Splicing the silence
Jolting our passive wait
Daring earsarmsfingerseyeslegsblood
To move,
To continue,
To struggle.

How insignificant is a life
A spirit force
Gathered and beaten back
Into the jungle
— That same area of darkness —
By guns and hate
By monopolies and money
By oil and greed
By impotence and power
By law and order
By lies and history

And yet how that life
Its words, its stories
Can reach my ears
Writing itself into my body

Like fists
That can move
The universe.

V

Works

Ken Saro-Wiwa's *Sozaboy*
and the Logic of Minority Discourse
Harry Garuba

In the last page of Ken Saro-Wiwa's posthumously published detention diary, *A Month and a Day*, the author briefly mentions an interesting but harrowing news story about: "132 Ogoni men, women and children, returning from their abode in the Cameroons, (who) had been waylaid on the Andoni River by an armed gang and cruelly murdered, leaving but two women to make a report." He ends the book with this chilling but prophetic statement: "The genocide of the Ogoni had taken on a new dimension. The manner of it I will narrate in my next book, if I live to tell the tale" (1995: 238).

Ken Saro-Wiwa did not live to narrate "the manner of it." On the 10th of November 1995, Ken Saro-Wiwa along with eight of his Ogoni kinsmen were hanged at the Port Harcourt prisons on the orders of the Nigerian military authorities. Their murder has become the principal site of discursive contestation between the hegemonic powers of the multinational oil industry and Nigeria's military despots on the one hand, and minority and environmental rights activists on the other. The murder of 132 people may be a more horrifying event than the killing of nine others but it is the power of representation which Saro-Wiwa so effectively harnessed that has made his hanging the converging point of the struggle for minority rights in the face of their ruthless suppression by a kleptocratic regime backed by oil interests.

In his various speeches, writings and other activities, Ken Saro-Wiwa had sought to draw discursive attention to the realities of the slow genocide of the Ogoni people and the degradation of their environment because he recognised the fact that the inability of the Ogoni people to represent themselves had made their situation more tragic and their circumstances more despondent. His mission, therefore, was to give voice to a silenced, marginalized minority who were not only being physically decimated as a people but who had also been representationally erased from national and international consciousness. This is why in the last sentence of the detention diary, he appears so concerned about narrating the 'manner of it', placing the emphasis on the manner of telling, of narrative and representation because he realized that in the postmodern world of multinational corporations, communications and commodities, reality is often processed for us through the images and narrative of them which we receive. Facts, in a sense, are always discursively packaged like commodities for the consumption of markets/audiences.

The phenomenal shifts in critical theory within the last two or three decades have led to the opening up of a new, uncharted space in the area of minority discourses and the power and problems of representation. Minorities of all shades have tried to chart their own unique forms of difference on its blank spaces as maps of their individual identities. Women, ethnic minorities, diasporic blacks and Africans, orientals, postcolonial nations, gays and lesbians, etc. have all tried to stake claims within this territory by rediscovering their difference and developing these as badges of identity.

Alongside these developments has grown a regrettable amnesia about the concrete, historical struggles of these minorities in their unending battle against the tyrannies of dominant groups and ideologies. The post-Saussaurean separation of signs from their signifieds and referents has led to the valorisation of language over reality, the privileging of culture over and above the material practices which create those cultures. The advent of post-structuralism and post-modernism with their emphasis on undecideability, self-reflexivity, relativity and contingency has further pushed a potentially liberating discourse into a sclerosized culturalism, arresting other developments in the direction of the material and historical.

The question of post-structuralism, post-modernism and history is a vexing one. Minorities seemingly offered by critical theory the voice to break their imposed silence find themselves unwittingly decentred from their own real, historical experiences. This, at least, has been one unfortunate development of certain strands of contemporary critical theory. The primary significance of Ken Saro-Wiwa's writings and his various activities on behalf of the Ogoni people, in this regard, has been to re-inscribe the concrete and historical into the linguistic world of floating signifiers and the culturalist mire into which minority discourses appear to be sinking. For Ken believed so much in the materiality of discourse that he seemed to have lived his life, in his last days, just to prove that point. He believed that his ability to take literature into the streets or, put differently, to take the streets into literature was his ultimate triumph against those who sought to silence him.

In this brief essay, therefore, I intend first to examine Ken Saro-Wiwa's *Sozaboy* as a novel that enacts the logic of minority discourse and then comment on how in the twists and turns of his life he appears to have fulfilled the dictates of that logic. The intention is not to prove how life imitated literature or how literature initiated life, but to show how both were so intimately interwoven that they become two events mediated by the same logic.

II

Virtually every article on *Sozaboy*, either as a first move or as its dominating manoeuvre, fastens upon the issue of language in the text. This may well be due to the fact that the author uses a variety of english which he describes as 'rotten English' and makes a point of drawing our attention to it both in the title of the novel and the author's note which precedes the narrative. The author's overinvestment in the language issue is borne out in this statement:

> Sozaboy's language is what I call 'rotten English', a mixture of Nigerian pidgin English, broken English and occasional flashes of good, even idiomatic English. This language is disordered and disorderly. Born of a mediocre education and severely limited opportunities, it borrows words, patterns and images freely from the mother-tongue and finds expression in a very limited English

vocabulary. To its speakers, it has the advantage of having no rules and no syntax. It thrives on lawlessness, and is part of the dislocated and discordant society in which Sozaboy must live, move and have not his being (Author's Note, *Sozaboy*).

This, of course, is an exaggeration for it is certainly neither correct nor true to affirm that the language of Sozaboy has no rules and no syntax. But every author's note performs the function of foregrounding certain kinds of questions and foreclosing others.

Critics are then led to accord primacy to the authorized question. And, in this instance, there can be no doubting the importance of the language question. Part of the de-canonizing and counter-canonizing gesture of postcolonial literature has been to question the hegemonic self-representation of the dominant discourse as encoded in a standard, formalized language handed down to the colonies from the metropolis. Bill Ashcroft, et al. in *The Empire Writes Back* say that "post-colonial writing abrogates the privileged centrality of 'English' by using language to signify difference while employing a sameness which allows to be understood" (1989: 51).

In employing 'rotten English' in this novel Ken Saro-Wiwa is indirectly saying that 'standard' english is incapable of representing the landscape and the reality that he seeks to portray. A different variety of english has to be invented to do the job. Even the favoured linguistic alternatives such as pidgin are also inadequate in conveying the full experience of Sozaboy whose education ended with a distinction at the level of the primary school leaving certificate. In emphasizing the social and experiential determinations of language he thereby focuses on the material character of linguistic usage. As Bill Ashcroft, et al. also say, "language is a material practice and as such is determined by a complex weave of social conditions and experience" (p. 41).

Glossing is usually one of the strategies of inscribing difference in minority texts. Often the indigenous or pidginized word is followed by a parenthetical translation which, as Ashcroft, et al. again assert, "may lead to a considerably stilted movement of plot as the story is forced to drag an explanatory machinery behind it" (p. 62). In *Sozaboy*, the author partially saves us from this by appending a full-blown glossary at the end of the novel.

The struggle for linguistic control within the text extends to the very act of writing itself. Even though the novel is a written text, *Sozaboy*, the narrator, consistently employs speakerly strategies to point at the oral nature of his narrative. Apart from his copious use of direct reportage and direct addresses to his readers/listeners, the novel begins by evoking a traditional African story telling scene — "knacking tory under the moon" (p. 1) — and ends with "Believe me yours sincerely" (p. 181). Between the beginning and the end of the novel, there is a constant tussle between the structures of the scribal narrative and the demands of orality.

Having disposed of the language issue, let us now turn our attention to the other questions which the text raises, the subordinate question which, I believe, deserves equal scrutiny. Perhaps, the most profitable way to read *Sozaboy* is to see it as an attempt to give appropriate form to the minority experience in a postcolonial state. The questions we need to ask of the novel, therefore, are those which lead us to see how the minority experience is narrativized.

Sozaboy tells the story of a young, naive primary school leaver who becomes an apprentice-driver in the bid to learn a profession and to become a man of his own. As the only child of his mother and a fatherless child at that, he has modest ambitions of obtaining a driving licence, becoming a successful driver and buying his own vehicle so that he can be of some help to his mother who both 'mothered' and 'fathered' him. Unfortunately, a military coup d'etat changes the normal run of events in the society and the course of his life. The entire community had initially welcomed the coup hoping that it will rid the society of corruption and check the venality of policemen and vehicle inspection officers who incessantly harass drivers by continually demanding bribes. However, the expectation that the new dispensation will usher in the millennium is quickly shattered as the soldiers prove to be more oppressive than the civilians who had been booted out of power unceremoniously. Unresolved conflicts and antagonisms in the society lead to a civil war and Mene, the narrator, finds himself joining the army. The rest of the novel is devoted to Mene's experiences as a soldier in the war.

Around this basic scaffold is built a rich, compelling story of the construction of human subjectivity, the ideological interpellation of individuals by dominant discourses, the transformation of reality into carefully processed and packaged images, the confrontation between real life experience and the expectations inscribed in the ideological test and its well-touted images, and finally the sobering realization of marginality and its consequences. In exploring these issues, Ken Saro-Wiwa unmasks the workings of hegemonic discourses and the logic of minority discourse.

We first encounter Mene soon after his formal education at school, during the next stage of his life which is his apprenticeship to a master-driver who is supposed to give him the training he requires to become a commercial driver. The socialization process, begun at the family level with his mother through the period of formal schooling in which he acquires some english, continues as he learns the trade at the hands of the master-driver who takes beyond the confines of Dukana to Pitakwa. His encounter with the world is 'processed' through the eyes of his mother, then his teachers, and at this stage the master-driver. In all of these he remains a voiceless but curious young man trying to grapple with the world on terms other than his own.

Helen Chukwuma (1992) in "Characterization and Meaning in Sozaboy" draws attention to the author's technique of pairing Mene with more experienced characters at every stage of the novel until he acquires a voice and begins to take his own decisions and act on his own.

We first encounter Mene as 'a young man and apprentice driver' (p. 1). This low status makes it impossible for him to exert any influence whatsoever on his mother or on members of the society at large. Mene is therefore paired off with his master-driver who gives him a sense of directions, with a promise of stability, professionalism and financial independence (p. 40).

His apprenticeship is brought to an abrupt end by the coup, and the beginning of the civil war starts him off in a new direction. As Helen Chukwuma puts it:

> In this part, Saro-Wiwa rests the professional aspect of his protagonist's development by grounding his vehicle and prolonging the process of its repair. This allows the author time to advance his character unto yet another dimension, still using his technique of pairing. Mene, in the absence of the lorry-driver, is paired off with

the young girl, Agnes, whom he meets in the African Upwine Bar.
(1992: 41)

Thereafter, he is paired off with the San Mazor, and then finally with Bullet. At every stage he is dominated by his environment and the images passed unto him by these more experienced characters.

Agnes, the rather brash young woman from Lagos, insists that he must enlist in the army before she can marry him because she needs a strong man who will be able to protect her. Agnes has completely internalized this image of soldiers as brave men with codes of honour and dignity, duty and selfless service and Mene is made to accept this image. His acceptance is aided by the fact that he is also in love with the uniforms of the soldiers, their smart salutes and parades, their weapons and show of power. Even though his mother fears for his life, this conflict between his mother's aspirations for him and Agnes' wishes is resolved in favour of the latter, and Mene joins the army after offering a substantial bribe. After being recruited, the Sergeant Major (referred to as San Mazor by the narrator) takes Mene in and educates him in the ways of the army. Apart from being a professional drill master he takes special interest in Mene because he realises that he is only an inexperienced young boy swept into the army by circumstances he does not fully understand. Mene's disorientation is further compounded by the General's speech to the recruits at the end of their training.

Luckily for him he has another mentor/father-figure in Bullet who smooths his way into regular service and the war. Bullet tries to explain to him why he is engaged in the various activities he finds himself performing.

He doesn't understand why they have to dig trenches, who the enemy is, and why one of them should come to them waving a white handkerchief. His bafflement is not helped by subsequent events such as the sharing of drinks and cigarettes, their captain's behaviour in hoarding the supplies meant for them, Bullet's humiliation by the captain after the theft, and Bullet's final shooting of the captain. By the time Bullet gets killed in an air raid, he is no closer to understanding.

Life after Bullet continues in the same manner. He is taken prisoner of war and only gains consciousness in the hospital where the soldier with the white handkerchief has now materialised as some kind of nurse treating the wounded. After Mene's discharge from the hospital he goes through a series of bizarre incidents, some fortunate and others tragic. His ability to drive saves him in the first instance and he is given a gun, military uniforms, and made a driver on the enemy side: a job he does conscientiously before he decides to quit the army for good after having served on both sides of the conflict.

Then he begins his own quest for his mother and his wife, the two oases of love left in that terrain of war. He wanders through the war ravaged country visiting refugee camps in search of mother and wife. At the last refugee camp where he finds a lot of people from his home town Dukana he is betrayed by his own people and again taken prisoner. But fortunately again the war ends just as he faces the firing squad. The executioner is the soldier with the white handkerchief who had treated him the last time at the hospital. This continually metamorphosizing soldier turns out to be Manmuswak, the amoral man he had met before the war at the African Upwine Bar.

After escaping from the firing squad he set off for home only to find himself rejected even in his home town. All the doors are barred against him and he has to take refuge in the church. After sleeping for some nights in the church, Duzia, the village cripple, seeks him out only to tell him that his mother and wife were killed in an air raid and that he Mene is also believed by the villagers to have died in the war. The villagers also believe that he did not die properly so his ghost has been haunting them wherever they go causing diseases and death. After consulting a medicine man, they were advised that they could only kill his ghost and bury him properly after certain sacrifices involving "money and seven white goats and seven white monkey blokkus and seven alligator pepper and seven bundles of plantain and seven young girls" (p. 180). Duzia therefore advises him to leave the village or risk being buried alive. Mene who had survived the war finds himself facing the prospect of being buried alive in the peace and he has to leave his own hometown in despair. He sums up his experiences in this manner:

And I was thinking how I was prouding before to go to soza and call myself Sozaboy. But now if anybody say anything about war or

even fight, I will just run and run and run and run and run. Believe
me yours sincerely. (p. 181)

At this point, his old ideas about the army now appear antiqua-
ted in the light of the new restructuring of consciousness occasioned by the facts of experience flying in the face of the images he
had imbibed, therefore leading to corrections in his knowledge of
the world.

Michel Pecheux in *Language, Semantics and Ideology* argues that
there are three ways in which subjects are constituted, and these are
by 'Identification', 'Counter-identification' and 'Disidentification'.
Identification involves willingly consenting to the images offered
by the dominant discourse while counter-identification involves
rejecting those images, and disidentification involves "working on
and against" the dominant ideologies (1982: 157–69).

Sozaboy passes through these three stages but finds himself
finally thrown into exile at the third stage. These three stages may
be said to constitute the inexorable logic of minority discourse.
After being framed by the images of the dominant ideology which
then passes itself off as the natural order of things, counter-identification and disidentification become so difficult to achieve or are
only achieved at great cost. Richard Terdiman in *Discourse/Counter-
Discourse* gives us an insight into the power and tenacity of hegemonic discourses:

> Not only are they unable to admit difference, in a sense they are
> incapable of imagining it. This is so for a simple reason. Once imag-
> ined, even so that it might be proscribed, difference acquires a
> phantom but fundamental existence. If it is countenanced at all, its
> legitimation, its inclusion within the canons of the orthodox, has
> to that extent begun. Thus even the work of proscribing it must be
> proscribed. (1985: 14)

In spite of this power of proscription and exile demonstrated in
Sozaboy, Mene is able to deconstruct the binarisms of the war by
fighting on both sides and ironizing the procedures governing the
discourse. In this regard, Manmuswak is the ultimate absurd symbol of this deconstruction. Acting without respect for boundaries

and divisions, he traverses and transgresses them all with an indeterminate character that privileges the contingent and — well — the amoral. Even knowledge comes to Mene, in the end, through the village 'idiot'.

In thus depicting the logic of minority discourse,Ken Saro-Wiwa's great feat in this novel is that *Sozaboy* can both be read within the ambience of the representational protocols of mimetic realism and also be seen as an allegorization of the minority experience in a postcolonial state.

III

The construction of a representational relation of coincidence between Sozaboy's story and the structure of the story of suppressed minorities can in fact be extended to the life of Ken Saro-Wiwa himself. Ken Saro-Wiwa always cuts the picture of a small embattled man confronting a material and discursive power far in excess of his ability to overcome. But Ken was born into an awareness of difference. Even though the carceral approach which dominating discourses adopt to subordinated ones, which the Nigerian government was later to adopt, had not become the practice at the time of the author's birth in Ogoniland, something close to a caste-like system of discrimination operated between them and their neighbours. So Ken Saro-Wiwa knew what he was talking about when he spoke of marginality and marginalisation. He was, so to speak, fashioned in the very crucible of minority discourse; and thus scarred by history.

It is no surprise therefore that after having passed through the first two stages suffering incarceration along the way, he refused the choice of exile at the third stage and was thus 'buried alive'. The gory details of his death need no recounting here. What is left is for other marginalised peoples to recognise the logic of minority discourse and continue to narrativize it while picking up the mantle of his material and discursive struggle.

REFERENCES

Ashcroft, Bill, Gareth Criffiths, and Helen Tiffin. *The Empire Writes Back: Theory and Practice in Post-colonial Literatures*. London and New York: Routledge, 1989.

Chukwuma, Helen. "Characterization and Meaning in Sozaboy." *Critical Essays on Ken Saro-Wiwa's Sozaboy: A Novel in Rotten English.* Ed. Charles Nnolim. London, Lagos, Port Harcourt: Saros International Publishers, 1992.

Pecheux, Michel. *Language, Semantics and Ideology.* (1975) Trans. Harbans Nagpal. New York: St. Martins, 1982.

Saro-Wiwa, Ken. *A Month and A Day: A Detention Diary.* London: Penguin, 1995.

———. *Sozaboy: A Novel in Rotten English.* London, Lagos, Port- Harcourt: Saros International Publishers, 1985.

Terdiman, Richard. *Discourse/Counter-Discourse: The Theory and Practice of Symbolic Resistance in Nineteenth-Century France.* Ithaca, N.Y.: Cornell UP, 1985.

Ken Saro-Wiwa:
Writer and Cultural Manager
Eckhard Breitinger

In the middle of the great debate about the language issue in African literature, Ken Saro-Wiwa very consciously and deliberately opted for a third choice. While Ngũgĩ wa Thiong'o with his Kenyan background argued tenaciously for the use of African languages only for African literatures, the West African writers defended the use of European languages in an Africanised variety. Ken Saro-Wiwa, being himself a member of the five hundred thousand Ogoni minority among the one hundred million Nigerians, very naturally adopted a pragmatic attitude towards languages: Between his own Ogoni minority language and the elite minority language English, he opted for the wide-spread inter-ethnic language of a strongly Pidginised English as it was used by the soldiers and traders in South-Eastern Nigeria. The 'rotten English' which Saro-Wiwa tried out for the first time in his novel, *Sozaboy* ranges somewhere between standardised and formalised Pidgin and Pidginised Standard English. Ken Saro-Wiwa's choice of this linguistic medium also meant that he was opening up a new front in the debate about popular culture. It is obvious that he wanted to reach beyond the limited audience of his own Ogoni constituency and beyond the limited audience of the university trained Nigerians, aiming to reach a broader middle class audience, comparable to, and yet quite different from the constituency of the Onitsha Market Literature. If we look at Tutuola's linguistic experiment as an attempt to regain ethnic specificity within the intra-ethnic medium of the English language, then Saro-Wiwa's linguistic medium is more in the nature of creating an intra-ethnic linguistic medium that constitutes a social class specificity within the rapidly changing class stratification of post-colonial Nigerian society. The aim was obviously to bring 'modern' literature to classes that had so far remained untouched by literary communication.

For the publication and distribution of his works, Ken Saro-Wiwa was faced with two unsatisfactory options, like all his other writer colleagues in Africa. He could either have his works published by one of the multinational publishing houses, with the effect that his works would be available in London or New York, but would be far too expensive for his real constituency at home, or he could seek the services of a local publisher with limited efficiency in managerial power, in particular in distribution and quality control. Local publishing could not guarantee overall availability on the Nigerian market, and the chances for international availability became rather slim. Ken Saro-Wiwa did submit *Sozaboy* to Longman Nigeria, only to be told that they were "hesitant to publish poetry and drama" (cf. *A Month and a Day*, p. 58). For a pragmatically oriented personality like Ken Saro-Wiwa, it became clear that he had to devise his own publication strategies, that avoided the shortcomings of the two systems available. An additional hindrance for accepting Saro-Wiwa's scripts for publication by multinationals was exactly his linguistic experiment and his attempt to achieve a new type of popular literature. On the other hand, it appears that Ken Saro-Wiwa's concept of popular culture, right from the beginning reached far beyond what could be achieved by publication in the print media only. Since he obviously aimed at conquering the popular culture market through all the available media, be it print, audio or video, he found that the available channels of publication and distribution were insufficient and that he had to design his own multi-media structures to achieve his goal.

Ken Saro-Wiwa's linguistic experiment met with very different critical responses. Enthusiastic reaction celebrating the innovative aspect of his writing in 'rotten English', predicting the development of yet another brand of African literature between the Europhone and African language literatures. There were the negative reactions in the old style of the Tutuola criticism, that this linguistic medium was 'inferior' English, and therefore projecting an image of cultural inferiority to the outside world. But even on the side of the enthusiastic critics, one could detect praises for the wrong reasons. Some critics saw Saro-Wiwa's 'rotten English' as yet another variety of the exoticism of African literatures, a critical point of view that appreciates specificity and diversity predominantly in concepts of otherness, viz. oddity. Ken Saro-Wiwa certainly did not intend to be odd or exotic, on the contrary, his concept was one of the cultural responsibility of the elite vis-a-vis society as a whole, a concept of sharing cultural values with the masses without cheapening these values. In fact, some of his colleagues and critics accused him of cheapening and not sharing values.

Ken Saro-Wiwa's development as a writer of popular literature and his involvement as a cultural activist, manager and practitioner, are closely related to each other. Since there were no structures and no facilities available for his kind of cultural communication, he had no other option than designing his own structures. After the frustrations with Longman, he set up his own publishing house, Saros International Publishers, with which he tried to combine the production quality of the multinationals and the low prices of the local publishing industry. It is difficult to tell to what extent Saro-Wiwa succeeded in solving the crucial problem of distribution, both nationally inside Nigeria and internationally. It is a fact, that the books of Saros International Publishers were available in Europe in the specialised book shops. From what we can gather from the various interviews and what he writes in his autobiographical record *A Month and a Day*, he must have handled all the editorial and managerial duties of publishing himself—learning on the job, as he confesses. It was only the actual printing and binding, the pure production side of publishing, that was handled externally. Saros International Publishers released up to a dozen titles a year, which is an astonishing output for a one-man part-time outfit.

Ken Saro-Wiwa had clear-cut strategic publishing policies. Most of the titles published by Saros International Publishers were connected to his television serial *Basi & Company*. Even in the print sector alone, he tried to serve the book market on all possible levels. In the first instance, *Basi & Company* was published as play script in the Saros Star Series for £ 3.50 (e.g. *Basi & Company – Four Television Plays*, Saros International Publishers, London, Lagos, Port Harcourt, 1988 or *Four Farcical Plays*, 1989). To attract a wider readership, the ideas of *Basi & Company* were translated into a more popular narrative version, a mix of drama, dialogue and narration. This was referred to as 'dialogue tale'. Saro-Wiwa also offered *Basi & Company* in a series of pure prose narration 'for younger readers', The Adventures of Mr. B. Series (e.g. No. 1, *Mr. B. Goes to Lagos*, No. 2, *Transistor Radio*, 48 pages, 1989) for £ 1.00, as children's book, but also in the Saros Junior Series of about 150 pages, sold for £ 2.95 (e.g. *Mr. B. is Dead*, Saros Junior Series 3, 144 pages, 1991) for the age group of young adults and secondary school students. He was thus serving the book market with specifically designed products for the earlier readers, young adults and middle class readers who read for pleasure.

Ken Saro-Wiwa's concept of a modern urban popular culture in Africa is best expressed through the publication of *Basi & Company* in the Saros Star Series No. 4 (1987) with the revealing sub-title *A Modern African Folktale*. In his editorial note Ken Saro-Wiwa recalls how intrigued he was as a child, when he assisted at the story telling sessions in his village, where he was entertained and educated with the tales of the trickster hero Tortoise. He depicts parallels between the old-time oral popular literature and the modern urban popular culture. He has endearing memories of the old style popular culture, but he also emphasises the inevitability for the manifestations of urban popular culture and the need to consciously shape that culture. On the level of form, Ken Saro-Wiwa discovers a close affinity between of the Tortoise tales and the modern television serials. Both share the episodic structure, where each episode focuses on the same hero figure and where each episode is narrated in a direct, monolinear, chronological fashion.

> As an adult, it has dawned on me that the form in which we heard the exploits of the Tortoise is very much of the genre of the television series. Consequently, in transforming the folktale into a contemporary idiom, I adopted the format of the television comedy series ... I have maintained this format in the belief that this accords better with African narrative methods than the European

novel with flashbacks, psychological analyses and progressive development of character.... (*Basi & Company: A Modern African Folktale*, Saros Star Series No. 4, Author's Note)

On the level of characterisation we can discern a clear affinity between the old trickster hero Tortoise and its modern counterpart Mr. B. Both of them are slick, street-wise, cunning, humorous and resourceful masters in the art of survival in a harsh and inimical environment. Both of them are heroes that attract our sympathies when they are suffering, our laughter when they are cheating, and our mild disapproval when they are betraying their fellow sufferers. Finally on the level of social and cultural communication, there is an obvious affinity between the old-style village setting and the modern urban setting of the less fortunate lower middle classes. The cultural and social need for entertainment, for comic relief, and an unobtrusive obstruction about shared cultural and moral values seem to be a basic need of the rural swamp dweller and the urban slum dweller. The parallels between these two forms of popular cultural/social communication is not simply one of chronological succession, in which the rural form dies down and the urban form takes over. In fact, the two forms co-exist at the same time in their specific cultural spaces, that exist separately but not entirely independently. Mr. B. himself is one of the recent arrivals from the village in the Metropolis. Ken Saro-Wiwa himself also catered for the rural cultural space with his collection of Ogoni folktales, *The Singing Anthill* (Saros Star Series No. 11, 1991).

Compared to the usual publishing policies, where the only viable business is seen in the publication of text books and set texts, Saro-Wiwa was practising a publishing policy that was clearly an implementation of his cultural philosophy. In creating a cultural infrastructure, that was capable of addressing the urban middle class, a culture that is clearly distinct from the practice of traditionalising folk culture, as well as from the manifestations of the internationalised pop culture.

In 1972, Ken Saro-Wiwa entered his play *Transistor Radio* for the radio drama competition of the BBC African Service. The play won one of the prizes, was broadcast in the African Theatre slot of the BBC World Service and was published in Michael Etherton's

Heinemann African Theatre anthology. *Transistor Radio* provided the key inspiration for Ken Saro-Wiwa's major contribution to Nigerian popular literature, the *Basi & Company* television series of the mid-1980s. It was also the departure point for Ken Saro-Wiwa's major achievement as a cultural organiser, as cultural activist and manager. With the BBC radio production of *Transistor Radio*, Ken Saro-Wiwa had experienced a standard of production, both on the technical and the directorial level, which he found difficult to maintain within the set-up and the studios of Nigerian radio. Once he developed the idea to expand *Transistor Radio* into a weekly serial and to enter Nigerian television on a regular weekly basis, he also had to face the organisational and managerial and financial deficiencies of Nigerian radio and television. Ken Saro-Wiwa obviously felt that, if he really wanted to have a show of *Basi & Company* on the screen every week, that he then had to retain control over all the aspects of the production, the broadcasting and even the marketing of that show. It is easily understood that Ken Saro-Wiwa wrote the script for *Basi & Company* himself. With his theatre background from his student days, it was also clear that he directed the play himself. That he set up his own production company, Saros International Productions, to shoot, edit, cut the films—i.e. that he kept total control over the technical side of the production — is rather exceptional in the field of television. Ken Saro-Wiwa also had to guarantee the funding and ensure the marketing and distribution of the series, i.e. he also had to handle all the commercial aspects of film and television production. As Saro-Wiwa recalls in *A Month and a Day:*

> I got involved in television production not through any design of mine, but by sheer accident.... It began as a joke, but once I got into it, I gave it my all as usual. I created, wrote, produced, financed and marketed a comedy series which ran for five years (October 1985–October 1990) on Nigerian network television.... Television production sharpened my writing skills and the flying success of the series *Basi & Co.*, established my reputation as a creative writer. (p. 58)

Ken Saro-Wiwa was obviously relying on his experiences as a government official (perhaps also as far as the unreliability of public services are concerned) and his experiences as a business man. He supplemented his creative spirit as a writer and his visions as a cultural activist with his enterprising spirit as a cultural entrepreneur.

Basi & Company is reported to have been a street sweeper, a show on television, which nobody wanted to miss. An estimated 30 million people saw the show each and every week. The stories about the resourceful, inventive, flunky Lagosian underdog, Basi, who never stops dreaming that he really could 'become a millionaire', if he 'only behaved like a millionaire' was certainly the most successful television serial, produced and broadcast by Africans in Africa for Africans. It is, to all our knowledge, the only African TV serial that successfully competed with the imported wares of *Dallas* or *Dynasty*.

At the height of the activities of producing and marketing *Basi & Company*, Ken Saro-Wiwa experimented with yet another form of distribution: newspaper serialisation. From 1985 Saro-Wiwa successively published his short stories, fresh from the typewriter in the *Vanguard*, which he afterwards published again in book form as a collection of short stories under the title *Prisoner of Jebs*. What is so intriguing about *Basi & Company* is that Ken Saro-Wiwa really lived up to Basi's motto of what it means to become a millionaire. Ken Saro-Wiwa succeeded in establishing a profitable enterprise in cultural industry, where he produced, processed and marketed his own creative inventions. It is the organisational and managerial talent, which he had taught himself, which he had trained and applied in the field of culture, which made him the logical choice of the Ogoni movement. Apart from his own cultural activities, Ken Saro-Wiwa was also highly active as newspaper columnist, a political commentator, a much sought for personality in shaping public opinion. In this capacity, he acquired another important skill, which became instrumental later in his Ogoni campaigns: the designing and managing of public relation campaigns.

From October 1989, Ken Saro-Wiwa wrote the column 'Similia' for the *Sunday Times*, a platform which he not only used for general political comment, but increasingly to advocate the cause of the Ogoni and the ecological war in the Niger Delta. Again Saro-Wiwa marketed his writings effectively when he published the collected essays he had written for the *Sunday Times* in his Saros Star Series (*Similia-Essays on Anomic Nigeria*, Saros Star Series 16, 1991, 200 pages, £ 8.95). In retrospect, he assessed his work as newspaper columnist as follows:

> The newspaper column widened my reading audience and spread my ideas to a considerable extent. Week after week, I made sure that the name Ogoni appeared before the eyes of readers. It was a television technique, designed to leave the name indelibly in their minds. Sometimes I would deliberately provoke readers or fly a kite in the acerbic and polemical column. (*A Month and a Day*, 65)

Newspaper serialisation as with *The Prisoner of Jebs* for creative writing, the column writing as a serialised form of essay writing for political comment, both in widely distributed weekly and daily papers, their republication in Saro-Wiwa's own publishing outfit reveals yet another strategy of distribution and marketing with which Saro-Wiwa approached the Nigerian book market. With the newspaper publications he used the available structures of public media to create and enforce the day-to-day effect for his political and ecological messages. Continuous high visibility and presence in the public media created the high grade of popularity for Ken Saro-Wiwa, which transformed his image in the public eye from that of a writer to that of a public figure. High visibility of Saro-Wiwa as public figure entailed growing publicity for his major messages: the ecological crisis in the Delta; the economic exploitation without remuneration in the Delta; minority representation or repression in the Delta. All these issues, as they were represented in Saro-Wiwa's writing after *Basi & Company*, dealt at first sight with the Ogoni agenda proper. A closer look revealed very quickly that all the issues raised in connection with the Ogoni nation were issues of national relevance, only that other groups had so far abstained or refrained from addressing them. This made it easy for the military governments to accuse Saro-Wiwa of Ogoni separatism and of depicting the Ogoni on the whole as a threat to Nigerian unity and Nigerian economic welfare.

To ensure permanent visibility and continuous presence in the public eye, Ken Saro-Wiwa planned the re-publication of serially written materials as follow-up activity. Serialisation in the papers guaranteed popularity, book publication with Saros International

Publications is used to give more permanence with greater focus on personalisation. Saro-Wiwa willingly profits from the popularity which he can gain for himself and his cause from the newspapers. He willingly gains windfall profits in popularity from existing public media. The conscious and strategic utilisation of these existing media rests to a large extent on the follow-up publication in Saro-Wiwa's own publication structures. Even the chronology of serial and monographic publication suggests that the two activities are planned to be mutually supportive in their publicity effect.

If one follows the development of Ken Saro-Wiwa's writing and managerial activities, a pattern of fast growing confidence and assuredness in the handling of public relations and the utilisation of available or self-generated publication channels reveals itself. There is also a very clear pattern from the purely creative personality in the first half of the 1970s, to the writer-cum-agent-cum-manager-cum-publisher personality in the early 1980s, to a person with a vision of cultural philosophy and an agenda of popular culture that becomes more and more pronounced until finally Saro-Wiwa's energies are totally absorbed by his political activism and the organisation and management of the Ogoni issue. In *A Month and a Day*, Ken Saro-Wiwa recalls his changing views on the role of the writer in the economically and politically besieged society of post-oil-boom Nigeria:

> ... it being my credo that literature in a critical situation such as Nigeria's cannot be divorced from politics. Indeed, literature must serve society by steeping itself into politics, by intervention, and writers must not merely write to amuse or take a bemused, critical look at society. They must play an interventionist role ... the writer must be l'homme engagé: the intellectual man of action. (p. 81)

It is also obvious that the skills and techniques, which Saro-Wiwa learned or even taught himself during his 20 years' career as a writer, cultural activist, but also as a civil servant/administrator and a business man, were instrumentalised in the new task to which he set himself from the beginning of the 1990s. The newspaper column 'Similia' in the *Sunday Times* marks the stage of transition. It is here that he first used the media power, which he could command to campaign for Ogoni issues.

At the end of the 1980s, Ken Saro-Wiwa had earned himself renown as an internationally known writer. Inside Nigeria he was a national figure as a "television comedy producer turning his pen from the comic to the serious" (*A Month and a Day*, 140), and he had a firm reputation as an internationally operating publisher and a nationally operating television and film maker, i.e. he was reputed as an intellectual—a man of ideas, and a man of action—the man with entrepreneurial and managerial skills and instincts, when he decided to devote his time and energies to the Ogoni cause. He was often accused of high jacking the Movement for the Survival of the Ogoni People (MOSOP), when he took over the chairmanship of that organisation. If we are willing to believe Saro-Wiwa's own testimony in *A Month and a Day*, he was not really high jacking a vibrant organisation, but he was inhaling a new spirit of life into an ailing organisation that was on the brink of death and even self-destruction. The almost total lack of political impact of MOSOP in the pre-Saro-Wiwian days, supports his assessment. Ken Saro-Wiwa bitterly complains about the educated Ogoni elite, that is highly corruptible and ever ready to sell out on the Ogoni cause for personal gains or preferment. Ken Saro-Wiwa's taking over of MOSOP and converting it into an efficient fighting machine for civil and ecological rights, seems to have constituted a new experience for the Nigerian military government. Being used to deal with organisations whose leaders could be bought and their movement harnessed to become part of the government convoy, MOSOP under Ken Saro-Wiwa proved to be unexpectantly different for Nigerian political standards. It could obviously not be bought, not be silenced and not be smothered with the usual 'diplomatic' manoeuvres.

It was Ken Saro-Wiwa's experience as administrator, as entrepreneur and manager, which recommended him as a leader for MOSOP. And it was Ken Saro-Wiwa, who duly injected his ideas and his organisational talent into the promotion of the Ogoni cause. It was him who designed a veritable public relations policy for MOSOP:

> I realised quite early the value of publicity to the protest march, and, indeed, to the entire Ogoni movement. I had ... learnt quite a

bit about how to promote an idea or a product during my television production days. The lesson came in very handy now. Television had made me the darling, so to speak, of the Nigerian media, including the junk press. And I had learnt how to use the print media, in particular, to promote my product. (*A Month and a Day*, 138–9)

His experiences in publishing, in serial production, in financing, producing, distributing print media products, is instrumentalised directly with one of the key instruments in the promotion of the Ogoni cause: the *Ogoni Review*. Ken Saro-Wiwa understood clearly the double need for a publication like the *Ogoni Review*, its importance to provide information for the Ogoni community proper, creating awareness of political and ecological facts, and providing resources for the evaluation of these facts; the importance of the *Ogoni Review* to forge the community into a unified and homogenous group that understands the necessity for sticking together; the importance for the *Ogoni Review* to create the feeling of togetherness, the spirit of communality; finally the importance of a publication outlet to project the image and the issues of the Ogoni to the rest of Nigeria and beyond in the hope to make them understand what MOSOP stands for.

Our publicity efforts turned the Ogoni people into avid readers of newspapers. Where previously they had not warmed up to newspapers, they now not only read newspapers but filed cuttings ... the *Ogoni Review* ... was sold at all our rallies in Ogoni and was distributed free to those on our mailing list. (pp. 140–1)

Mobilising the Ogoni population to stand up and fight for their rights and the protection of their homeland is one aspect of Saro-Wiwa's success as a manager. Through his personal contacts with leading media figures in Nigeria, he successfully demonstrated his skill in organising a public relations campaign on the national level with a continuous presence and visibility in the press. He also managed to extend his public relations campaign onto the international plane through many contacts as a writer and international publisher. BBC Africa Service was one of his major outlets. But he also approached in a well statefied campaign all the relevant environmental and human rights organisations from Greenpeace to PEN, from Amnesty to Unrepresented Nations and Peoples Organisation. He even succeeded in bringing the Ogoni cause before the United Nations Human Rights Commission and several other international bodies. The international resonance which Ken Saro-Wiwa successfully engineered, was probably what annoyed the military government most. Inside the country, they could always put down the lid tight or allow a controlled letting off of steam; outside the country on the international plane, they had no chance to monitor or even suppress Ken Saro-Wiwa's MOSOP campaign.

In one of his letters, smuggled out of prison in March 1995, Ken Saro-Wiwa diagnoses the dictators' fright by the word:

> Sixty-five days in chains, many weeks of starvation, months of mental torture and, recently, the rides in a steaming, airless Black Maria to appear before a Kangaroo Court ... where the proceedings leave no doubt that the judgment has been written in advance.... The men who ordain and supervise this show of shame, this tragic charade are frightened by the word, the power of ideas, the power of the pen, by the demands of social justice and scared of the power of the word that they do not read. (*Mail and Guardian*, May 26 to June 1, 1995)

The case of Ken Saro-Wiwa shows clearly that it is not only the ideas, not only the word, but Ken Saro-Wiwa's extraordinary efficiency and capability in making the word go round, in giving a voice to the Ogoni people and in making sure that this voice can be heard all the world over.

> My experience has been that African governments can ignore writers, taking comfort in the fact that only few can read and write, and that those who read find little time for the luxury of literary consumption beyond the need to pass examinations based on set texts. Therefore, the writer must be ... the intellectual man of action. He must take part in mass organisations. He must establish direct contact with the people and resort to the strength of African literature

— oratory in the tongue. For the word is power and more powerful is it when expressed in common currency. That is why the writer who takes part in mass organisations will deliver his message more effectively than one who only writes waiting for time to work its literary wonders. (*A Month and a Day*, 81)

REFERENCES

Saro-Wiwa, Ken. *Sozaboy: A Novel in Rotten English*. Port Harcourt: Saros International, 1985.

———. *Basi & Company: A Modern African Folktale*. Port Harcourt: Saros International, 1987.

———. *Similia: Essays on Anomic Nigeria*. Port Harcourt: Saros International, 1991.

———. *A Month and a Day*. Intro. William Boyd. London: Penguin, 1995.

Ken Saro-Wiwa
Abiola Irele

In his doctoral thesis on the literature of the Nigerian civil war submitted to the then University of Ife, Chidi Amuta advances, as the main plank of his argument on the significance of this literature,[1] the idea that it marks the critical turning point in the development of a truly national literature in this country. It is not difficult to understand his line of reasoning, for the point on which his emphasis falls is that the civil war itself, as a historical event of the greatest magnitude in our national life so far, represents both a watershed and a point of new departure in the process of national formation among us. It has inevitably determined a corresponding line of development in our literature towards a less 'ethnic' and a more 'national' orientation of themes and concerns.

The importance of the civil war resides of course in the fact that it provides a major point of reference for the evolution of a national consciousness in this country not merely in terms of the relation of this consciousness to a perceived sense of a common involvement which took root while it lasted and began to mature in its aftermath, but more fundamentally, in terms of an awareness that has also emerged of the play of social forces in the process of national formation itself. There is undoubtedly a new nationalism abroad among us, but it is less a result of a definitive settlement of the national question than a function of the social determinations of our national life, as well as of their extensions into the realm of ideology. It is especially this phenomenon that recent literature in Nigeria has tended to reflect in a convergence of thematic preoccupations, despite the diversity of forms employed and of the approach of each individual writer.

From the point of view then of its historical significance and its social and ideological implications, the civil war has come to have an import that goes further and deeper than the question of maintaining the territorial integrity of the Nigerian state on which it was fought. It touched directly upon an issue that has remained with us ever since, and which has acquired at this moment a peculiar intensity, that of the nature and complexion of the human society that we intend to create within the framework of the political entity that we have accepted as a common reference, as a bounding context in which the life and destiny of every one of us are totally implicated. If Nigerian literature has any significance today, that significance can be said to turn on this unique issue.

Paradoxical as it may seem, it is in the literature of the Nigerian civil war, and especially that produced by the writers on the Biafran side, that this issue has so far received its more insistent examination. There is a real sense in which this particular body of works stands today at the very centre of what one may call the 'Nigerian question', in the comprehensive reassessment of the Nigerian situation that it presents under the pressure of a national crisis. The real interest of this literature resides not in its documentary vale as a record of certain events that affected the lives of millions of our countrymen and women; not in its quality, for much of it was of a middling standard; but rather in the astounding testimony it provides of the peculiar nature of the bond that tied Biafra to Nigeria. The remarkable fact of this literature is the sober appraisal it undertook of the Nigerian inheritance of the leaders of the secession and the grave limitations it imposed upon the effort to make the secessionist state a reality founded upon new social values. The contention that underlies Madiebo's (1980) account of the Biafran experience in his *The Biafran War and the Nigerian Revolution*[2] brings out in an indirect but defined way the point of this seeming paradox. As he seems to me to argue, Biafra was a symbol of disaffection towards Nigeria as it was devised and bequeathed to us by the British coloniser, and the secession signified a quest not only for an alternative political arrangement but also for a new and more harmonious social order. In this view, the Biafran secession was intended as a revolutionary break from Nigeria, as a creative and purposeful new beginning.

The admirable sincerity with which the Biafran writers portray the experience of the civil war indicates why this ideal could not be realised. The same ethnic and social contradictions that plagued Nigeria reappeared within Biafra, and the evidence of the literature suggests that the most pervasive disabling of these contradictions was the marked cleavage between the elite and the common people. There seems no doubt from a consideration of the evidence that the secessionist effort was prevented from being a 'people's war' by this singular factor, and there is a tragic irony to Biafra that the literature of the civil war has made even clearer to us today, for if there was a genuine commitment of millions of ordinary individuals to the secessionist cause — roused to a pitch as much by deeply genuine grievances as by a strident propaganda machine — this commitment now seems to have been the manifestation of a false consciousness, insofar as the war itself was being prosecuted on behalf of interests that bore no real relationship to their lives, but had everything to do with furthering the power and privilege of a restricted group who had the direction of the secessionist effort.

The point that emerges from these considerations as they are forced on us by the literature of the civil war has a curious interest. In the composite tale of corruption, intrigue, self-seeking and even sheer incompetence on the Biafran side — along side the heroism, dedication and sense of sacrifice — enacted by the novels and other literature of the civil war, we are offered a picture that is decidedly *Nigerian*. The indictment that is implicit in this tale of an elite that was unwilling and unable to effect a radical transformation of its values that the occasion called for retains of course its relevance, and its application to our present situation can be measured by the real scale of the damage that Biafra has come to represent. If ever there was such a thing as a Biafran revolution, it was one that was betrayed from within. In the event, federal guns did no more than bring back into a common fold, such as it was and has remained, a people that had been kept all along even to the core, profoundly Nigerian.

To read Ken Saro-Wiwa's (1985) *Sozaboy*,[3] the latest addition to the literature of the Nigerian civil war, is to be persuaded more than ever of the truth of this observation. To be sure, the perspective that his novel projects on the war is in many respects different from that of the Igbo writers whose works, for obvious reasons, dominate this phase and area of our national literature. For one thing, Saro-Wiwa is concerned in this novel primarily with the experience of the common people caught up in the war. His choice of an obscure apprentice driver as the hero of the novel underlines a point that none of the Igbo writers has made with sufficient force: the fact that the civil war occasioned an involuntary involvement of masses of individuals in events of whose drift and meaning they had not the slightest idea. Saro-Wiwa's Sozaboy is forced to enlist on both sides of the conflict as these events impinge on his life and direct his fortunes, and we can be sure that for him, as for many like him who were pulled into the vortex of the war, the abstractions in which the issues on which it was ostensibly fought counted for nothing at all. There is a decided shift of focus therefore in Saro-Wiwa's novel that is significant. It not only concentrates upon that level of experience at which the war produced its most devastating effects, it offers a broader canvas in such a way as to inscribe this experience on the larger tragedy of our national crisis.

It is obviously an advantage that Saro-Wiwa himself hails from one of the minority areas that found itself enclosed within the secession in the early phase of the civil war. Moreover, his participation in the federal war effort as administrator of Bonny shortly after its liberation provided him with a direct insight into the turmoil that the war inflicted upon ordinary lives, and it is this material that he has now transmuted into affecting art. It was said at the time that, next to Ukpabi Asika, the then Civilian Administrator of the East, Saro-Wiwa occupied the most dangerous post in the world. The impact of an assignment of such fearful responsibility on the sensibility of the young university teacher that he then was, does not require a great effort of the imagination to comprehend. The immense disruption of ordinary lives, the suffering and the brutality occasioned by the war to which he was witness clearly made a deep impression on him.

The poems collected in his volume entitled *Songs in a Time of War*[4] represent an effort to convey this impression in artistic terms. As with J.P. Clark's (1970) *Casualties*,[5] these poems offer a mental record of a momentous collective drama, so as to bring them within the grasp of the singular consciousness. It cannot be said however that Saro-Wiwa's poems succeed as those of Clark, who had a direct experience of the war in the same way as Saro-Wiwa, in giving to this experience the definition in metaphor that the poetic form requires. The feeling in his poem lies too much on the surface and the language is too obviously contrived to elicit a satisfactory response to what Saro-Wiwa urges upon us.

With the fictional presentation of this same experience, on the other hand, Saro-Wiwa achieves a different effect. I believe it is fair to say that we have in *Sozaboy* something of a masterpiece, in which the trauma of a shattering experience has been held at the proper distance necessary for its sublimation into a work of rare artistic power, embodying at the same time a statement of great human import. There are, to be sure, passages in the novel that make for an unevenness of tone and effectiveness, but the large sensitivity to life as much in its quotidian ordinariness as in the intensities of its dramatic moments which Saro-Wiwa displays in his novel seem to compensate amply for these passing defects in what is, after all, a first novel. At all events, there is an overriding force of suggestion of the narration that impresses Saro-Wiwa's fictional universe upon the imagination as indeed upon the sensibility.

It is especially in this regard that the Nigerian quality of Saro-Wiwa's novel manifests itself most convincingly. This quality inheres in the setting, characterisation, narrative movement and most evident of all, the language of the work; indeed, the idiom that Saro-Wiwa employs here, and which he calls 'rotten English' resumes the sense and direction of the novel. As he puts it in the author's note at the head of the book, this language is "disordered and disorderly" — in other words, the expression of a world that is yet to find an abiding compass in a grounding order of values. The bewildering nature of the social and moral universe in which Sozaboy is called upon to establish a sense of his identity is made evident from the outset. His youthfulness and the obvious energy with which he takes his life into his own hands are mocked by the shifting movement of manners and attitudes that he encounters all around him. The war which he seizes upon to provide him with a centre of consciousness of his own being turns out to be the ultimate dissolvent of what remains of what has all along been made plain to us as his fragile personality.

Nonetheless, war and the series of grim adventures that he goes through offer him the theatre of a precious education in life, even something of a spiritual adventure. Like Medza in Mong Beti's *Mission to Kala*,[6] Sozaboy undergoes a development that modifies his initial spontaneous and uncomplicated approach to life into one that becomes governed by a reflective consciousness. And the most remarkable feature of this novel for me is the way in which the language evolves to enforce this development of the main character, becomes in fact central to the unfolding of the process of growth of his mind.

On this question of language, it is apparent that Saro-Wiwa has run the gauntlet of two risks involved in his deliberate choice of idiom of expression for his hero. The first is that of consistency of register, and there will no doubt be reservations about the appropriateness of some of the turns of phrase that he attributes to his hero. The mixture of levels that often occurs in the novel is apparent in a passage such as this:

> And as I do not know anybody in that place, I said to myself that after all said and done, they are all enemy sozas. But if they are enemy sozas, why did they not kill me that time when they see me for inside bush? How about all those that they are killing everytime with bomb and gun? Why should they sorry for me and not sorry for those people? Or praps they want to do me some very bad thing after I have get well, so they do not want to kill me now. Or praps they do not like to kill soza who is not well. Or soza who is not fat like llama. And as I am not well and I am not fat, they will not like to kill me yet.[7]

But we can, I think, take it that this language communicates sufficiently enough to make us forget what may be regarded as a stylistic lapse. The second risk is more imperilling, and relates to the comic associations which pidgin and less standard forms of English tend to take on in our literature, much as dialect forms do in contemporary Yoruba drama, for example. The risk here, of course, is that the serious intent of Saro-Wiwa's novel could be missed. But it is evident that the choice of idiom here goes beyond that of the novel. This is no longer, as with Gabriel Okara's *The Voice*, or Amos Tutuola's novels, a personal dislocation of the structure of English to suit a generalised African mode of expression, but a creative handling of an existing language, a collective property whose sinews reflect the areas of strength characteristic of a Nigerian — that is a *national* — mode of expression. It is only in Frank Imoukhuede's pidgin poems that we encounter a similar purposive use of this mode to reflect the distinctive way of life and outlook that we recognise as our own.

What is even more impressive in the case of Saro-Wiwa is the veritable triumph that he seems to me to have wrestled out of the discordance offered by his chosen medium. For he has made it to serve the profound intent of his novel: both to capture the authentic feel of life at the level of society at which the language of his novel functions as the regular medium of communication, and to stamp upon his portrayal of this life the seal of a 'high seriousness'. The register of language in this novel corresponds to the register of the existence which it explores, and the critical realism of Saro-Wiwa's fiction inheres in the progressive modulation of its idiom from a comic key of expression to one capable of sustaining a note of intense pathos that culminates in the moral at the very end of the book. This moral, as it turns out, widens the scope of Saro-Wiwa's comment on the events of our civil war into a statement on the precariousness of the individual's existence.

When we consider the broad canvas on which Ken Saro-Wiwa projects his narration of Sozaboy's adventures in his novel of the Nigerian civil war, and the general human significance that, as I have earlier suggested, these adventures come to assume, it becomes evident that the most rewarding approach to the novel is to read it as the expression of a clearly defined national consciousness as it begins to manifest itself in our literature. In Saro-Wiwa's novel, this consciousness is articulated through an exploration of the ordinary train of everyday preoccupations which give to social life its human complexion and provide, as its ultimate determinations, the very sense of the flow of history.

The relation of fiction to historical fact in *Sozaboy* indicates this particular orientation of Saro-Wiwa's imaginative grasp of social forces in the particular context of our national life. The events of the civil war are not dwelt on in themselves, but remain as a general background to a tale of massive disruption of life at the particular moment in which it breaks like a storm over the heads of the common people. The setting and the language of the novel serve to emphasize the novelist's preoccupation with presenting as complete a range as possible of those aspects of the Nigerian experience that account for its specific feel and character, in such a way as to give a concrete quality to the evocations of the tragic impact of the civil war on the course of ordinary lives. The frame of reference of the novel thus extends beyond the historical experience of the civil war to embrace the whole area of life and expression into which it intrudes with devastating consequences.

The use of the same setting and of the same minor characters of Sozaboy in the series of short stories that forms the first part of the collection entitled *A Forest of Flowers*[8] confirms this orientation of Saro-Wiwa's fiction, suggesting as it does that the war novel itself has as its formal and contextual background the realities that make for the felt texture of the total experience we meet with in these stories. Moreover, the shift of setting from the rural environment in the first part of the volume to the urban milieu in the second part, with its passably grotesque modernity that we recognise as presently distinctive of the national character, underlines Saro-Wiwa's commitment to a determined fictional purpose: to give us back a reflection of our lives and of our times with the clarity and definition we require for the perception of our collective self and situation in their manifold character.

The organisation of the volume into two distinctive but related parts intimates us at once with this purpose. The first story in each part, which also provides the sub title to the series at the head of which it stands, serves as an indication of the atmosphere of the stories that follow and as a principle of their integration into a whole. Each of those keynote stories — 'Home Sweet Home' in the first part and 'High Life' in the second — is deliberately made to point up the orientation of fictional representations into which they lead. This is especially the case with 'Home Sweet Home' which introduces us to the closed world of the backwoods village of Dukana, the single setting for all the eight stories in the first part of the volume. The location of characters and situations in this setting links these stories with the novel *Sozaboy* and gives them a coherence both of atmosphere and of formal design and intent. With 'High Life', the urban setting and the consistent tone of satire that comes through much of the writing constitute the formal properties that unite the eleven stories in the second part of the volume, providing at the same time the informing spirit of a more varied presentation of characters and situations. The structure of the volume thus becomes in itself a telling index of the intention that presides over its conception.

That this intention is ironic and critical, there can be no doubt. All the stories focus on aspects of life in Nigeria that are indicative of the inner movement of transition and the various forms of accommodation to this movement that individuals are forced to adopt; taken together, they constitute a series of vignettes that compose a comprehensive picture of the dislocations that are characteristic of a changing society. In 'Home Sweet Home', which tells the story of the return to the village of a young school girl on holiday, we are given a double perspective upon the state of mind of the narration as a device for the presentation of life in the village. There is an intimate tone to the narration, while at the same time the objective character of life in the village is made evident. The narrative device thus enables us to enter into the process of the detached consciousness that the author brings to his evocations of the rural environment in the first part of the volume.

The irony here resides in the contrast which becomes apparent between the sharply etched quality of Saro-Wiwa's evocations of life in the village and the implied judgment upon its negative implications which these evocations contain. In 'A Family Affair' for example, we are made to witness a drama of social honour whose tragic repercussions ring through our minds long after we've left the story, and to contemplate the full extent of the implacable code of this rural community in its hold upon collective attitudes. What we see is a picture of a communal solidarity that has quite lost its sense of bearing upon the needs of the individuals; of a rigid adherence to conventions of life whose relevance to the contemporary situation is, to say the least, seriously in doubt.

The remarkable thing about these stories is the total absence of any kind of romantic involvement on the part of the author with the world he presents — a point on which I shall comment later. There is a clarity of detail in his evocations which suggests a familiarity with the environment and the category of characters he employs for his stories. The unrelenting realism of his writing however precludes a suggestion of affective commitment. It is true that his frequent notations upon the material conditions of the people's lives — notations which build up a picture of sheer destitution — point to a basic sympathy for the kind of relegated community that these people typify. It is also true that we get a sense of engagement with the simplicity of life in this environment. But this never leads to a positive consideration of a way of life which revolves around the stark confinement to a natural mode of existence that we are made aware of as the objective definition of this simplicity.

For the impression that we are left with as we come away from Saro-Wiwa's presentation of the rural environment in the first part of his volume is the crushing weight of tradition upon the rural community. In the circumstances in which we are made to encounter this community and to obtain some insight into the attitudes of the people who embody its commanding values, this aspect of life in the traditional context emerges clearly as a disabling factor. It is not only the harsh quality of life that Saro-Wiwa dwells on, but the anomaly that he makes obvious of the inflexible attachment of the community itself to a way of life that is both outmoded and in a fundamental sense objectionable. This is so because the conventions that regulate conduct in the community that he presents leave no room for those common human sympathies that temper social constraint and make for a comfortable sense of individual involvement in a collective order. In these stories, set as they are in the perspective of social and cultural transition, we are made aware of the disparity between received modes of existence and the direction towards a new dispensation.

It is the emerging shape of this new dispensation that Saro-Wiwa sketches for us in the stories that make up the second part of his volume. We meet here with the boisterous world of Nigerian modernity inhabited by the multitudes displaced from the rural environment by the pressure of economic and social factors and the promise of a new life in the urban centres of our country. There is considerable interest in the fact that the lead story in this section is not only entitled 'High Life' to suggest the newly accelerated pace of life in the new dispensation, but is also written in an idiom equivalent to that which is employed in *Sozaboy*. As with the novel, the jostling of linguistic structures in this novel corresponds to a parallel situation in the state of mind of the character whose bizarre adventure is recounted in the story. That the confusion dramatised here in situation and language is an effect of the social environment is the point that the stories that follow demonstrate.

Saro-Wiwa presents us in these stories with virtually a cross section of the social categories and human types that crowded upon the national area of our lives and its corners, as we have experienced our new social situation and continue to bear with its tensions in recent times. Indeed these stories take the form of individual portraits of characters who are the varied embodiments of contemporary Nigerian experience. Saro-Wiwa's mode of presentation is just as varied, moving from the mordant irony of a story like 'Acapulco Hotel' to the genuine pathos of 'Robert and the Dog'. The social commentary that is contained in these stories discovers itself only by implication in the vivid rendering of situations and manners, endowed with a discreet quality by the urbane of Saro-Wiwa's writing and the technical mastery of the short form that he displays throughout.

It cannot but strike the alert reader who considers the relationship between the two series of stories in this volume that there is an option, discoverable in its organisation and execution, for the modern dispensation. It is not so much that the writer is less critical of the urban world of his creation that he is of the rural, but that we do get the distinct impression of a greater tolerance towards the disorders of the former than to the rigours of the latter. The different effects of the irony in the two parts of the volume suggest such an impression. Where in the second part it is mocking, and even at times mild, directed at a familiar world with which it is possible to negotiate a satisfactory form of accommodation, in the first part it takes on a character that is unmistakably grim. The critical perspective here focuses upon a world that is closed in upon itself, within which neither the individual nor his mind's will is allowed any appreciable range of expression.

The fact is that it is not only a physical and social world that we encounter in Saro-Wiwa's presentation of the rural setting and of the peasant community in the first part of the volume but also a mental universe. It becomes evident as we go through these stories that the authorial mind that is at odds with the order of values which determines a certain human essence in this environment. The point seems to me important for an appraisal of the angle of perception which Saro-Wiwa adopts for viewing the traditional background of our contemporary social and cultural situation, as indeed of the specific orientation of the entire collection of his short stories. We may take it that the content of the first part of his volume corresponds to what, following Chidi Amuta, we can designate as the ethnic level of the writer's consciousness. If this is so, the ironic stance that he assumes towards his material and the critical implications which this suggest must represent a firm rejection of the customary association of this material with the movement of revaluation of the traditional culture and background which has been a dominant feature of African literature.

It is instructive in this respect to consider the nature of Saro-Wiwa's evocations, for they mark a radical departure from one of the most established of our literary conventions. I have already commented upon his realism and the connotations this produces in his writings. What is even more remarkable here is the absence of those anthropological references that, for better *and* for worse, our writers have relied upon to give character to their evocations of the traditional world. There is nothing here of the elaborate ceremonial life that we have been accustomed to as the hallmark of this world — no communal dances, no ritual, no festival enacted, save the sullen confinement of lives to a primordial scale of existence. The ultimate irony of Saro-Wiwa's stories is that of the title of his book. If the forest that dominate these lives has any flowers, it also holds our terrors that seem to be more firmly lodged in the heart of the community which is physically enclosed by its menacing presence.

There seems to me a sense in which therefore Saro-Wiwa's stories represent an advanced stage in the movement towards a new realism in African literature. In the Nigerian context, his fiction has come as a singular expression of a process of *transvaluation* through an expansion of the writer's consciousness beyond its ethnic horizons and ideological conditioning. From this point of view, the second series of short stories can be seen as a necessary complement to the first — as an extension of the sociological perspectives of Saro-Wiwa's portrayal of the rural and traditional background. The passage from the context of the first part of the volume to that of the second implies a crossing over, as it were, from the ethnic to the national frame of reference, symbolic of the mental process that is at work in the conception of the whole volume.

The conclusion then that imposes itself upon me, as I consider Saro-Wiwa's fiction in its revelation in these books, is that we have in this writer a major new figure of our national literature. The direction already taken by him, the resources of the imagination that his work evinces, the skill that he deploys in the crafting of his texts — all these indicate a promise that I have every expectation he will come to fulfil.

NOTES

1   This was in 1984. Also see Chidi Amuta 'History, Society and Hero-ism in the Nigerian War Novel', *Kunapipi*, 6.3 (1984): 57–85.

2   Alexander A. Madiebo, *The Nigerian Revolution and the Biafran War*, Enugu: Fourth Dimension, 1980.

3   Ken Saro-Wiwa, *Sozaboy: A Novel in Rotten English*, Saros International, 1985.

4   Ibid., *Songs in a Time of War*, Port Harcourt: Saros International, 1985.

5   J.P. Clark-Bekederemo, *Casualties: Poems 1966–68*, Harlow: Longman, 1970.

6   Mungo Beti, *Mission to Kala*, London: Heinemann Educational Books, 1964.

7   Saro-Wiwa, *Sozaboy*.

8   Ibid. *A Forest of Flowers*, Port Harcourt: Saros International, 1985.

Poetry

SEWING A PATH FROM THE TATTERS
Olu Obafemi

Mountains heap inside my bowels,
Ridges of words
Tumble to the lip
Of my embittered pen.

Ridges,
Upon which are planted
Seedlings of events
Tumble
On the flat face of my jotter.

I find an avalanche
Of crowding events
Tearing through the wind
Like famished tiger in the presence of prey.

These mounds must harvest
The history of tomorrow.

But,
The pain
Of the dryness of the earth
Stands stoutly
Between the ridges of words;

Thoughts
Clash in the breathless pace of events
And the mind—
Being and seeing—
Does not find the mortar
For crushing the corn.

The events of the season
Heavy and countless
Like the multiple teeth of Adepele

Can we, like the weaver-bird,
Weave thoughts
Among the labyrinth?

Yet,
This season of the mind—
Like a hill
Pressaging a greater storm
After a whirlwind—
Must crush the throng of events
Into a rolling ball.

Those whose ears
Weave meaning from a crowd of sounds
Must put a head
to the tatters of time
And sew a path
Through the torrent of crises.

SONG OF THE SEASON
Joseph Ushie

We begin here another stanza
of the song of the season,
our song of sighs sung in whispers
until the tongue blisters, until
the throats dry up and the dry
earth is wet with our tears.

We begin here another stanza
of the reigning song with the felling
of another silk cotton tree by the
axe of our gods of war.

We begin here another stanza
of this song of the season, attired
in sable uniform, mourning another
Prometheus, Kenule Saro-Wiwa.

Brave to the death, you were the
lamb that stared the invading
leopard in the face. Anchored
on truth, you stood stoutly as
the people's pillar and they all
leaned on you like climbers on iroko.

But you are gone! Fresh feast
for the ants in shallow mass grave.
You, your priceless brains, your lion heart,
our tears for the people, all.

Shocked, the ever-journeying wind
reared not her head this day; the
birds hid in their nests, the rivers
slowed down their pace, the ants
wept aloud, the owls hooted
themselves hoarse and the
dogs barked their throats dry.

MY RED BERET
(for Ken Saro-Wiwa, 1941–1995)
Charles Burmeister

I smile
big big smile
in my red beret
as I hold on
to shiny-oh shiny machinegun
in mighty fast technical.[1]

And I be prouding like numbawon big man
because I see mary[2]
with tits shake like calabash
who make my little man stand up.

And she see my red beret
and my big shiny-oh,
and she give me eye
wide like the full full moon.
And I thank jesuschristamen
for being sozaboy.

Then the world turn topside down,
when G.I. come
with choppa buzz like bee
and roaring A.P.C.,
and make technical look like beetle
and machinegun nothing.
And all the time noos-croo
scurry behind G.I.
like marys with calabash tits.

And big big G.I. yell,
"Tenshon!
Azjuwar!"

And we run away like mouse
into the bush in our little beetles.
And the G.I. go to the hungry pickaninny
    with mountain of chop[3]
like sand bags to the flood.

And I remember
before before
my father say
thru his teeth
as he chop his chop,
"Never see a skinny man with a gun."

And he go on chop his chop,
while the pickaninny cry,
and the dirt is dry
like pussy of plenty old mary.

Then big big numbawon white man come.
And the pickaninny with peanut head
make sing sing for numbawon G.I.
because he bring chop.

But numbawon reach with reaching hands,
and kiss with wet lips and
scare little mary pickaninny away.

Then, "Tenshon!
Azjuwar!"
And numbawon Mr. Bush
tok big big grammah,
"Continuing on all fronts"
and "Extending goodwill to your people,"
while tiny small pickaninny
with peanut head and poking tummy
wait for chop.

And out in the bush
I wait
long long wait
like for plenty old mary to walk.
I wait for G.I. to go home,
so I can see calabash tits shake
with jesuschristamen
and wear my red beret.

But the G.I. stay long long time,
and still pickaninny chop like cricket,
and the dirt is dry like pussy of plenty old mary,
and the pickaninny bones chatter in the night.

NOTES
1 *technical* – a truck with a machine gun mount.
2 *mary* – woman, girl, female.
3 *chop* – food or to eat, e.g., chop his chop = eat his food.

CROSSROADS
Jacqueline Onyejiaka

We stand at the crossroads today
Spectators to uncertain freedom
We have been silent,
But we shall be silent no longer
We have been mules,
But we shall be mules no longer
You smiled your pasty smile
While you plotted our plunder
But today before the whole world
We shall come forward as heirs
And claim what is rightfully ours —
The land of our fathers.

CONFESSION FROM A SEX CLINIC
(on reading Jonathan May)
Femi Dunmade

My dear,

> They committed our anthem to sexist language
> and etched lasting images of a father and youths
> the mother who gave them birth unmentioned
> they call us to serve only our fatherland.
>
> Father's face is a Sunday School teacher's
> sweet and innocent he claims the land is ours
> and will to us be the same as that name
> mother calls him...
>
> Ask me not what the name is
> remember the picture on our story book
> remember Oh dear! that great big buck
> his fine spread-on antlers smears of blood
> thirsting for more from his fawns
> in the heart of Southern Sahara.
>
> I no longer need to tell you
> who a horny bastard is
> where a father seeks to maim his children
> who dare seek some interest on a motherland
> held in trust to his strange allies.
>
> If you read (between) my lines
> keep my identity from being public knowledge
> I only give to you a parable-in-history
> take a clue from Ogonis' agonies.

THE SEA
Jonathan Hart

He once saw her by the sea
As it swelled as the sun rose
And the moon dreamt on the other side
As he remembered how they ran

On the beach, as if they could leap
Over stones from Europe to Africa.
When they locked him up, they both felt
Blind, and the cusp dissolved

Like sand before the tide. When they
Hanged him, his mouth bled
Like oil on the beaches, and they
Buried him, like a platform, with excuses.

WHEN RAIN FALLS
Abdul-Rasheed Na'Allah

Refrain: In ruwan sama ya faɗo, ya jiƙe ƙasa
           Ya taru a rijiya, a samu na sha

The Parrot has sang this song before,
In homage to a friend in snowy fore.
Our eyes, this karo,[1] look down the more.

Refrain: In ruwan sama ya faɗo, ya jiƙe ƙasa,
           Ya taru a rijiya, a samu na sha.

It's me, Parrot, Master of the lore.
Come oh you,
your steps at the floor.

Refrain: In ruwan sama ya faɗo, ya jiƙe ƙasa
           Ya taru a rijiya, a samu na sha

When the rain falls,
the earth is wet
Our wells 're full
Our throats 're soak.

In ruwan sama ya faɗo,…

Yes, my tale be told:
This land's eyes have seen much dust
Its seas and oceans have lost their limbs,
To the marauders who loot its trust.
This land must seek its rims:
Or else it drowns, in this drought of whims!

In ruwan sama ya faɗo,…

My fellow kin, lend me your ears
If I wake early in the morning , I sing a thousand songs;

Failure to wake early, I sing in hundreds.
The Parrot's doses aren't intoxicating dungs:
Fruits-bear trees, I water.

In ruwan sama ya faɗo,...

Ho rain, this land is starved of you!
Come forth and wet our mouths.
Come, our wells want a private talk with you
Our throats want their appointments fulfilled.

In ruwan sama ya faɗo,...

All you,
almajirai,[2]
and you akawun-gwamnati[3]
who eat files daily on your desks,
And those makers of ridges on the land,
All you carvers, smiths, weavers
You fellow painters who paint boldly on the slates
Even you who stray the abuja streets
For you, a tiding!

In ruwan sama ya faɗo,...

When the rain falls,
It'll wash the streets.
Its mighty flood,
Will clear off all remnant-gutters
That survive its piercing wind.

In ruwan sama ya faɗo, ...

Water must flow!
'Yan uwa,[4]
Honey must spring.

In ruwan sama ya faɗo,...

Yes,
When the rain does fall,
We'll drink to our fill,
And make our fields,
In this, our own dear native land.

In ruwan sama ya faɗo, ya jike ƙasa
Ya taru a rijiya, a samu na sha.[5]

NOTES

1   Hausa word for 'this round', or 'this next attempt', or 'this next meeting.'
2   Hausa word for 'the poor' or 'beggars'.
3   Hausa word for 'government workers', 'civil servants'.
4   Hausa phrase for 'my people'.
5   Stanza six translates this refrain.

SONG OF HOPE
Olu Obafemi

Though we know
Those who cut our bellies
Of anger meant for
The throat of a cow,
We do not stretch our hands
To strangle the air.

We know too well that
Those who take the lean meat
From out of our watered mouths;
Those who feed us with left-overs
From the general(s) table
Mean us to weep —
Weep our eyes blind
With vain tears.
We do not cry.

We do not dull the edge of our eyes
With the strain of weakness:
Instead
We brace ourselves;
Tie the bottoms of our hopeful brooms,
Link our arms,
Link the fine edges of our heavy cords
To sing the song of hope.

We do not mourn;
We mend our shattered dreams
And sew our voices
To sing a hopeful song.

We gather our splintered dreams
To remember in the swell memory
The precious moments
Of our collective dreams.

We do not open our mouths
To the foul wind
Nor cry of a forgotten prodigal.

Instead
We sing the song of hope.

VI
Politics, Satire

Civil Critiques:
Satire and the Politics of Democratic Transition in Ken Saro-Wiwa's Novels
Frank Schulze-Engler

Literature bides its time, preparing the minds of the public for the ripe moment, whenever that may be.

Ken Saro-Wiwa, Similia

At present, any attempt at assessing the political significance of Ken Saro-Wiwa's writings will necessarily have to begin with his involvement in the eco-political struggle of the Ogoni against the environmental devastation perpetrated by Shell and other oil multinationals and the political oppression engineered by Nigeria's military rulers. It was this struggle that — as his posthumously published Prison Diary *A Month and a Day* amply testifies to — absorbed most of Saro-Wiwa's energies and increasingly shaped his life during his last years. It was this struggle that transformed Saro-Wiwa from a popular Nigerian writer into a global political player, whose unprecedented media presence was instrumental in putting the plight of the Ogoni onto the international human rights and environmentalist agenda. And it was this peaceful struggle that posed such a delegitimizing threat to the ruling military junta that they decided to utilize the very kangaroo courts Saro-Wiwa had so bitingly satirized in his *Prisoners of Jebs* for an act of cold-blooded judicial murder, thus signalling their grim determination to block the democratic transition that had begun in Nigeria in the late 1980s and early 1990s at all costs.[1]

Yet, Saro-Wiwa's commitment to and involvement in this transition began long before the Movement for the Survival of the Ogoni People (MOSOP) was founded in 1991. Most of his earlier writings were trenchant critiques of contemporary Nigerian society — of authoritarian military rulers as well as corrupt civilian politicians, but also of the docility with which large parts of the population seemed to accept their fate and of the self-destructive greed, stupidity and bigotry that in his view permeated the whole of society and was as widespread among the powerful as among the powerless. The popular, often humorous vein in which this satirical vision was put across helped to broaden the audience for his civil critiques (as did his move beyond more conventional literary forms into new media like television), but did not diminish the radical anger that informs most of Saro-Wiwa's writing. In its most bitter moments, his satirical critique seems on the brink of losing faith in society's capacity to heal itself, but time and again it shrugs off despair to carry on with its laborious task of bringing the absurdity of a society into the open that often enough seems to have resigned itself to its seeming fate.

It was as popular satirist that Saro-Wiwa made his most important impact on Nigerian society in the late 1980s and early 1990s, and — as I hope to show — it is the radical, uncompromising stance with which he insisted on taking the whole of society to task that constitutes the most important legacy of his writing for the development of Nigerian literature in English and for the critical role of literature in the politics of democratic transition.

My analysis will focus on those works Saro-Wiwa himself called his 'novels': *Sozaboy*, *Basi and Company*, *Prisoners of Jebs* and *Pita Dumbrok's Prison*. Actually, only one of these prose writings, *Sozaboy*, shows some of the features conventionally attributed to the novel form: it tells a consecutive story, has a coherent plot and provides a central hero (or rather anti-hero) figure whose development — and disillusionment — the reader is invited to follow. Both *Basi and Company* (based on Saro-Wiwa's popular TV series of the same title) and *Prisoners of Jebs* (which arose out of a weekly newspaper column) consist of short satirical pieces strung together in a more or less consecutive time-frame, but lacking all the other characteristics referred to above. *Pita Dumbrok's Prison*, a sequel to *Prisoners of Jebs*, comes closer to the conventional novel-format, but hovers somewhere between an action thriller (the novel actually begins with a parcel-bomb killing), a political treatise and the surreal satirical patchwork so successfully explored in *Prisoners of Jebs*. All of these works, however, are characterized by a sustained involvement in the politics of civil society: they debunk authoritarian structures that are reproduced at all levels of society, they mock the inflated state that seeks to subjugate the whole of society but founders on its own inefficiency, they scorn the culture of violence that has been nurtured by consecutive military regimes, they castigate the systematic violation of human rights and the erosion of the rule of law, they satirize the ignorance, the self-destructive values and the 'culture of cheating' that permeate all layers of society and they deplore the loss of individual initiative and responsibility that constitute the most important resources for an alternative future.[2]

An early example for the prevalence of these concerns is *Sozaboy*, Saro-Wiwa's first novel, written in what the author himself termed 'rotten English', a composite language "made up of three registers — his mother tongue, Kana; 'broken English', that is, the unsystematic use of strings of English words; and Standard Nigerian English."[3] Saro-Wiwa made the social and political dimensions of this amalgamated construct used by his narrator-protagonist Mene abundantly clear in his 'Author's Note' to the novel (see the 'Author's Note' in *Sozaboy*; also quoted in Garuba in Section Five). It can thus hardly come as surprise that the political and social evaluation of *Sozaboy*'s 'rotten English' has become a central issue in the critical reception of this novel. While some critics have seen the novel as "an attempt to break the norms of the English of [the] elite class and allow in another voice"[4] and as "the product of two impulses: the impulse to rebel against the norms of English set by the elite oppressors and the impulse ... to communicate to an audience larger than the usual novel-reading elite,"[5] others have pointed out the self-ironizing and satirical dimensions of Saro-Wiwa's linguistic device:

...Saro-Wiwa and his narrator do not speak the same language, and

the great distance between them in the given socio-historical context is reproduced in the fictional relationship between author and
narrator. Far from making Mene his spokesman, Saro-Wiwa subjects him to an all-embracing ironic treatment.... Although Mene
takes great pains both to ensure that he maintains close contact
with the audience at all times and to thereby make the relationship
between story and audience as direct as possible, the truth of the
matter is that the audience is urged, as it were, by the "Author's
Note" right from the start to resist these advances, and can become
further distanced from narrator and story by the alienating effect of
authorial irony.[6]

Since Saro-Wiwa himself, in an essay on 'The Language of African
Literature', made it quite clear that to him 'rotten English' was a
communicative experiment which he had no wish to repeat,[7] and
Sozaboy systematically undermines populist notions of linguistic
'Homecoming', there seems to be little need to associate that novel
with the literary appropriation of a 'communally owned Creole'.[8]
Instead, I would like to focus on the remarkable qualities of *Sozaboy*
as political satire.

Sozaboy has often been described as a deeply moving anti-war
novel. While this characterization is undoubtedly true, it is hardly
sufficient to denote the full significance of Saro-Wiwa's satirical
project. Behind the apparent simplicity of the tale and its narrator
lie multiple layers of bitter irony and radical satire. Thus, to begin
with the most obvious instance, the narrator-protagonist Mene —
who enthusiastically joins the Biafran Army to become a 'sozaboy',
survives the horrors of the Nigerian civil war, embarks on a prolonged but ultimately futile quest for his mother and his wife and
finally returns 'home' only to be driven away again as the ghost of
an unwanted past — is a deliberately constructed simpleton whose
narration is shot through with ironies that he himself cannot perceive and who time and again becomes the butt of the author's
satirical intentions.[9] These are not only directed — as one might
expect — against powerful war-mongers, cruel soldiers and corrupt
profiteers, but also against the 'good people' of Dukana, Saro-
Wiwa's fictional composite 'Ogoni-town', who unwittingly become
willing agents of their own destruction.

Interestingly enough, Dukana also appears in Saro-Wiwa's short story collection *A Forest of Flowers*, where in a story entitled 'Home, Sweet Home', the narrator describes his homecoming to his fictitious birth-place in the following terms:

> ...I was glad that I was going to live in Dukana and be part of the community. For Dukana is home, and as everyone will proudly tell you in these parts, 'Home is Home'. This cryptic saying means that it is far better than all those places you have visited or read about. That the dirt in which it wallows comfortably is to be preferred to the paved streets of the best cities of the world. ... And how could anyone disagree? For to disagree was to be disloyal to communal wisdom and to be disloyal to that wisdom so carefully distilled through the ages was arrogance. And arrogance is a deadly sin in Dukana....
>
> Some, taking a cursory look at it, would have considered Dukana a clearing in the tropical rain forest peopled by three or four thousand men, women and children living in rickety mud huts and making a miserable living from small farmlands in the forest or from fishing in the steamy creeks around the village. Some such, not being of Dukana origin, would hold that the absence of a health clinic, of a good school, of pipe-born water, of electricity, was a blight on the town, and would think it primeval. Such ill-informed, malicious people might look at its emaciated, illiterate population and assert that there was malnutrition, that disease was rampant, that life for its inhabitants was brutish and short. (1986: 2)

The ironic perspective on Dukana, which is rendered in a lighter mode in the short story, acquires much harsher qualities in the novel. *Sozaboy* begins with jubilant scenes of celebration in Dukana after the townspeople have heard of the military coup that has toppled the old government. In retrospect, the innocuous opening sentence ("Although, everybody in Dukana was happy at first") vibrates with sinister overtones as it becomes clear in the course of the novel that the same military violence that Dukana is celebrating will ultimately usher in its total destruction.

From the very beginning, there is thus a latent undercurrent of authoritarianism and violence in Dukana, which gathers force with the mobilisation rally presided over by the corrupt Chief Birabee, the enthusiasm with which the townspeople greet Mene's decision to become a 'Sozaboy' and the general identification of military violence and male sexual prowess: the heroic war tales from Burma recounted by the old veteran, Zaza, predictably climax in his sexual exertions with white women (p. 33), Mene's young wife Agnes urges him to prove his manhood by becoming a soldier (pp. 65–6) and in the army Mene is taught to develop an erotic relationship with his gun: "Love am, respect am, keep am clean every time.... Sleep with am as you sleep with your wife or your girl friend" (p. 74).

It is against this background of willful ignorance that Mene's tribulations oscillate between satire and tragedy. It is by not disagreeing and by remaining loyal to the dominant values of his community that Mene becomes involved in the war in the first place — a war which is rationalized as the heroic defence of his community but which ultimately destroys it. The heroism quickly vanishes: the corruption and violence in one's own army turn out to be as lethal as the mysterious 'enemy', and the 'eternal soldier' Manmuswak ('Man must eat') who at one stage becomes something of a father figure for Mene, later cooly massacres unarmed prisoners. When, disillusioned about military heroism, Mene meets the dispersed remnants of his townspeople in a far-away refugee camp, the erstwhile simpleton seems to be the only one who has actually learned something from the war experience: while the starving Dukanians-in-exile still toe the line of Chief Birabee and Pastor Barika, the sobered-up sozaboy discovers that this infamuous duo works hand-in-glove with corrupt military commanders and piles up food and luxury goods behind their tent. He has learned to disagree with the community leaders and sees through the grand promises of a better life once the war is won, commenting wrily: "So I asked myself that if we do not win the war then what will happen?" (p. 155). In a bitterly ironic reversal at the end of the novel, Mene finally returns to his home town only to be ostracized by the community he once set out to defend. Because his haunting presence in the ruins of Dukana disturbs the Chief- and Pastor-ridden townspeople who want to settle back into their old routine, he is denounced as a ghost, blamed for all the evils that bedevil the town in the after-math of war and has to flee into uncertain exile: "...if porson who does not know Dukana people hear this tory, they will just laugh and say that it is nonsense tory. But Dukana is not like that. The people are wicked more than. Anything can happen in that town" (pp. 180–1).

Thus the most important feature of Saro-Wiwa's later satirical prose is already present in his first novel: radical anger about igno-rance bred by poverty and oppression. Despite the bleak ending of *Sozaboy*, the novel is not characterized by a misanthropical con-demnation or arrogant dismissal of the 'common man', but rather by a stern refusal to fall in line with populist myths of the 'good people' as a resource of wisdom and good will.

In his essay-collection *Similia*, which brings together contribu-tions to a regular newspaper column in the Nigerian *Sunday Times* written between 1989 and 1990, Saro-Wiwa spelt out some of the political principles underlying his writing. Commenting on the polemical style that had become his trademark not only in the *Similia*-column, he wrote:

How else do you wake the sleeping elephant? Poke it with a needle? It will not feel it. A million needles will not rouse it from the sleep of three decades. Ever since Nigeria was born, it has been sleeping grandly. So much so that, as I say, flies, ants, maggots and all such agents of corruption have presumed it to be either dead or dying. To wake the big, bad beast from its stupor, a sledge hammer is needed.[10]

Saro-Wiwa made it quite clear that as far as he was concerned this 'sledge hammer' needed to be applied to all aspects of society in order to fight a new type of 'barbarism':

...The prurience of Nigeria has been such that truth has become a pariah and cheating a way of life in schools, universities, govern-ment departments, even in homes. A culture of cheating can only lead to barbarism. And that must be "Similia's" well-founded fear, and the destruction of this barbarism, the goal of its aggressive-ness.[11]

Years later, in summing up his final speech of defence before the court that was to sentence him to death, Saro-Wiwa made a similar point:

> As we subscribe to the subnormal and accept double standards, as we lie and cheat openly, as we protect injustice and oppression, we empty our classrooms, degrade our hospitals, fill our stomachs with hunger and elect to make ourselves the slaves of those who subscribe to high standards, pursue the truth, and honour justice, freedom and hard work. (p. 109)

Yet, in 1990, Saro-Wiwa seemed convinced of the eventual success of his literary mission:

> I am sure that by clear thinking, hard work, honest endeavour and a struggle for social justice, we will rouse the sleeping elephant and send him rumbling through the forest of our despair to light, hope and civilization.[12]

For a brief period of time, one possible way of achieving this rousing feat appeared to be the Directorate of Mass Mobilization for Self-Reliance, Social Justice and Economic Recovery (MAMSER), of which Saro-Wiwa became Executive Director in 1987. This body set up by the Federal Government under General Babangida was to strengthen civil values in Nigerian society, as Saro-Wiwa wrote in *Similia*:

> ...MAMSER seeks to destroy the culture of silence which has enabled a few people to ride roughshod over the cherished beliefs of a people; to arrogate to themselves what is the property of all; to lie and cheat with impunity; to waste and squander national resources and, in the end, lead the nation to perdition.[13]

In this necessary task of social reconstruction, Saro-Wiwa counted particularly on a new generation of younger Nigerians who seemed to possess some of the civil traits necessary for the democratic transition:

They argue and fight for a better nation. When they find anything going wrong, they complain to the authorities. They write to the newspapers and they form organizations and associations with like-minded people to fight collectively for a better society.[14]

Even if (or perhaps, because) Saro-Wiwa's involvement with MAMSER was short-lived (he resigned from his post as Executive Chairman after just over a year in 1988),[15] these remarks show clearly that he saw his literary activities in the wider context of the politics of civil society and democratic transition. Since these politics differ significantly from the decolonizing discourse that in the past decades has provided the dominant paradigm for many intellectual fields (including literary scholarship), I would like to briefly sketch some basic features of these politics before returning to an analysis of Saro-Wiwa's satirical prose and its involvement in them.

At the centre of the democratic transition lies the radical break with what Issa G. Shivji (1985) has described as "developmentalism," i.e. the notion that, given the necessity of rapid development, politics is a luxury in postcolonial Africa.[16] Having inherited "the colonial leviathan with all its authoritarian tentacles" (Zeleza, 1994),[17] the successful anticolonial movements identified politics exclusively with the state:

The equation of politics with the state was rooted in the homogenising ambitions of nationalist ideology and the nature of the reforms implemented in the twilight years of colonial rule. The political monopolies of the one-party state and military rule were incubated in nationalist ideas that posited the independence struggle in essentialist and exclusivist terms. After independence, now that the dreaded colonialists, the "them," had apparently gone, it was time for the "us," the "people," to build and develop the nation. Pursuit of separate class, social, cultural or gender interests, could be dismissed as "sectional" and, therefore, delegitimised.[18]

Thus, according to Frank A. Kunz,

> ...the first phase of independent African statehood, stretching from independence until recently, was a state-centric era of the 'Engagement Paradigm', when state consolidation was the number one item on the agenda.... In civilian and military regimes alike, this state-centric era was characterized by an essentially top-down administrative approach to state-society relations, the net effects having been 'de-politicization' and 'de-participation'.[19]

This state of affairs resulted not only in undemocratic political systems or in human rights violations, but, as Peter Anyang' Nyong'o (1987) has pointed out, crippled the very developmental progress it was meant to enhance:

> At the centre of the failure of African states to chart viable paths for domestic accumulation is the problem of accountability, the lack of democracy. The people's role in the affairs of government has dimished, the political arena has shrunk, political demobilisation has become more the norm than the exception in regime behaviour, social engineering for political demobilisation (i.e. repression) is the preoccupation of most governments; all this has come about to cement one notorious but common aspect of all African governments: the use of public resources as possibilities for viable indigenous processes of development is neglected or destroyed altogether. *There is a definite correlation between the lack of democratic practices in African politics and the deteriorating socio-economic conditions.*[20]

A 're-politicization' and a 're-participation' are thus vital elements in overcoming the acute socio-economic stagnation that so many African societies are suffering from. It is against this background that the distinction between the state (and its military, policing, legal, administrative, productive, and cultural organs) and the non-state (market-regulated, privately controlled or voluntarily organized) realm of civil society and the politics associated with defending, stabilizing and enlarging it, has been gaining an increasingly higher profile in the African context.[21]

As far as the role of intellectuals in this process is concerned, Jean-Francois Bayart (1986) has come forward with some rather sceptical conclusions:

Civil society can only transform its relation to the state through the organisation of new and autonomous structures, the creation of a new cultural fabric and the elaboration of a conceptual challenge to power monopolies. This can only be achieved by means of ideological and institutional 'mediations', and 'mediations' of new categories are nothing less than schemes for the reconstruction of identity and the plural invention of modernity. ...[B]ecause they more readily lend their services to the state than to its challengers, African intellectuals (with few exceptions) have failed to provide civil society with the original conceptual instruments required for its advance. Even when they have had the courage to offer themselves to the leadership of the resistance, they have in no way been able to transcend the epistemic gulf between the state and society. They continue in terms of the state's conceptual logic.[22]

While this statement may be generally true, it seems hardly applicable to a writer like Saro-Wiwa who consistently involved himself in the politics of civil society and, in his essays as well as in his fictional writing, battled on behalf of individual creativity and responsibility with "the state's conceptual logic" and the political, social and cultural deformations it had produced in society. These political concerns which had already surfaced in *Sozaboy* are particularly pronounced in his subsequently published satirical writings.

At first sight, *Basi and Company* seems to have very little in common with his earlier novel. The satirical episodes about Mr. B. and his friends who seek to trick a living out of their Lagos neighborhood are comical, humourous and light in tone. Yet a number of chapters of this urban 'African folktale' based on the popular serial produced by Saro-Wiwa for Nigerian TV deal with obviously political matters such as the manipulation of election results, the absurdities of party politics and the abuse of political power, and even those chapters that initially seem politically quite harmless do in fact offer trenchant social and political critiques underneath the apparent comical surface. The focus of Saro-Wiwa's concerns is the preponderance of norms, values and forms of social behaviour in Nigerian society that hamper sound development and further authoritarianism. What emerges from *Basi and Company* and other of his satirical writings is a farcical dialectic between rulers and ruled: the rulers are not simply violent villains, but also symptoms of a general malaise of society, which they — together with the ruled — continually reproduce. In one of his *Similia*-essays, Saro-Wiwa used a *Basi and Company* character to explain this problematic:

> Then there are those who, like Dandy of "Basi and Company", say, 'I must have my piece of the action. Everyone is doing it, why should I be left out?' They wait in ambush, hoping that one day it will be their turn to join in ruining the country. "Turn-by-turn-Nigeria-Limited". Such people are opportunists and they are as dangerous as wild animals.[23]

Some of the most striking examples of this dangerous opportunism are to be found in the chapters 'The Candidate' and 'The Party Secretary'. Because virtually all characters in *Basi and Company* are perenially unsuccessful trickster figures whose intricate plots and ploys inevitably fail and turn against them, the individual episodes are held in satirical suspense: despite the colourful realism of setting and dialogue no 'real' trouble or violence is to be expected and the more sinister aspects of the 'culture of cheating' are balanced by numerous instances of delightful comedy for which the intricate schemes and counter-schemes provide an ideal setting. Yet, the satirical critique comes into its own when the reckless bar-owner Dandy attempts to ambush the tottering body politic by becoming Governor of Lagos; or when Basi, who is always on the lookout for his first million, becomes party secretary in order to acquire government contracts for services never rendered but well paid; or when Madame, Basi's landlady and distinguished member of the 'Amerdolian Club', invests her money in one crooked deal after the other. The real scandal in all these cases is not so much that these latter-day tricksters almost succeed, but rather that they seem to act in full accordance with the governing values of society. It is this hegemony of self-destructive norms which have been internalized by rulers and ruled alike, the 'culture of cheating' referred to above, that is the real target of Saro-Wiwa's satirical craft.

This is also true of *Prisoners of Jebs*, Saro-Wiwa's most sustained political satire, that revolves around an imaginary island prison set up by the Organisation of African Unity (OAU) to stow away political prisoners from all over Africa. As a high percentage of the inmates are provided by Nigeria, Jebs prison eventually comes to resemble a farcical microcosm of Nigerian society. The 53 satirical episodes that make up *Prisoners* were originally published in a weekly column in the Nigerian *Vanguard* between January 1985 and January 1986. Since Saro-Wiwa used the short satirical form to comment on topics of the day, *Prisoners of Jebs* is full of allusions to contemporary African and particularly Nigerian politics.

The absurd world of Jebs Prison, presided over by the equally ambitious and corrupt Director and peopled by an incredible variety of political, criminal and comical inmates provides an ideal setting for satirical critique. One of the most important targets in *Prisoners* is the theft of public funds and property: the acclaimed prestige project soon runs into severe financial straits because the Director takes large sums from the prison treasury and hides them in his garden, the ceiling of his bedroom and in his mattress, while his employees embezzle equally large amounts with the help of innumerable fake 'Local Purchase Orders'. In a memorable speech to the assembled prisoners, the Director explains the mystery of the vanished prison funds in the following terms:

> 'In Nigeria, hundreds of millions of naira, indeed billions, have accustomed themselves to the trick of disappearing. A trick which has been encouraged by certain influential Nigerians. I am sorry to inform you that from all available evidence, our millions have decided to act like their Nigerian relations.'
>
> 'And who are the influential people in the Prison who are encouraging the Prison's millions to misbehave?' asked the Guinean prisoner.
>
> 'I am ashamed to say that I know them very well. They are in my office. They are all Nigerians', replied the Director.
>
> 'And what do you propose to do to them?' asked the Ghanaian prisoner.
>
> 'I'm afraid there is nothing I can do. Because in their country, assisting the millions to disappear is no crime. The men and women who aid this magical act are regarded as heroes of their revolution,' said the Director. (1988: 21–2)

Another important malaise addressed is the systematic undermining of the rule of law and the perversion of the judicial system. *Prisoners of Jebs* is full of topical allusions to contemporary justicial scandals involving high-ranking soldiers, businessmen, judges and lawyers. The maladministration of law is embodied in the figure of Jeromi the Kangaroo, who is imported from the Southern Hemisphere and establishes his own system of administrating justice, first in Nigeria and later in Jebs. In a passage registering the prisoners' reaction to the Kangaroo's visit, the light and mocking tone that characterizes most of *Prisoners* gives way to a more sombre note as Saro-Wiwa describes the effects of the 'Kangaroo justice' that a few years later would engineer his own death:

> The prisoners were not only full of wonder and amazement. They were afraid of the Kangaroo. Because apart from his power over individuals, he was a terror to the social fabric of individual nations. Because society exists on the notion that there is right and wrong and that the demarcation between them is clear and unmistakable. But when a kangaroo makes it possible for right to become wrong and vice versa, then the nation reaps a harvest of turmoil. (p. 55)

Other targets of satire include the inefficiency of the state apparatus and the armed forces, symbolized by a batch of high-ranking generals who fall asleep as soon as they enter Jebs prison, the criminal energy among the rich and powerful embodied in the drug-trafficking Madame Kokane and Miss Smuggle Kokane, and the hegemony of the three major ethnic groups in Nigeria, who appear as 'Wazobians' in Jebs and, because of their reckless in-fighting, spoil the great prison football fiesta.

Saro-Wiwa states in the 'Author's Note' to *Prisoners of Jebs* that he did not know from the outset which direction the story would take. A good example of this 'work in progress'-character of *Prisoners* is the introduction of Pita Dumbrok into the story. As Saro-Wiwa explains both in the 'Author's Note' and in one of the numerous footnotes appended to the text, he originally introduced this character because he was angry about a young journalist called Pita Okute who had published a very critical review of *Sozaboy* in the *Vanguard*. Exercising his writer's licence in a rare case of immediate fictional retribution for a critic's attack, Saro-Wiwa had 'Pita Dumbrok' imprisoned in Jebs and hung in a cage on a pole high above the parade grounds where he could watch everything, but for several installments was confined to chirping the key sentence of Pita Okute's review: 'silly plot, silly plot'. At a later stage, however, Pita Dumbrok becomes more reflective, learns to understand the Prison, voices some important insights and finally becomes the only prisoner to be saved when Jebs sinks beneath the sea—and the main character in *Pita Dumbrok's Prison*, the sequel to *Prisoners of Jebs*.

Prisoners also throws an interesting light on Saro-Wiwa's views about his own role as satirical writer. In Chapter 32 'A Satirist, A Scare and a Chief', he introduces himself into the story. The Director becomes aware that his exploits are being monitored from Nigeria by a certain Ken Saro-Wiwa and wants to know from Pita Dumbrok — just released from his bird's cage — about this distant antagonist:

> '…He is learning to be a satirist.'
> 'What does a satirist do?'
> 'He holds up a distorting mirror before people. Some people look into the mirror, see their reflection and get scared.'
> 'Good Heavens!' moaned the Director. 'I'm finished. The man is dangerous!'
> 'Very,' agreed Pita Dumbrok. 'And he spends his time picking holes in everything under the Nigerian sun: a chief's foolish cap, a thieving governor's walking stick, Customs officers' uniforms, University professors' hoods, a journalist's pen, a wrecked naval boat's deck. The Nigerians in and out of prison are sick of him. He's giving them sleepless nights.' (pp. 103–4)

As the story continues, they have every reason to lose their sleep. While Jebs is in a pretty bad state, Nigeria is even worse, and the rivalry between Nigeria and the incumbent Prison Republic becomes more pronounced. Many Nigerians feel that their situation is worse than in prison and, in a quasi-religious procession implore the Director to admit them to Jebs. A satirical climax is reached when the Nigerian government, pressed for funds, attempts to sell the country either to ITT or Britain, but cannot find a buyer, while the Jebsian President-Director considers invading Nigeria, but desists because he wouldn't know what to do with this prize. Finally, the military government decides to destroy the rival prison island and sends Nobel laureate Wole Soyinka to Stockholm to procure the necessary Dynamite. But the Professor, a mysterious, wise character who has all along acted as the Director's advisor and bears strong resemblances to the key protagonist in Soyinka's *The Road*, pre-empts this move and sinks Jebs to the bottom of the sea.

Three years later, Jebs Prison reemerged in *Pita Dumbrok's Prison*, a sequel to *Prisoners of Jebs* that combined the satirical farce of the original story with a novelistic thriller-plot. As a novelistic experiment, *Pita Dumbrok's Prison* is not particularly successful, since the thriller-parts do not combine very well with the satirical sections written in the original *Prisoners* style: once realistically portrayed, serious secret-service agents and journalists become engaged in a quest for a farcical place like Jebs, the techniques of the suspense-oriented realistic novel lose credibility and the 'realistic' scenes can easily get boring.

Yet, as satire, *Pita Dumbrok's Prison* elaborates as effectively as ever upon the themes already tackled in *Prisoners of Jebs*. A completely new development made possible by the inclusion of more serious language registers is the elaboration of what might be called a historical programme which is set out in a pamphlet circulated by Pita Dumbrok, who after having returned to Nigeria from Jebs, is hounded by the secret police and has to go underground. He suggests that the whole nation should search for Jebs and utilize this search as an impetus towards democratization; his central notion of unity in diversity seems to strongly echo Saro-Wiwa's growing concerns with ethnic minority rights:

> I suggest that we unite and form indestructible bonds in this quest. I am aware that the natural divisions of our peoples into different languages and cultures has been used by the enemy to stymie our efforts. The perceived wisdom is that these divisions should be obliterated so that we can have a unified aim. Those who make that prescription lie to their teeth. For if this were not so, Englishmen should be French, the French should be German, the Italians should be Portuguese and so on and so forth. If they are not, why is anyone suggesting that Yorubas must be Igbos, Igbos Hausas, Kikuyu be Luo and so on? Our strength lies in our variety. (p. 114)

The most impressive satirical passages are to be found at the end of the novel, however, when Biney and Andizi, two young journalists engaged in the quest for the resurfaced Jebs, encounter seven islets that epitomize all those public and private vices that Saro-Wiwa untiringly fought against. Interestingly enough, these passages develop their striking, truly Swiftian satirical force only after the author has isolated the protagonists from the more realistic plot by making them lose their way in dense fog and having their canoe move "as if steered by an unseen hand" (p. 222).

The first of these, the islet of laziness, is extremely fertile and full of orange-trees, but inhabited by destitute, starving beggars who only eat the readily available oranges when they are picked, peeled and put in their mouth for them by passing strangers. The second, the islet of happiness, is inhabited by people who only dance, drink and fornicate, and whose decrepit houses are surrounded by stinking gutters. The third islet has been ravaged by civil wars ever since foreigners introduced different religions, while on the fourth dishonesty rules and all honest people are immediately arrested. On the fifth islet, the travellers meet thin men carrying obese masters on their arms who maintain their rule by means of deafening laughter; on the sixth, they are welcomed by the only literate person among an island population that prouds itself on being unable to read and write. The inhabitants of the seventh and last islet have dedicated themselves to the money-goddess Moolah and spend their lifetime hunting for money.

Seen in retrospect, the common denominator of Ken Saro-Wiwa's satirical writings seems to lie in the author's unflinching commitment to unpalatable civil critiques, even at the risk of taking a lonely stand or alienating public opinion. However, the intense political involvement in the Ogoni struggle during the last years of his life, while clearly in line with his long-standing commitments to democratization and minority rights, may have modified some of his earlier held beliefs. An indication for this could be seen in the following passage from *A Month and a Day*, where Saro-Wiwa seems to see the political role of writers in terms of direct political involvement in mass organizations rather than in terms of critical writing:

> ...literature in a critical situation such as Nigeria's cannot be divorced from politics. Indeed, literature must serve society by

steeping itself in politics, by intervention, and writers must not merely write to amuse or to take a bemused, critical look at society. They must play an interventionist role. My experience has been that African governments can ignore writers, taking comfort in the fact that only few can read and write, and that those who read find little time for the luxury of literary consumption beyond the need to pass examinations based on set texts. Therefore, the writer must be *l'homme engagé*: the intellectual man of action. He must take part in mass organizations. He must establish direct contact with the people and resort to the strength of African literature — oratory in the tongue. For the word is power and more powerful is it when expressed in common currency. (p. 81)

Given the evidence of Saro-Wiwa's own writing which explored the political effectiveness of a popular satirical genre with great success as well as his long-standing commitment to a decidedly literary culture as a vehicle of democratization and civil change, one cannot help noticing a certain tension between this somewhat populist emphasis on 'interventionism' and 'orature' and his own earlier literary theory and practice. Saro-Wiwa himself seems to have felt a little uneasy about the apodictic normative nature of the above statements, as the following cautionary remark testifies to:

The only problem I see is that such a writer must strive to maintain his authenticity, which stands a chance of being corrupted by the demands of politics. A struggle will necessarily ensue, but that should conduce to making the writer even better. (p. 81)

Given the enormous versatility and wide-ranging creativity that Ken Saro-Wiwa displayed in his earlier writings, it would have been most fascinating to witness the outcome of that struggle in his own creative writing. However, the ignominious judicial murder he and his co-activists fell victim to ended not only a brilliant political, but also a no less brilliant literary career.

The legacy of Saro-Wiwa's satirical writings lies in the insight that the movement towards democratic transition will have to address the basic social illnesses of Nigeria, of which its military rulers are symptoms rather than prime causes. There can be no doubt that the present impasse can only be overcome and hopefully restored if the present murderous junta is removed from power. An even greater challenge, however, will then lie ahead: the long, arduous task of civil reconstruction.

The moment of democratic transition arrives when the masses turn into people — free and willing to choose, to disagree, and to determine their own lives. It is to this moment, which after cruelly disappointed hopes seem once more to recede into the future, that Ken Saro-Wiwa's satirical writings owe their ultimate allegiance.

NOTES

1   For a detailed analysis of the Ogoni struggle in the context of the blocked transition to democratic rule in Nigeria see Osaghae, 'The Ogoni Uprising'; for a general account of the Ogoni struggle see Saro-Wiwa, *Genocide in Nigeria* and *A Month and a Day*.

2   For a more detailed analysis of the relationship between literature and the politics of civil society see Zeleza, 'The Democratic Transition in Africa and the Anglophone Writer' and Schulze-Engler, 'Chinua Achebe and the Politics of Civil Society in Modern African Literature' and 'Literature and Civil Society in South Africa'.

3   Cf. Zabus, 'Mending the Schizo-Text': 124; for a comprehensive account of the relationship between 'rotten English' and different forms of transcribing Nigerian pidgin see Mair, 'The New Englishes and Stylistic Innovation': 280–4.

4   Cf. Okereke, 'Patterns of Linguistic Deviation in Saro-Wiwa's *Sozaboy*': 10.

5   Ibid.

6   Cf. Koroye, "*Sozaboy*: First Person Narration and Mene's 'very bad dream'": 90.

7   "With regard to English, I have heard it said that those who write in it should adopt a domesticated 'African' variety of it. I myself have experimented with the three varieties of English spoken and written in Nigeria: pidgin, 'rotten' and standard. I have used them in poetry, short stories, essays, drama, and the novel. I have tried them out in print, on stage, on the radio, and with television comedy. That which carries best and which is most popular is standard English, expressed simply and lucidly. It communicates and expresses thoughts and ideas perfectly" (p. 157).

8   Cf. Zabus, 'Mending the Schizo-Text': 126.

9   Willfried Feuser has quite rightly pointed out the narratological

parallels between *Sozaboy* and the 17th-Century *Simplicius Simplicissimus*; cf. 'The Man from Dukana': 63. For a closer analysis of the narrative construction of *Sozaboy* see Awosika, 'Narrative Style in *Sozaboy*', Koroye, '*Sozaboy*: First Person Narration and Mene's "very bad dream"' and Inyama, 'Point of View in Saro-Wiwa's *Sozaboy*'.

10   'A Cannibal Rage', *Similia*: 166–7.

11   Ibid.: 167.

12   Ibid.

13   'Who is Mobilizing Whom for What?', *Similia*: 16.

14   *Ibid.*: 17.

15   For an account of Saro-Wiwa's involvement with MAMSER see *A Month and a Day*: 59–61.

16   Cf. Shivji, *The State and the Working People in Tanzania*: "The central element in the ideological formation in post-independence Africa has been, what we call, the ideology of developmentalism. The argument of this ideology is very simple: 'We are economically backward and we need to develop very fast. In this task of development we cannot afford the luxury of politics.' ... Even Marxist scholars and 'politicians' echo the ideology of developmentalism, albeit in their own vocabulary" (pp. 1–2).

17   Cf. Zeleza, 'The Democratic Transition in Africa and the Anglophone Writer': 479.

18   Ibid.: 480.

19   Cf. Kunz, 'Liberalization in Africa': 225.

20   Cf. Anyang' Nyong'o, 'Introduction': 19 (emph. in the orig.).

21   See, for example, Bayart, 'Civil Society in Africa', Bratton, 'Beyond the State', Chabal, *Political Domination in Africa* and *Power in Africa*, Diamond, 'Introduction: Roots of Failure, Seeds of Hope', Fatton, 'Liberal Democracy in Africa' and *Predatory Rule*, Nyang'oro, 'Reform Politics and the Democratization Process in Africa', Osaghae, *Between State and Civil Society in Africa*, Rothchild, *The Precarious Balance*.

22   'Civil Society in Africa': 120.

23   'Who is Mobilising Whom for What?' *Similia*: 17.

REFERENCES

Anyang' Nyong'o, Peter. "Introduction." *Popular Struggles for Democracy in Africa*. Ed. Peter Anyang' Nyong'o. London: United Nations University/Zed Books, 1987: 14–25 (Studies in African Political Economy).

Awosika, Olawole. "Narrative Style in *Sozaboy*." Nnolim, *Critical Essays*: 64–72.

Bayart, Jean-François. "Civil Society in Africa." Chabal (1986): 109–25.

Bratton, Michael. "Beyond the State: Civil Society and Associational Life in Africa." *World Politics* 41.3 (1989): 407–30.

Chabal, Patrick, Ed. *Political Domination in Africa: Reflections on the Limits of Power*. Cambridge: Cambridge Univ. Press, 1986 [African Studies Series, 50].

———. *Power in Africa: An Essay in Political Interpretation*. New York: St Martin's Press, 1992.

Diamond, Larry, "Introduction: Roots of Failure, Seeds of Hope." Diamond, Linz and Lipset: 1–32.

Diamond, Larry, Linz, Juan J. and Lipset, Seymour Martin, eds. *Democracy in Developing Countries, Volume Two: Africa*. Boulder & London: Lynne Rienner Publ., 1988.

Fatton, Robert Jr. "Liberal Democracy in Africa." *Political Science Quarterly* 105.3 (1990): 455–73.

———. *Predatory Rule: State and Civil Society in Africa*. Boulder & London: Lynne Rienner Publ., 1992.

Feuser, Willfried F. "The Voice from Dukana: Ken Saro-Wiwa." *Matatu* 10 [*Contemporary Nigerian Literature*, Ed. Willfried F. Feuser], 1987: 52–66.

Inyama, Nnadozie. "Point of View in Saro-Wiwa's *Sozaboy*." Nnolim, *Critical Essays*: 102–7.

Koroye, Seiyifa. "*Sozaboy*: First Person Narration and Mene's 'very bad dream'." Nnolim, *Critical Essays*: 82–101.

Mair, Christian, "The New Englishes and Stylistic Innovation: Ken Saro-Wiwa's *Sozaboy: A Novel in Rotten English*." Us/Them: *Translation, Transcription and Identity in Post-Colonial Literary Cultures* (Cross/Cultures, 6). Ed. Gordon Collier. Amsterdam/Atlanta: Rodopi, 1992: 277–87.

Nnolim, Charles, Ed. *Critical Essays on Ken Saro-Wiwa's* Sozaboy. Port Harcourt: Saros International, 1992.

Nyang'oro, Julius E. "Reform Politics and the Democratization Process in Africa." *African Studies Review* 37.1 (1994): 133–49.

Okereke, Augustine. "Patterns of Linguistic Deviation in Saro-Wiwa's *Sozaboy*." Nnolim, *Critical Essays*: 9–15.

Osaghae, Eghosa, Ed. *Between State and Civil Society in Africa*. Dakar: Codesria, 1994.

———. "The Ogoni Uprising: Oil Politics, Minority Agitation and the Future of the Nigerian State." *African Affairs* 94 (1995): 325–44.

Rothchild, Donald and Chazan, Naomi, eds. *The Precarious Balance: State and Society in Africa*. Boulder: Westview Press, 1988.

Saro-Wiwa, Ken. *Sozaboy: A Novel in Rotten English*. Port Harcourt: Saros International, 1985.

———. *A Forest of Flowers*. Port Harcourt: Saros International, 1986.

———. *Basi and Company: A Modern African Folktale*. Port Harcourt: Saros International, 1987.

———. *Prisoners of Jebs*. Port Harcourt: Saros International, 1988.

———. *Pita Dumbrok's Prison*. Port Harcourt: Saros International, 1991.

———. *Similia: Essays on Anomic Nigeria*. Port Harcourt: Saros International, 1992.

———. *Genocide in Nigeria: The Ogoni Tragedy*. Port Harcourt: Saros International, 1992.

———. "The Language of African Literature: A Writer's Testimony." *Research in African Literatures* 23.1 (1992): 153–7.

———. [Summing-up to his 40-page defence statement]. *P.E.N. International* 46.2 (1995): 109–10.

———. *A Month and a Day: A Detention Diary*. Introd. William Boyd. London: Penguin, 1995.

Schulze-Engler, Frank. "Chinua Achebe and the Politics of Civil Society in Modern African Literature." *The African Past and Contemporary Culture*. Eds. Erhard Reckwitz, Lucia Vennarini and Cornelia Wegener. Essen: Die Blaue Eule, 1993: 169–83 (African Literatures in English, 8).

———. "Literature and Civil Society in South Africa." *Ariel* 27.1 (1996): 21–40.

Shivji, Issa G., Ed. *The State and the Working People in Tanzania*. Dakar: Codesria, 1985.

Zabus, Chantal. "Mending the Schizo-Text: Pidgin in the Nigerian Novel." *Kunapipi* 14.1 (1992): 119–27.

Zeleza, Paul Tiyambe. "The Democratic Transition in Africa and the Anglophone Writer." *Canadian Journal of African Studies / Revue Canadienne des Études Africaines* 28.3 (1994): 472–97.

Ken Saro-Wiwa
and the Politics of Language
in African Literature
Adetayo Alabi

One of Chinua Achebe's preliminary remarks in his paper 'Politics and Politicians of Language in African Literature', presented at the University of Guelph in 1987, is that the presentation, which would have been impossible twenty-five years before, was possible then because of "the eruption of African literature, shedding a little light here and there on what had been an area of darkness" (p. 3). What Achebe does not say expressly, however, is that the eruption of the previous twenty-five years was not an eruption of "African literature" but that of African literature in non-African languages. In other words, African literature predates the eruption referred to. Similarly, Achebe does not add categorically to his observation about the eruption of African literature in non-African languages the fact that the crisis of language erupted along with these literatures.

The problems and controversies surrounding the choice and use of non-African languages for African literatures, what Abiola Irele calls a "radical anomaly," are as old as these literatures.[1] This 'radical anomaly' was, perhaps, first formally acknowledged during the 1962 Makerere conference of 'African Writers of English Expression'. Shortly after the conference, Obi Wali published his undoubtedly provocative paper 'The Dead End of African Literature'.

It is Obi Wali's contention that a significant achievement of the 1962 conference was the recognition that "African literature as now defined and understood, leads nowhere" (p. 13). His controversial position stems out of the contradiction inherent in writing African literature in non-African languages. This new trend, according to Wali, "lacks any blood and stamina, and has no means of self-enrichment" (p. 13). Consequently, this outward looking approach to an internal phenomenon is the pursuance of "a dead end, which can only lead to sterility, uncreativity, and frustration" (p. 14). He, therefore, concludes that "any true African literature must be written in African languages" (p. 14).

Needless to say, Obi Wali's arguments generated a heated controversy among scholars of African literature.[2] One of the most sustained reactions to Obi Wali's assertions is offered by Chinua Achebe who argues against the suggestion that an authentic African literature cannot be written in a non-African language.[3] He takes this position after foregrounding the importance of a writer's mother tongue and acknowledging the contradictions inherent in writing African literatures in non-African languages.[4]

Ngũgĩ wa Thiong'o is another very important and sustained contributor to the language controversy in African literature.[5] His contributions to the debate follow a rather long period of silence from Obi Wali, who triggered off the discussion. Ngũgĩ's postulations on the language of African literature have been particularly dramatic because his career as a scholar and writer started with an important investment in the English language. He renounced the investment, however, by changing from using English for his creative writing to using Gikuyu. He now uses both English and Gikuyu for his explanatory essays depending on the audience.

Ken Saro-Wiwa is also a productive contributor to the language controversy in African literature. Like Ngũgĩ and Achebe, his contributions are not only on the theoretical level but on the level of creative writing. Saro-Wiwa's argument on the language question is in a way a combination of the positions of Achebe and Ngũgĩ. In 'The Language of African Literature' (1992), Saro-Wiwa argues for the use of any language for African literatures, and as a creative writer, he uses both indigenous and foreign languages for his creative writing.

The initial process of linguistic choice for Saro-Wiwa was an easy task. Growing up in Bori, Nigeria, he spoke Khana — an Ogoni language, and took part in oral literary activities of the community in the language. At this point in his life, the language question wasn't an issue. It became an issue as he grew up, going to school. At the primary school, he had access to both Khana and English with English functioning as the language of instruction for most of his classes and Khana operating as a pre- and post-school language. As he puts it, English was the language of learning while Khana was the language of play (p. 153). The equation changed when he had to leave his Khana speaking area for Government College, Umuahia. Since he was the only Ogoni boy in the school, with other students from Igbo, Ibibio, Ijaw etc. speaking areas of Nigeria, he was lucky to have English because that was the language he could communicate in with the other students. It was only because of English that he wasn't isolated in the school; hence he describes the language as "a unifying factor at the school" (p. 153). Since the only language he spoke at school, the only language with books in the school library, was English, he didn't have a choice but to start using English for his creative writing. He says:

[t]here, at Government College, I began to write poems, short stories, and plays in English, the language which as I have said, bound us all together. There was no question of my writing in Khana because no one would have understood it. (p. 154)

At the University of Ibadan, the situation wasn't different for Saro-Wiwa. He wrote in English since nobody at the university would have understood his native Khana. It was actually during his Ibadan days that he encountered Obi Wali's argument on the language of African literature as discussed earlier. Saro-Wiwa wasn't fascinated by Wali's argument because, as he argues:

as long as I [Saro-Wiwa] could speak and read English, it was easy to relate to the rest of the country — away from my Ogoni home. So English was important. Not only as the language which opened new ideas to me, but as a link to the other peoples with whom I came into contact during my day-to-day life. (p. 154)

Saro-Wiwa interrogates the notion of African literature by arguing that a common history and colour should not necessitate the lumping together of African literature as a unit. Since there are several languages and cultures on the continent, each language has its own literature, many of which are oral. Despite the existence of African literatures in various African languages, "the need to communicate with one another and the rest of the world, and the fact of colonialism (which is also real) have forced us to write in the languages of our erstwhile colonial masters" (p. 155). He is contented with the reality of the language question because if he wrote in Khana, he would be able to speak with only about 200,000 people who mostly do not read and write, unlike communicating with 400 million people in English. To him, English "is a worthy tool, much like the biro pen or the banking system or the computer, which were not invented by the Ogoni people but which I can master and use for my own purposes" (p. 156).

Saro-Wiwa takes up issues with Ngũgĩ wa Thiong'o on the concept of decolonizing the mind and his decision to write in his native Gikuyu. Saro-Wiwa argues that writing in English cannot colonise his mind. As he puts it, "I am, I find, as Ogoni as ever. I am enmeshed in Ogoni culture. I eat Ogoni food. I sing Ogoni songs. I dance to Ogoni music. And I find the best in the Ogoni worldview as engaging as anything else" (p. 156) . What Saro-Wiwa's argument overlooks is the fact that like Ngũgĩ, Saro-Wiwa was a man of different worlds that he mastered coordinately. Perhaps Ngũgĩ's concern is with formally educated Africans who can not vouchsafe for their languages the way both Saro-Wiwa and Ngũgĩ can.

Still on the language issue, Saro-Wiwa argues that "there is no need to blow this matter out of proportion" (p. 156) since many writers have been writing in their mother tongues with even newspapers in many African languages like Yoruba and Hausa. Despite his reservations on Ngũgĩ's position, Saro-Wiwa also writes in Khana, his mother-tongue. He was actually writing a novel in the language before his death. He argues that his novel in Khana is not to prove a point, unlike Ngũgĩ, but to provide another reading material for his mother who has only the Bible to read in Khana. His experimentation in the language is possible because like many of his other works, he can self-publish the book unlike Ngũgĩ who can be translated into English easily because of his international status as a writer. Although Saro-Wiwa's novel in Khana is not to prove a point, it advances Ngũgĩ's argument significantly. Since one of the reservations against the use of African languages for African literature by some people is their contention that the languages are not fully equipped and sophisticated enough for writing and adapting to contemporary technological developments, Saro-Wiwa's novel in Khana, like Ngũgĩ's in Gikuyu, Fagunwa's in Yoruba, etc., illustrate the fact that all these languages are as dynamic and resourceful as any other languages.

Saro-Wiwa also takes up issues with the suggestion that Africa should adopt an indigenous continental language citing Soyinka's suggestion for the adoption of Swahili. Saro-Wiwa argues that the suggestion is not only impracticable, but lacks either intellectual or political merit arguing that "once a language is not one's mother tongue, it is an alien language" (p. 156).

To Saro-Wiwa, "African literature is written in several languages, including the extra African languages of English, French, and Portuguese" (p. 157). It is interesting that Saro-Wiwa refers to English, French, and Portuguese as "extra African languages." To him, therefore, although these languages originate from outside the continent, they are now indigenous to the continent because of the differences in the varieties of the language used on the continent and their original homes. According to him, there will always be African literatures in these languages and the fact that they have been on the continent for so long and spoken by many Africans qualify them for "a proper place among the languages that are native to the continent" (p. 157).

Like Achebe, though Saro-Wiwa favours the use of these languages, he supports their use in Africa in a way that differentiates them from how they are used in other places. He has experimented with three varieties of Nigerian English namely pidgin, 'rotten', and standard varieties. Standard Nigerian English, according to Saro-Wiwa, is popular and expresses ideas simply and lucidly. This will be the variety of English spoken by formally educated Nigerians. Pidgin, on the other hand, resulted from the encounter between English and Nigerian languages and has developed into a language of its own. It has actually become the first language of many people in the Delta area of Nigeria. Its diction is made up of words from both English and many Nigerian languages. Saro-Wiwa defines 'rotten' English in his novel *Sozaboy*. In his note to the novel, he informs the reader that 'rotten' English is the result of his interest in "the adaptability of the English Language and of [his] closely observing the speech and writings of a certain segment of Nigerian society." The rest of this essay will analyse the language of *Sozaboy* and the effectiveness of Saro-Wiwa's experiment.

Sozaboy is a literary account of the Nigerian civil war from Mene's perspective, a naive apprentice driver turned soldier. He starts out very enthusiastic about the war because it provides him with an opportunity to make more money, as an apprentice driver, since there are more people travelling from various parts of the country to Dukana and Pitakawa. Despite his mother's reservation about a career in the army for him, he finds support in his wife, Agnes, and bribes his way into the army. He fights in various places like Iwoama for both sides of the war. During the war, he undergoes tremendous suffering on the battlefield, in Kampala, from Manmuswak etc. He experiences hunger, thirst, and depravation as he fights and searches for his family. Ultimately, he grows from an enthusiastic soldier who was happy to join the army to a critic who detests war, and towards the end of the story, he describes war as a;

> very bad thing. War is to drink urine, to die and all that uniform that they are giving us to wear is just to deceive us. And anybody who think that uniform is fine thing is stupid man who does not know what is good or bad or not good at all. All those things they have been telling us before is just stupid lie. (p. 114)

Mene's confusion and the disaster that comes with the Nigerian civil war in *Sozaboy* is foregrounded in the first two lines of the book: "Although, everybody in Dukana was happy at first" (p. 1). This construction at the beginning of the text is a fragment. The fact that the opening unit of the book is a fragment, an incomplete sentence, is not accidental. It is the narrator's method of foregrounding the fragmentation of the society and the crisis that comes with a war of this magnitude. It is also a strategy devised to highlight the linguistic choices made in the text, the variety of 'rotten' English earlier referred to and the educational background of the narrator.

The impression that the reader (at least this one) gets from reading the fragment that opens the book is that the narrator speaks a specific variety of English which will not qualify as standard English. This possibility is quickly confirmed as the reader encounters the first full sentence of the novel: "All the nine villages were dancing and we were eating plenty maize with pear and knacking tory under the moon" (p. 1).

The atmosphere evoked from the first full sentence is rural, and this explains the diction of the sentence and the variety of English that it belongs to. Words like "knacking tory" are Pidgin while the rest of the words in the sentence are standard English words. There is, therefore, a combination of a variety of standard English and Pidgin in this sentence. The next sentence throws a little more light into the linguistic choice in the book: "Because the work on the farm have finished and the yams were growing well well" (p. 1). This is not just another fragment but a fragment in broken English — a variety of English which shows a very limited exposure to the English language. It is not until later in the novel that the choices of words for narration and conversation are explained by the educational and social status of Mene, the narrator.

Mene introduces himself as "young man and apprentice driver" (p. 1). This introductory remark identifies him as a member of a very low and impoverished social class. His education which he talks about in the following chapter complements this. He attended St. Dominic's school where he passed his elementary six with distinction. Due to financial problems, he cannot proceed on an educational career. Instead, he becomes an apprentice driver. Since his educational attainment is only at the most preliminary stage, his knowledge of English which he must have learnt at school must be limited. In the same way, since he is only an apprentice driver, he doesn't need an excellent mastery of English to perform his job. The variety of English his education and social status allow him access to can at best be the rotten variety which Saro-Wiwa defines as a combination of words from Pidgin, broken English, and occasional instances of idiomatic expressions.

Due to his social and educational classes, he is an appropriate protagonist and narrator for a novel that the author sets out to write in rotten English, the variety of the language that Mene is exposed to. Similarly, Mene's social status as a poor apprentice driver pitches him against the affluent both on the linguistic and social levels. On the linguistic level, for example, he differentiates between his own limited exposure to English from their comprehensive encounter with the language. These people are the ones causing the trouble in the country. As Mene puts it naively, "Before, before, the grammar was not plenty and everybody was happy. But now grammar begin to plenty and people were not happy. As grammar plenty, na so trouble plenty. And as trouble plenty, na so plenty people were dying" (p. 3). Examples of speakers of standard English causing trouble for the others are the Chief Commander General and his entourage — "[f]ine fine tall men in fine fine uniform" (p. 77). Because of the Commander's exposure to English, he speaks the standard variety. For example, when addressing the new soldiers at their passing out parade, he speaks standard English, what Mene calls "fine fine grammar." He says: "You boys have got excellent training. You must be brave and proud of your country.... We shall overcome. The Enemy will be vanquished. God is on our side" (p. 78). Some members of the oppressed group also speak some form of standard English as one of the varieties of English available to them. An example is Bullet who employs standard English to give orders to the soldiers under his command. For example, when giving Mene instructions, he orders: "Now, you hold your gun on the ready. Release the safety catch and keep your hand on the trigger. Keep cool. And keep your mouth shut" (p. 93). On other occasions, he speaks 'rotten' English.

Since those who speak standard English like the Chief Commanding General are the rich people in the society and those who exploit the peasantry, the exploited speakers of 'rotten' English expose their greed and high handedness. This is why Bullet and Mene are able to expose the corruption of their commanding officer who keeps all the alcohol and cigarettes meant for his soldiers to himself. Though he is exposed, Bullet, Mene, and others are severely punished in Kampala and Bullet is even forced to drink urine (pp. 100–3). Similarly, Mene as an exploited person is able to expose Chief Birabee's corruption and his attempts to swindle his people. Chief Birabee and Pastor Barika's later attempt to get Mene arrested also shows that they occupy different positions from him on the social ladder.

The use of 'rotten' English, a combination of Pidgin, broken, and standard English, is interesting in *Sozaboy*. In many passages in the book, the three varieties of English occur in one paragraph. Sometimes, people code-switch from one to the other or code-mix them. Take the following speech by Chief Birabee for example: "My people, listen to me very carefully. (S1) As all of you know, there is plenty trouble now. (S2) True, the trouble never reach Dukana yet. (S3) But plenty of trouble dey all the same. (S4) Everywhere in our country. (S5) Government no like trouble. (S6) So therefore, nobody here must give trouble" (S7) (p. 6).

Chief Birabee's speech starts with a high variety of standard English. He switches from this to a lower variety of English that is close to broken English in S2. The variety used in S2 is lower than S1 because of the use of the word 'plenty'. If he stuck to the variety used for S1, plenty would have been substituted for by words like much, a lot of, etc. Similarly, 'As all of you know' would have been substituted by 'As you all know.' In S3, there is a switch to Pidgin. This is betrayed by the use of 'true', an adjective and a noun functioning as an adverb and the combination 'never reach'. S4 is also in Pidgin as betrayed by the use of 'dey'. The use of 'plenty' in the sentence also compliments the use of 'dey'. 'All the same' that ends the sentence is in standard English. S5 is a fragment in Standard English, another fragment that highlights the crisis in the society. S6 is in Pidgin as betrayed by the use of 'no like'. There is a shift to broken English in S7 as 'so' and 'therefore' are combined. The remaining part of the sentence also suggests that 'trouble' is an item that can be given and not what can be caused.

Saro-Wiwa remains a very important contributor to the language debate in African literature. His experimentation with the English language is unique and represents day-to-day use of various varieties of English by different members of the Nigerian speech community. His ability to create characters that approximate the use of language by different people depending on their social and educational positions in the society is remarkable. His attempt to write a novel in Khana, his mother tongue, also advances the importance of writing in the mother tongue. Though he is unable to communicate with a lot of people in his mother tongue because of limited speakers of the language, his attempt is praiseworthy because of the unique communication possibility between him and the few that he can communicate with. Whether the Nigerian government allowed him to finish his novel in Khana before executing him is another issue that we will ultimately find out.

NOTES

1   See Abiola Irele, 'African Literature and the Language Question', *The African Experience*: 44. While David Westley's 1992 bibliographic essay, 'Choice of Language', traces the history of the language controversy in African literature written in non-African languages, his 1987 paper, 'African-Language Literature', discusses African literatures in English translation.

2   For some of the immediate reactions to Obi Wali's paper, see Barry Reckord, Ezekiel Mphalele, Gerald Moore, Wole Soyinka, and Denis Williams' letters, *Transition* 3.11 (November 1963): 7–9.

3   Chinua Achebe argues that African literature can be written in any language, but when it is written in a foreign language, a domesticated variety of the language should be used. For details, see 'The African Writer and the English Language', *Morning Yet*, 55–62: 'Politics and Politicians of Language in African Literature', and Adetayo Alabi 'Same Language'.

4   See 'Politics and Politicians': 3, where Achebe argues that "[n]o serious writer could possibly be indifferent to the fate of any language, let alone his own mother tongue," the preface to *Morning Yet*, and p. 62 on the contradictions inherent in writing African literature in non-African languages.

5   Ngũgĩ wa Thiong'o argues that African literature can only be written in African languages. For details, see *Decolonising the Mind, Moving the Centre*, and Adetayo Alabi 'Rewriting the Law of Cultural Precedence'.

BIBLIOGRAPHY

Achebe, Chinua. *Hopes and Impediments: Selected Essays*. New York: Doubleday, 1989.

———. *Morning Yet on Creation Day*. London: Heinemann, 1975.

———. "Politics and Politicians of Language in African Literature." Ed. G.D. Killam. *Historical and Cultural Contexts of Linguistic and Literary Phenomena*. Proceedings of the Seventeenth Triennial Congress of the Federation Internationale des Langues et Litterateurs Modernes. August 18–25, 1987. Guelph: University of Guelph, 1989: 3–8.

Alabi, Adetayo. "The Novelist as Linguist: A Comparative Study of Selected Works of Chinua Achebe and Ngũgĩ Wa Thiong'o." Diss. University of Guelph, Canada, 1993.

———. "Rewriting the Law of Cultural Precedence: Ngũgĩ's Return to the Roots." Conference Paper, "Ngũgĩ Wa Thiong'o: Texts and Contexts," Penn State University, April 7–9, 1994.

———. "Same Language, Different Reality: Achebe and the Africanization of English." Conference Paper, First International Conference on World Englishes, University of Illinois at Urbana-Champaign, March 31–April 2, 1994.

Bamgbose, Ayo. "English in the Nigerian Environment." Conference Paper, British Council/University of Ibadan Conference on English Language and Literature, December 14–18, 1993.

Gibbs, James. "Ola Rotimi and Ken Saro-Wiwa: Nigerian Popular Playwrights. " Ed. Granqvist, Rauol. *Signs and Signals: Popular Culture in Africa*. Acta Universitatis Umensis. Umea Studies in the Humanities 99. Sweden: Umea University, 1990: 121–35.

Inyama, N.F. "Ken Saro-Wiwa: Maverick Iconoclast of the Nigerian Literary Scene." *New Trends and Generations in African Literature Today* 20 (1996): 35–49.

Irele, Abiola. *The African Experience in Literature and Ideology*. London: Heinemann, 1981.

Moore, Gerald. "Letter to the Editor. " *Transition* 3.11 (November 1963): 9.

Mphalele, Ezekiel. "Letter to the Editor." *Transition* 3.11 (November 1963): 7–9

Ngũgĩ wa Thiong'o. *Decolonising the Mind: The Politics of Language in African Literature*. London : James Currey Ltd., 1986.

———. *Moving the Centre: The Struggle for Cultural Freedoms*. London: James Currey; Nairobi: EAEP; Portsmouth N.H.: Heinemann, 1993.

Niang, Sada. "Linguistic Deviation in African Literature." *Dalhousie Review* 68. 1–2 (1989): 111–36.

Nnolim, C.E.N. Ed. *Critical Essays on Saro-Wiwa's Sozaboy*. London, Lagos, Port Harcourt: Saros International Publishers, 1992.

Reckord, Barry. "Letter to the Editor. " Transition 3.11 (November 1963): 7.

Saro-Wiwa, Ken. "The Language of African Literature : A Writer's Testimony." *Research in African Literatures* (Special Issue on the Language Question) 23.1 (Spring 1992): 153–8.

———. *Sozaboy*. Port Harcourt, Nigeria: Saros International Publishers, 1985.

Soyinka, Wole. *Art, Dialogue and Outrage: Essays on Literature and Culture.* Ibadan: New Horn Press, 1988.

———. "Letter to the Editor." *Transition* 3.11 (November 1963): 9.

———. "We Africans Must Speak With One Tongue." *Afrika* 20 (1979): 23.

Spencer, John, Ed. *The English Language in West Africa*. London: Longman Group Limited, 1971.

Ubahakwe, Ebo, Ed. *Varieties and Functions of English in Nigeria*. Ibadan: African University Press, 1979.

Wali, Obi. "The Dead End of African Literature." *Transition* 10. 3 (1963): 13–5.

Westley, David. "African-Language Literature in English Translation." *Research in African Literatures* 18. 4 (1987): 499–509.

———. "Choice of Language and African Literature: A Bibliographic Essay." *Research in African Literatures* 23. 1 (Spring 1992): 159–71.

Williams, Denis. "Letter to the Editor." *Transition* 3.11 (November 1963): 9.

Zabus, Chantal. "Mending the Schizo-Text: Pidgin in the Nigerian Novel." *Kunapipi* XVI.1 (1992): 119–27.

Poetry

THE MOSQUITO AND THE EAR
Wumi Raji

The tale once was told
of Mosquito and Ear,
one subject, the other king
in the land of Ajose.

Before Ear,
the people shared
one food basket,
one soup pot,
one water pot.
Ear took over,
emptied the basket,
refilled it with ashes,
stored away the soup,
defecated in the pot,
urinated in the water.
The people's cry of loss
met with the king's scorn;
as people starved,
as people thirsted,
the king swam in opulence.

Children wept,
women wailed,

men groaned,
people died —
till they resolved:
dismantle the throne,
banish the king.

Ear fled to the land
where Head was king;
refused entry,
he became a sentry.

But Mosquito had pledged:
no respite for Ear;
he would trail him,
assail him
with the crimes of the past.

So Mosquito whines,
So Mosquito screams
close, close to Ear:
close, close
to Ear's inner ear.

THE NIGERIAN COCKROACHES
Abdul-Rasheed Na'Allah

Cock what, d' you call them?!
These Cock-cruel-ches
Have soaked their heads
In the calabash hidden under my bed
And drank my storage for tomorrow.

As they approached my door, my arms I opened wide
Thinking them good neighbors.
Bala, Obialo, Anana
My children all, and
Basiratu who bore them
All ushered cockroaches into
Our house.

Ye pa!
At the crowing of the Cock,
We learnt
That the cockroaches aren't our species
Those Nigerian cockcroaches are born through their mothers'
mouths.
They soaked their
        heads deep
Into our fura and nono.
They drank our storage
        for tomorrow.
And when we asked,
They lashed us,
with a wired-cane.

THE MILLION NAIRA MARCH
Tayo Olafioye

The military has been busy
curing its ringworms
while leprosy afflicts the nation
this myth of action.
Those poor market women
and the silly Local Councils
marshalled to the march with fifty naira bribes
Heads of households held by the balls
behaving like silly little girls
hiding in the brush.

I tip my hat at awe
in total profound speechlessness
for the military's ability
to spin these propagandas of disgrace
tilting the eyes of misfortune
to foreign enemies of the land, real or imagined.
That's clever and dandy —
only one problem, a sticky itch:
The man who has only one cowrie in his pocket
but tells the world he has two,
will be left at the end with his lies
after he has spent the only one in the pocket.
Who really is the fool —
the foreigner or the indigine without honour?

Propaganda is no food or comfort
Your people are hungry
Oh, dispenser of misery
the world laughs at you,
Look at yourself in the mirror.

ZOMO AND BUSHIYA[1] IN THE NIGERIAN FOREST
Abdul-Rasheed Na'Allah

The wind today is roaring in rage;
Did anyone murder
his child?

The rain is hitting the earth
in such annoyance,
the earth's skin hurts her.

The hill is hastily
sparkling its lava,
as if hurrying for a battle.

Zomo — the rabbit raps within his hut
smoothing his skin with his palms
taking some doses into his dreamland.

Bushiya, the thorny animal
shrieks from the tearing hands of the raging wind,
He yells from the precipitating rocks of the angry rain.

Bushiya, did you murder
the wind's child?
Did you seize the eyes of the rains' siblings from their sleep?

Bushiya, do you not hear
That whoever lifts a dead aparo[2]
Lifts troubles!

Your art is not strange in this land:
Zomo — the rabbit tells his story:
How you murdered his sleep.

"One day," started Zomo his tale:
"Came Bushiya, in his soaked apparel:
'Zomo my friend, just for the night'."

And zomo having heard
The roaring wind,
Granted his strange visitor the night a stay.

Soon, Bushiya
suffocated Zomo right into the flesh
With his bodily pins!

Groans all-through the night:
Begging for a mercy from the visitor.
But the snoring Bushiya lapped his sleep, like a cat does his milk.

Zomo's courtesy now his grief:
As the sun took its stand to heat up the day,
Bushiya said "Zomo, go to hell!"

A new proverb Bushiya coined:
"He who is uncomfortable in an abode
Takes a journey to a new one."

Zomo was now
To take a jaunt
From his house of birth.

Zomo's domicile
Vacated for Bushiya
While Zomo roamed the streets.

If you don't know this song
It's the popular tune in Nigerian forest
The military Bushiyas send our Zomos to the streets!

NOTE
1   Zomo and Bushiya are Hausa names of two kinds of animals in the
     rabbit family. Bushiya, unlike Zomo, has a thorny skin.
2   Yoruba name for a type of bird.

MADE IN NIGERIA[1]
(for Ken Saro-Wiwa, the Ogoni people
and all the exploited people of the world)
Eze chi Chiazo

The logic of survival lives
at the edge of teeth and claws
sharks and lions can tell better
they have inferior brains

we have better brains
to use longer claws and stronger teeth
to scratch and scrape the skins
of our neighbours that they will die
in their own pool of blood

we are not brutes?

perhaps it is time to know
we have gone too far
too near

to the brutes, teeth growing
sharper, longer
words, h-o-oo-w-wl-l-l

II

can we ever learn
none is the others' prostitute
that never closed laps for…

or is the mind not strong enough
to blunt our teeth to
saw off the claws of the cannibals
to learn?

i hear the loud laughter of our past
like the hyena scorns a dying lion

the tears shed on the ship decks
in the sugar plantations
deep in the belly of the earth
under the heavy loads
ah, brother, slaves
have turned to slave dealers

the tears swell into a sea
ready to engulf us
in an apocalyptic feast of the
brutes

NOTE

1   Taken from 'This is our Life', a compilation of poems currently in
    press.

VII
Interviews with Ken Saro-Wiwa

They are Killing my People[1]
Ken Saro-Wiwa

K en Saro-Wiwa, irrepressible iconoclast, agitator and propa-
gandist spoke on the forms and content of Ogoni struggles
saying his people live in the middle of death.

*Can you link your person and the minority rights struggle in a historical
continuum?*
I have written about it in books, I was born of Ogoni parents into
the problem that is now looming. I began to see these things as a
child. The Ogoni people were independent before 1901 and were
finally absorbed into the Nigerian colony by the British in 1913.
From then till 1947, they demanded for their own native authority
and it's very difficult for them. For over 35 years, they waged this
struggle. Eventually, they got it in 1947. Then I was only a six year-
old.

That lasted only for 10 years, 1947 to 1957. I was in a position to
see the Ogoni people really doing things for themselves under colonial rule. And I saw a successful society. But from 1957 onwards, it
was all disaster. In the book *On a Darkling Plain*, I show how in 1957,
precisely during the election into the Eastern House of Assembly, as
a five year-old schoolboy in Government College, Umuahia, I was
taunted and teased by the Igbo cooks about being Ogoni and I
never forgot. I knew that from that moment onwards, I would have
to fight for the dignity and rights of the Ogoni people.

I actually started as a 16 year-old. I know that by 1958, I had
started writing to the *Eastern Outlook*, the paper in Eastern

Nigeria, raising the things that were happening to the Ogoni people as a result of the oil find.

I had even started writing stories at that time about this particular subject. So all through my life at University College Ibadan, (I left Umuahia in 1961 and went to Ibadan in 1962) in the three years that I was there, I began to see what dangers the Nigerian system posed to the Ogoni people. By that time, of course, Nigeria was independent. But if you are one of two boys from Ogoni at the University of Ibadan, you began to see yourself in isolation. And you know that the country was not an answer to the problems of your people. I enjoyed Ibadan, where I made a network of friends from across the country. But even at that time, I did begin to see that it was necessary for the Ogoni people to have autonomy.

Why?

Well, in order to come to full realisation of their potentials. Each time I came back home, I knew that the Ogonis were a depressed community. Each time scholarship results were announced, you would find only one or two Ogoni boys winning scholarships. So it was clear to me that we were on our way out. Fortunately for us, the crisis had been fully involved in the struggle for the creation of Rivers State which we felt would isolate us from the power block in Eastern Nigeria headed by the Igbos. So it was quite easy taking part in that struggle for a Rivers State which I did very happily when the war eventually came. There was no doubt in my mind that I had to be on the federal side. With the 12-state structure there was now hope that many of the things we were looking for could be achieved.

Unfortunately, this did not prove to be the case. After the civil war was won, all the gains we made were gradually eroded. Gowon seized the offshore oil in 1970. Then they started tinkering around with the commission of inquiry on how to take away the oil royalty. I sensed danger. And by 1973, I was so alarmed that I knew I had no faith in the government of that period any more. Then I started protesting which led to my dismissal from the government of Rivers State.

By 1974, we started asking for a split of Rivers State so that within a Port Harcourt State, we would now be able to function; the smaller units like the Ikwerres and the Ogonis would now begin to have greater access to funds and development. Of course, all that was a failure. We started the clamour for states. But it is strange that today, almost 20 years after, many other states have been created but none which would have given us opportunity.

The environment was being degraded and people were being driven from their land. Today there is a colony of 18,000 Ogoni in Cameroon who have been driven off their land, and off the fishing ports, because the oil companies have taken the farming land and have messed up places we used to fish.

Well, to make this argument for a small group of people requires a lot. It was clear to me because each time I raised the matter, my audience was hostile. That is, other Nigerians. It did not matter whether they were top military brass or people in academia whom I knew very well. Or even politicians whom I also knew well. All of them were hostile.

The moment you mention anything about minority rights, they all get hostile. It was necessary for me to strengthen myself in order to fight that battle, a sort of going back in order to jump better. And that was what I did between 1974 and 1984.

I went into business and tried to earn money while maintaining my authenticity. There the sort of business I chose was trading, buying and selling, no need to wheel and deal. I still had an eye on what was happening politically. So I even contested local government elections and tried to get into the Constituent Assembly in 1977. I failed because I was cheated out of a seat in the assembly.

In any case, I was busy trading and trying to earn money. By 1984, I felt I had earned enough money for the purpose I wanted to live for. I then took to writing. I was always writing about things I had thought about even as a schoolboy. Most people do not know this. But a lot of my writings have to do with the situation of the Ogoni people in Nigeria.

I looked at Ogoni and found that the entire place was now a wasteland; and that we are the victims of an ecological war that is very serious and unconventional.

It is unconventional because no bones are broken, no one is maimed. People are not alarmed because they can't see what is happening. But human beings are at risk, plants and animals are at risk.

The air and water are poisoned. Finally, the land itself dies. That is what is happening to the Ogoni people.

Then when you think that the Ogonis are very rich, they were created very rich by God. And then black people themselves who are always complaining that there is racism, they are being cheated, they practice even more of this racism on our own society. Then I knew it was time to put on my boxing gloves before I die and raise this matter and get a resolution. If it is not done, I would not know how to face my own children, to say that we come from the richest part of Nigeria, a place with fertile land, with water and clean vegetation, oil and gas, that this very people cannot go to school. How was I going to explain it? That I am an educated man and I'm seeing soldiers, bandits, actually coming to take away this stuff and develop their own home while pretending that they are running Nigeria. Oil has brought nothing but disaster to our people. That we are an ancient people; we've been there from remembered time, and we successfully organised that society. So, don't look at oil. Let's see what we can do for ourselves. Unfortunately, the things that we used to live on — the land, the sea — have now been entirely polluted. So, we can't go back to agriculture. So, we have a basic dilemma there. If oil money is not being used to sustain the development of the Ogoni people and all that money is being transferred to Abuja to build a new city or to Sokoto or to Maiduguri to send everybody there to school, and the Ogoni people cannot even go to primary school, then you have a basic moral dilemma. The question of social justice which occupies all writers — and those questions which occupy writers, sensitive people throughout the ages — I am faced with them and my reaction has been to tell the people thus far and no more. You must fight for your own liberation, even from your kith and kin.

Now you are sounding like the late Boro yet you once said the problem Isaac Boro had was that he didn't build a mass movement. How did you get MOSOP to the masses?
I am not sounding like him. No, he did not have a mass movement like I have. Isaac Boro went out on what his biographer called a quixotic experiment which bemused his people. I am recreating the Ogoni people, first and foremost, to come to the realisation of what they have always been which British colonisation and Nigerian

indigenous colonialism try to take away from them. So, my effort is very intellectual. It is backed by theories, thoughts and ideas which will, in fact, matter to the rest of Africa in the course of time. It derives a lot from Obafemi Awolowo whose views on this matter were very clear and were very closely articulated. So, anybody talking about Boro, doesn't know what to say. Boro came out and said, "we are going to disengage the Niger Delta from the rest of Nigeria." I said, "No, you don't have to do that. We should try and continue to be in the same country so long as there is social justice and there is fairness, and there is equality of opportunity — it is going to be good for us. I like to belong to the country of Wole Soyinka and (laughs) Fela Anikulapo Kuti and Kole Omotoso and Niyi Osundare, J.P. Clark, Elechi Amadi, Chinua Achebe. That's good company for me. I would not be removed from that. But I demand justice. I am prepared to work for this justice and there are several ways to it. I believe that an informed citizenry will stand up against dictatorship, will stand up against social injustice. And the first thing to do is to mobilise all our people to realise that.

So, my philosophy is entirely different from Boro's. Of course, when you come out with a new idea, particularly in a country where people are not reading, you are open to all sorts of interpretations, because what I'm saying is not new; Awo said it long ago.

Path to Nigeria Freedom and *Thoughts on Nigeria Constitution*, 1966-47-66 of *The People's Republic* – Awo had detailed these in a closely-knit study. I have featured it, somewhat, because Awo thought that the smaller groups should be together in order to run a state, but all the big groups should be one each, and I said no. You don't force them together. Everybody, speak for yourself. Do you want to be in this sort of set-up? If you don't want to, say it. Say why you don't want to do that. And don't be worried about your size. What's size got to do with it? (Laughs) You know, I did a study on the Ogonis, and I found that, in terms of area, they are bigger than 21 nations that are represented in the UN, in terms of population, they are more populous than 37 nations in the UN. So, you cannot use size in denying a people the right to self-determination within the same country, whereas to some people you are giving a surfeit of self-determination. Why should the Yoruba be in six states? Why should the Hausa/Fulani be in eight.

You seem to be frustrated that the creation of states has not resolved the Ogoni problem. What is your current platform?

We are asking for autonomy. This means the right of the Ogoni people to rule themselves. The right to use their resources for their own development. The states the military has been creating since 1967 are not states. It is a fraudulent act. You cannot split certain people into a multiplicity of states, and force other people to live together. And then you ask those living together to pay all the bills of the others you have split into a multiplicity of states. That is a massive fraud. It is not acceptable. We want a new society where every ethnic group is independent. It can do what it likes with itself. It can hold hands if it wants to with the rest of the country. What we are saying in effect is that Nigeria was put together by force and violence. But now, each group should be free to choose what it wants to do for itself.

The Ogoni people are not asking for the sort of states Babangida has created because they are leprous. Those are not states. There is nowhere else in the world where this thing is done. In a multi-ethnic state how can you say that the Ogoni people cannot have eight states, like the Hausas. Why? You ask the Ogoni people to pay the bills of the Hausa states, provide them with television, radio, roads? That is slavery. That is what the Ogoni people have said "no" to. We don't want that. We want social justice. However, if within what is happening now, a state is created along the lines of the states that are operating now, it is one step forward.

At least, it allows the Ogoni people to mind their own affair. Not that you put them in a hybrid Rivers State where before they do anything for themselves, they have to see what the Ijaws want to do for themselves. The Rivers State does not work at all. It is very unfair of this government to have left this state like this since 1967, the only state that has not been split out of the states that were created in 1967. It is not fair.

Are you looking for a confederal arrangement or is secession the answer for you?

We would rather see a confederal arrangement. I am not a secessionist. I think that Black people are in such bad shape worldwide that they need to cooperate with one another. I said it and I mean it.

I don't want to break that link. I would like to see it continue. But I want it continued with justice.

A confederal arrangement is the best arrangement for a multi-ethnic state like Nigeria. There are so many languages, so many cultures, so many peoples.

But was your arrest and detention not related to fears that the Ogoni people might secede?
It would be stupid. Why would 500,000 Ogoni people want to face 80 million people, especially in a fascist state like Babangida's? It would be suicidal. I could never contemplate such a scheme for the Ogoni people.

One of the central tenets of the Ogoni Bill of Rights is that we want adequate and fair representation as of right in Nigerian national institutions. That is central. If you are going to the Nigerian Defence Academy, we want as a right to have a number of places there. In the unity schools we want places there as of right. If you keep Rivers State as a whole, most times we would not have anybody in those institutions.

That is what we are asking for. Not secession. My mind has always been for the salvation of the Black man. I can see that happening if we are all co-operating. But under a just system. My quest is for social justice, not for a break-up of the country.

I have warned that the people breaking up the country are people like Babangida, Obasanjo when he was in office, and Gowon. They are the ones breaking up the country by their actions. I am the one protesting and trying to save the country. But a lot of people who don't read would not recognise that. I am the statesman, they are the ruiners of the state.

This government is afraid of the ideas I am giving people about their rights, their environment, their right to the oil. They are afraid it will destroy the fraudulent system they have set up. As usual, when falsehood sees the truth, it tries to hide. Instead of facing the message, they are looking for the messenger. It is easier to destroy the messenger than to destroy the message, so they are looking for the easy way out.

All the SSS[2] people were asking was we want to see the flag of the Ogoni people; the symbol.

But they have not gone to worry Hausa people about the flag. The symbol of the Bank of the North is an Arewa sign. They know what it means. Nobody has confronted them. They haven't asked those who constructed State House, Abuja why they used the Islamic symbols there. But they are worrying me.

I feel very insulted by it. The Ogoni have been admitted into the Unrepresented Nations and Peoples Organisation based at the Hague. Everybody there has a flag. Not everybody there is looking for independence. Some, like the Ogoni, are looking for social justice within their country. Others are looking for outright independence. Others are looking for assistance to do certain things within their society. I showed the SSS all these things. I gave them all the literature. We developed a symbol for Ogoni identity and the government gets scared because we are minorities whom they have been cheating all these years. They haven't tried to solve even one out of the problems the Ogoni people have put before them — not the absence of developments, not oil royalties, nothing.

The Oil Mineral Producing Areas Development Commission (OMPADEC) under ex-security chief, Alfred Horsefall, is seen as an attempt to address your concerns. What is your attitude to it?
OMPADEC is illogical, an insult and an injury. If you have your own money, why would government set-up a commission to run your money? The money they give to Kogi and Sokoto states is money from our oil. Have they got an Ogoni man to help them spend the money? That is not the business of government. They are treating us like babies here. They even have some Fulani people sitting on that commission. It is an insult. When Babangida says I give you three percent, who told him that what we need is three percent? The oil is ours, 100 percent. All we can do is pay tax to the government. The petroleum profit tax is enough to keep the government alive. They must allow us have rent and royalties as landlords. We must run the type of government we want. Not surrounding us with troops as they are doing. OMPADEC is an insult. Babangida himself knows it and that is why he put an ex-security man in charge. It is like he is using it to bait us and destroy our will to resist this injustice.

Who is more culpable for this state of things between the oil companies and the government?
What I find is that the oil companies would like to do anything that is lawful. If the laws were properly set out, they would obey the laws. But our own government is so irresponsible that the oil companies are happy to exploit that irresponsibility to advantage. The laws are made so lax so that people can profit from corruption. The Nigerian government makes laws to cheat its own people. In any case, they don't even feel that the people in oil producing areas are their own people.

How are neighbouring oil producing communities relating to your struggle?
They are getting interested. They have been coming to me for advice as to how they can organise their fight.

The best thing to do is to allow the landlords who suffer the degradation, the disturbance, to establish the laws that will bind the companies and government which can tax the proceeds. There is no way you can take 30 billion dollars out of a territory and you put nothing back. It is so immoral. By the time I finish, Nigeria is going to be ashamed standing before the council of the world.

What is the attitude of the Rivers State Government to your struggle?
I have not seen any clear policy from the government. What we heard is the governor saying the Ogoni people must be careful. I don't know if he was correctly quoted. He said he had handed the matter over to the security agents.

But this is not a security matter. It is a matter of dialogue. It cannot be resolved by the use of force but by clear thinking and discussion in the interest of the country.

The Rivers State House of Assembly recently passed a resolution asking for more money than the Ogoni people requested. They asked Shell to pay four billion pounds sterling as royalties and rent for the oil and gas they have exploited. That assembly includes representatives from all over the state. That speaks for the popular feeling around the state.

The latitude to protest without intimidation may...
That's not true. All these guys in Abuja or Lagos — the NNPC[3] are still here — they don't care. For them, all that is just there is a mining lease, you go ahead. And Shell arrives in the place, they have a paper from the federal government. If you talk, then they go to the federal government and take troops and start shooting you.

Have they?
They have. They killed them last Friday.

How did it happen — the killing?
Last Friday, they shot at least 10 people, including a mother of five.

But you insist on a peaceful movement?
Yes, I do, what are we going to do. Our stand is purely moral, that is all we have. We are only using the weapons that are available to us. I myself am a man of peace.

The best thing for the country is confederal. Yes, that is the best. Because you have seen that federation has failed. Why do you fail so often and keep doing the same things? When you do that you look stupid. You must be stupid if you fail so often and just keep at it. So, forget it, everybody, go to your home. Use your resources for yourself. Contribute to the things that we do in common. It's simple. But because all people have their eyes trained on oil, they have gotten so greedy, they do not even remember that all our neighbours who have no oil are better off than ourselves. So, there must be something wrong, when all you are thinking about is revenue sharing, revenue sharing. Where is the contribution? So, because you think you have revenue to share you can run six parliaments where there should be one, six bureaucracies where there should be one. And, meanwhile, you are just destroying the fabric of the parliamentary society.

It is increasingly being interpreted in Nigeria that things are falling apart and may be, degenerating to a Liberia-like extent. Is it not a way of dismantling the entity known as Nigeria?
I keep saying that people are not made for states; states are made for people.

So, you must not think that there is this thing called Nigerian and it's untouchable, no matter what happens.

You mean it should be dismantled?
Of course, why not? The Soviet Union was set up about the same time this man was amalgamating Nigeria. It's gone. Yugoslavia is gone. Therefore, you have to be very careful. You must so organise the place that you must stay together. Because if you don't do that, the dynamics of history will tear it apart. That is what I've been at pains to teach my country man — to teach my country men that look, you're not in a sacrosanct situation. And that the things you do may lead to disintegrations. So, be careful because the dynamics of history will not allow you to go on and on and on. You will get somewhere and the whole thing will collapse. So, when I do this historical analysis they say, "Oh, Ken Saro-Wiwa wants this place to disintegrate."

No I'm doing an analysis. All you need do is go back into history and see what happened to states that refused to allow principles of social justice, including Sodom and Gomorrah!

Is it the strident tone that makes them suspect that your case has a latent secessionist implication?
They are just being silly. Our case is that no group should arrogate power to itself on account of size. Power belongs to the ethnic groups. That's why I'm saying I'm on the right path. Because, in any case, if you look at what the Igbos did in Biafra when they felt they were threatened, all the power that came out, the suffering that they were able to endure because they believed in themselves, then you can see the beauty in this — extending to everyone else. Don't deny to the small groups, because you think they are few they cannot argue for themselves. That is the problem with the country.

But you did not support Ojukwu's secession bid then…?
(Cuts in) That's because he was trying to steal a country — to take the rest of us. (Laughs) But if he had come out and said: "Look, we the Igbos we have suffered so much in Nigeria, we can't take it. We must be on our own." I would have said, "Carry on, boy. Go ahead."

If someone said that now — if Ojukwu said that now would you count on his support?
No, not at all. If he says "Ogoni people, stand on your own. We will stand hands together and see what we can do," then I can listen to that. But my message is actually to the whole country. Let each stand on its feet and let's hold hands to see what we can do for each other and for all of us collectively. I think it's a good message.

You composed the Ogoni anthem for your people.
Yes, the Ogoni liberation song. It is not the anthem yet. (Laughs) Not yet....

And, one of the questions that the SSS people did ask your men in Lagos was simply that, "Look if your man composed this liberation song - as Zik initially did for Biafra...."
No, but that's wrong. Let us understand the history. There was Biafra first before there was a national anthem ... Oh yes, Ojukwu made it clear he was leaving Nigerian federation. He was creating a new country. And that new country needed an anthem. (Laughs) You do not become free because you have an anthem. (Laughs)

How do you reconcile these: Calling for the right for self determination and secession?
But self determination does not mean secession. Self determination means that you choose. You come to the Ogoni people and say "You want to be in Rivers State." They say "No, we don't want to be in Rivers State. We want to run our own state." What's wrong in that?

But it means you are still opposing the present arrangement.
Of course, why not? Who else has not done that? All those people who were demanding states — is it not a revolt against the present system?
   If you ask for states, what are you doing?

Will the state solve all the problems?
It will not solve all, it will solve some. Why are they denying it?

I wonder if you want to comment on the artistic dimension of this your new involvement, and if you want to choose between heroism and martyrdom, how is it to be handled?

No, I think writers are led into different things. In my case, it has made me an activist, not every writer needs this kind of activism. You react to your situation. If I were Yoruba maybe I would not be an activist because there are certain things that are available. But I live in the middle of death and incomprehension from the rest of the society. Even antagonism; the day I lectured in Abuja, someone came to me and said, "Look, Mr. Saro-Wiwa, you're being selfish." And I laughed and said, "You have no oil you can have a state? I'm not the one who's being selfish." So if you're a writer, even in that sort of society, like the Ogoni society, then I think you must go into activism because if you're not into activism, then you're irresponsible.

Has there always been a heavy security presence in your area? Or is it a product of recent agitations?

They are now intensifying their presence because the people now know and are saying 'No'. What they were stealing surreptitiously, they are now stealing openly. That was always my hope, because now all the world can see it. The international community can see it because there is nowhere else in the world where you put armed soldiers beside foreign companies to steal the resources of the people.

The Ogoni struggle has been non-violent, but with the recent shootings, do you truly have the strength to restrain angry youth?

Yes, successfully. Violence is not the answer to a fascist government. We must continue a non-violent struggle. It is very expensive to do that, it is hard. But it is the only way that our way can proceed. There is no other way.

So you don't fear a desperate recourse to sabotage?

There is no point in it. If you sabotage the oil companies, it is our own land you destroy. We know how to tackle the fascist government in Nigeria.

We will never resort to violence. But we will tackle the irresponsible leadership of this country. In any case, environmental degradation is a very high form of violence. How do you tackle that? Are you going to take up a gun and start fighting oil spillage and gas flaring? Our struggle has been well-defined and has been well thought out. I assure you it is going to be successful.

Even the way the government is behaving now is a sign of success. They are jittery and there is no way they can go on in the next three years. But we shall win.

How would you assess successive governments since independence?
In relation to the Ogonis?

In relation to the nation.
They are all the same. They have all failed. The only possible exception I can think of is perhaps Buhari's government which was short lived, patriotic … I think Babangida's government was the most woeful.

Will you prosecute the soldiers who fired at your people?
Our lawyers are looking into it. Willbros, the company that invited the soldiers, is still there. I am not even sure Army HQ knows that its troops are being used to protect people making profits. We will examine it and take appropriate action.

NOTES
1   Excerpts from an interview with Ken Saro-Wiwa entitled "They Are Killing My People." Orignally published in *The News*, 17 May 1993.
2   State Security Service.
3   Nigerian National Petroleum Corporation.

We Will Defend Our Oil With Our Blood[1]
Ken Saro-Wiwa

On January 3, the Ogoni people of Rivers State staged mass but peaceful protests to vent their anger at the despoliation of their land through oil-production activities. Their area is one of the leading oil producers not only in Rivers State but in the country. The rallies were attended by over 300,000 Ogoni. Even those living in 'exile' came home to be part of the momentous assertion of Ogoni nationalism. Their complaint: their land has been systematically destroyed by the oil companies which, in collusion with successive Nigerian governments, have been stealing their prized natural resource — crude oil — without the people getting commensurate compensations for their losses — unproductive farmlands, polluted waters and general environmental degradation.

One of the prime movers of the Ogoni protest was Ken Saro-Wiwa, prolific writer and film producer who has been trying in the past four years to draw attention to the sorry lot of the oil producing areas in general and Ogoni land in particular. Two weeks after the historic (from the perspective of the Ogoni and their supporters) event, Saro-Wiwa, president of the Association of Nigerian Authors, spoke to a team of TELL editors including Nosa Igiebor, editor-in-chief, Onome Osifo-Whiskey, managing editor, Dare Babarinsa, executive editor, Ayodele Akinkuotu, senior associate editor, and Don MacWarra, staff writer, who himself is an Ogoni.

The interview took place in TELL's boardroom and lasted for two hours. It could have gone on much longer especially because Saro-Wiwa's authoritative command of the issues made it so absorbing. It had to be terminated reluctantly by the editors to enable him to rush to the airport to catch his flight to the Hague, Netherlands, where he attended the General Assembly of the Unrepresented Nations and Peoples Organisation, one of the international fora Saro-Wiwa is using to publicise the plight of his people who, according to him, are being deprived of their God-given natural resources forcibly. Excerpts:

About four weeks ago Ogoni people held mass rallies to protest the continued exploitation of their natural resource which is oil. To what extent would you describe the whole exercise as addressing the issue?
The rallies finally took place before the whole world. The protest is against the insensitivity of successive Nigerian governments. What has been happening is equivalent to slave trade, because the collusion of the rulers of Nigeria with oil companies is intolerable. So, the Ogoni people staged a mass rally and the exciting thing about it was that men, women and children even the disabled, came out to say no. Against the instruction of the government, against the security people, they took a stand for the outside world to know and to see what they have been saying in words now demonstrated in action.

Can you amplify this exploitation?
Well, basically, the oil belongs to the landlords. Ogoni is older than Nigeria; any of the communities producing oil is older than Nigeria; the oil is their property. First of all, the matter of royalty. That's very central; royalty by definition is what is paid to you for minerals extracted from your soil. The Nigerian government has no reason whatsoever to appropriate royalties to itself, and it has been doing so to all Delta people — minorities — who produce oil. If the oil has been in any of the majority areas, in Hausa/Fulani country or Yoruba country, they would never have seized these royalties. And they have always done this because in the words of the present secretary of petroleum, P.C. Asiodu, "these people are so small, they will never threaten the welfare, the economic welfare of Nigeria or

its stability" — so it's a case of open naked exploitation. Secondly, the harm that has been done to the environment is enormous. There is no part of the world where oil has been mined and the land remains the same thereafter. In Nigeria, because of the total lack of care in oil exploitation and because the rulers of Nigeria are in collusion with the oil companies, the environmental damage done to the Delta is totally irreparable. The entire Delta is now a wasteland. That of Ogoni is so obvious because it's a very small area. You have 1002 people per square mile in Ogoni, the Nigerian national average is 300, and therefore the situation in Ogoni is immediately obvious to any newcomers. The oil is on their farmlands. It is not in the swamps. The oil companies have been running over all these farmlands the pipelines, the gas flares, access roads to the oil wells, oil well themselves — all these have completely destroyed the Ogoni countryside because as far as SHELL is concerned (SHELL is the major prospector in Ogoni), the land, whether residential, forest or farmland, means nothing else, but land that has to be exploited. Therefore they can get into villages without bothering and as far as the rulers of Nigeria are concerned they only have a map in front of them. This is an open map cut into oil-mining leases and the oil companies can get in there once they have a paper from Lagos or Abuja and do whatever they like. And the poor peasants have no protection whatsoever, and so long as the country is getting its money that's alright by the rulers of Nigeria. Then a very funny thing comes along after government has taken $30 billion from Ogoni: it turns round and tells Ogoni people that look, you are in debts.

How did you arrive at this figure, $30 billion?
It is very easy to calculate. We know the total number of barrels that have been taken out of Ogoni since 1958. That is no secret. And we know the cost of oil per barrel per year throughout the different years. Between 1958 and 1964 for instance, they took about $600 million out of Ogoni and that was about 125 million barrels of oil calculated at an average of $4 per barrel. I believe more have been taken away. All the gas is property, is money; they flare gas, they have wasted all that. So the federal government takes away $30 billion and invests not one cent in Ogoni. Then it turns round and

tells Ogoni people — you are in debt — Nigeria is indebted to the tune of about $30 billion and Ogoni people have to pay that debt. They sell Ogoni oil for $20 per barrel and then turn around to ask Ogoni people to bring out N20.00 for $1.00. Where are Ogoni people going to get the money from all their farmlands having been taken away? That is the level of injustice, and at the same time you can see those who are benefiting from this oil like Borno, Sokoto or Kebbi States. They have free education from primary through tertiary levels but the Ogoni people cannot go to school, not even primary school. That is a case of genocide.

Well, in your present struggle, what role did Rivers State government play?
The governor was admittedly in a very difficult situation — he has the responsibility to maintain law and order. As a politician I do not know exactly how he might have felt. But the important thing is, he did not want the protest march to take place. Quite clearly, I discussed with him at length and it's not the first time I have discussed with him over the issues that affected Rivers people. But in this particular instance, he made it quite clear he did not want the protest march to go on. Also because of January 2 and all the events that were anticipated, there should be no protest march throughout the country. But the Ogoni people were determined after the 30 days (ultimatum) we gave the oil companies expired, they carried the argument further to show their total disenchantment with the oil companies and with the federal government itself.

One other community that is badly exploited in this country like Ogoni is Isoko community in Delta State. Just like Ogoni people, there is actually no federal presence there. Were your people in contact with other oil-producing areas in respect of making this struggle a collective one since your interests kind of coalesce?
Well, you have to understand that in a struggle of this nature, it is very dangerous in a military regime, when you are facing people who are benefiting heavily from the system and are using military decrees against even peaceful demonstrations. So, there are many communities who will like to do what the Ogoni people have done and I imagine that they do not have either the leadership or the courage to do it. It costs a lot of money, even organising the protest

itself; not to talk of the publicity and psychological work that went ahead of it which has been like five years work on my part and on the part of the leaders of Ogoni. So, basically, the philosophical underpinnings are available in the books I have written. For instance, I have made no secret of the fact that the situation of the Ogoni is shared by the Ibibio, Isoko, Urhobo and in fact, the Edo are coming to face it now because they are beginning to find oil there. The Igbo to some extent, and also the Ijaws to a very large extent. So the ideas are broad; people have to catch on to them.

Did some of these communities send representatives to the rallies?
No. I think most people could not have believed the rallies would hold, given the attitude of the government at the time and, in any case, it wasn't even desirable that they should be there. This was an Ogoni affair and it is only for other communities to learn from what we have done. I believe there must be peaceful protest, the rights of people in the oil-producing areas are being abused. These people are being driven to extinction and it's their responsibility to stand up and say no to it in the same way as the Ogoni people have done.

You accused the leadership of the country of genocide and of slavery. One will think the rulership of Rivers State is sympathetic to your struggle considering that most parts of Rivers State have the same kind of experience you are having?
Well, it is very difficult for me to speak for the government. I think they should speak for themselves.

From your experience what kind of mandate. Or were they just being pressured by the federal government ...?
I do my work as a writer, as a human rights activist and environmental campaigner. The case of government is a different matter all together. Rivers State is multi-ethnic and there are many forces working there; there are also so many forces working in Nigeria at this time when there is so much confusion. Are we in a democracy? Are we in a military regime? Just what are we doing? Or are we in a state of anarchy? In which case everybody is free to interpret the laws in whatever way they like? If I were the governor of Rivers

State, I would find myself in that dilemma as well, and therefore I am not blaming the governor of Rivers State for standing against the demonstration. It was for him, as chief security officer of the state, to judge the situation as best as he could. But it was my responsibility and the responsibility of the Ogoni people and Ogoni leadership to do precisely what they wanted to do and to take the consequences for whatever action they took. If the Ogoni leadership, the leadership of the Movement for the Survival of the Ogoni People (MOSOP) had said no, Ogoni people would probably have lynched them.

It was said the Ogoni people were under considerable pressure from the security apparatus not to hold the march. Precisely what did take place in Ogoni during that time?

The pressure was before the march. On Christmas Day for instance, the president of MOSOP, G.B. Leton, was invited by the state director of the SSS. And when he told me, I volunteered to go with him and we held a discussion. They were trying to honour me actually on December 27 (the Elite Social Club) with the first Ogoni national merit award. And this was on radio. So, I think it scared the security people. So, they called me, the president of MOSOP and I went and we held discussions. The director of the SSS said, "look we are worried about this," and we said no, this is a usual end of year activity and there is nothing. The people must be allowed to enjoy themselves and to do the things they have always done. Well on December 26, the preparatory meetings that were being held were disrupted by the police and the chiefs were so worried that they made representations to the security authorities. And after we had done everything, we were able to hold the ceremonies of the 27th. Thereafter, the security authorities knew we were also planning the protest march of January 4 but were not quite sure we were going to do it. But in fairness to the state director of the SSS, he did make arrangement of the Ogoni leadership to get to Abuja and speak with the director-general of the SSS. We told them that we were not doing anything in secret so we didn't see anything wrong. We told the security operatives in the state that a march was going to be held on January 4, and that it was going to be peaceful. And I accordingly reported the matter to the state director of the SSS and

I subsequently spoke to the governor about it, at which point he called a proper meeting and the state commissioner of police, the director of SSS, the governor and his deputy were present. They made it known to me that it was not advisable to hold the march and that they will not support it. We knew before then that since the 10th of December, after our letter to the three oil companies had gone out, the police had been massed around Ogoni. And we also knew a company of soldiers was around. But we were prepared to march in spite of that. And I did warn that there will only be violence if the state practiced violence. The Ogoni people wanted to let the world know that something was wrong. Beside, it was the international day of the world's indigenous people and we were using the opportunity to celebrate that fact.

What would you really say is the success of the march?
It is tremendous. In the first instance, we have shown the outside world that the Ogoni are determined brave people that would never go under, and that they are not going to allow themselves to be victims of this genocide. There is tremendous awareness in Ogoni now, and right there, there is no woman or child who does not know as of today that the Nigerian government is cheating them, and that the ethnic majorities in Nigeria are cheating them, and that they have no right to be doing what they are doing. They also know that the international oil companies are practicing international '419' and that something has to be done to stop it. The people are determined. And I think that in future you are going to see a lot of activity on the part of the Ogoni to assert their right of the property.

Very recently the government set up a commission for dispersal of special funds to oil producing communities. Has the commission been in contact with you?
Well, they don't have to be in contact with us actually. They are obeying the voice of Abuja as far as the Ogoni people are concerned. Three percent of their property is rubbish. Is three percent going to restore the land? What does it do? Is it going to restore the fishes in the rivers? What the government is faced with is the fact that they should stop stealing. What they are doing is terribly

unfair. It does not happen in any other part of the world. In fact, the government should be ashamed to announce to the rest of the world that they are giving back three percent of the resources of people in a federation to the owners of the land. And at the same time, you have a majority of the ethnic groups split into six and oil money is being shared according to equality of states, land mass, all the elements of cheating that you can ever think of. Any group of people who can openly do this to any section of their own people have lost the moral authority to govern that group of people. As far as Ogoni people are concerned, there is no government to deliver us. We have vampires on top of us. We are prepared to fight to the last cup of blood to ensure that this stops. And the royalties which the government owes us will have to be repaid. That is why the country should stay together so that those who have taken this money over the last 35 years, even if it takes them 100 years to pay, they must repay to succeeding Ogoni children. And they have to pay back the money because they have to learn that cheating is wrong.

So what is your agenda for achieving this?
We are involved in passive resistance. We are appealing to the United Nations that the matter is beyond the care of the Nigerian government. They don't know what to do. Everything is beyond them. They cannot even tell the oil companies to stop flaring gas. The oil companies are willing to re-inject the gas into the soil but the Nigerian government says no, poison our people instead and let's take the money. So the thing is beyond the Nigerian government. They don't even know how to pay royalty to the owners of the land. So what can they do?

Is it that the government is not paying royalty or that they are not willing to give the people a fair share?
That is what I mean. They are unwilling so I should say they are ignorant. They don't know how to pay the money back; so if they can't do such elementary things, how can one expect them to take care of human lives? Since the oil companies are multinational entities and the rest of the world is interested in the environment, the United Nations should come in and save the Ogoni people and

the Delta minorities because the rest of the country is incapable of doing it.

How does it work? Because we do know you have campaigned vigorously in UN circles for its involvement. How do you envisage the UN to work in this type of situation?
Under United Nations regulations e.g. Procedure 1503, anybody can take it against a government, like the federal government of Nigeria, and I am going to do that next April. This is presented to the Sub-Commission of Human Rights on the Prevention of Discrimination (against) and Protection of the Minorities, and the sub-commission will then examine it very strictly. If they can see a consistent pattern of violation of rights they will then make reference to the Nigerian government and action will start from there. But there is no doubt that genocide is a very serious crime and is viewed as such by the United Nations. When I present the case of genocide against the Nigerian government formally ... I haven't done so formally; at this moment I have been doing all the preparatory work and doing the publicity that is going to lead to that. And hoping that in the interim, the Nigerian government will get sufficiently alarmed, then their conscience will be stricken in some small measure to do something.

Many people have been saying that you use the word genocide very loosely. Can you substantiate?
There is a clear definition of genocide by the United Nations: anything done to destroy a group of people. Now, if you take the Ogoni case for instance, you pollute their air, you pollute their streams, you make it impossible for them to farm or to fish, which is their main source of livelihood, and then what comes out of their soil you take entirely away and you say we will give you 1.5 percent or 3 percent, but we are not going to give it to you. We are going to keep it somewhere else where other people will take care of it. Mark you since 1979, this money has never been paid to any of the people there. Now, if more people in Ogoni are dying than are being born, if Ogoni boys and girls are not going to school, not primary not secondary not university, if those who manage to scale through cannot find jobs; if when they find jobs they don't get promotion

because promotions don't even go by any standards at all, then surely you are leading the tribe to extinction. Ogoni people are going extinct. I have seen it. If you get to the Eleme Kingdom in Ogoni for instance, you put the petro-chemical there, you put NAFCON, you put the refinery, you put the airport, the people cannot sleep at night. If anything happens at the petro-chemical anytime, as happened in Bhopal (India), all Eleme people will be dead. If you get to Ibobu for instance, there is a blow-out that happened there 20 years ago. The land is totally unusable and it has ruined their only source of drinking water.

But these are said to be federal presence?
No, they are not federal presence but presence of death. Because if you get there, the landlords cannot even find jobs in the petro-chemical companies.

Can you cite anywhere procedure 1503 of the UN has helped any community?
There are many instances, even the Kurds (Iraq) you are hearing of now used that. I do not think the UN is the panacea for the world's problems. Ogoni people must themselves fight for their own salvation. I believe they are doing that now. They are very very ready. The country is going to know that because Nigeria will shoot, kill every Ogoni man, woman and child before she takes any more of that oil. And the Ogoni people are going to lie on the oil fields, on the fuel stations bare-handed and invite the Nigerian government to send their soldiers and police to go and kill all of them. You are going to see that very soon. It is coming.

A so-called National Conference called by the federal government took off in Abuja this morning, (January 17) and this is exactly what a lot of people have been calling for—a National Conference that should address all issues among which is those concerning minority groups, especially the oil producing areas. What is your position on the National Conference and your feeling about what is going on in Abuja?
What is happening in Abuja now is a seminar and not a national conference. I was in fact invited to deliver a paper at the seminar but I am not available. It is true that they have invited all the

Nigerian big weights and not necessarily in academics to that conference. The seminar cannot be called a national conference at all. What we are asking for is a sovereign national conference, which is to say that all the parts of the federation, mostly ethnic groups because Nigeria is a federation of ethnic groups, who have agreed to come together as one to run the Nigerian nation-state. All those should get together now and find out what we can do to save the country. Not the gimmickry of the quixotic experiment which Babangida is carrying on now and ruining all of us in the process. We want all groups to get together and decide what they are going to do with themselves, whether to stay together or whether to part in peace, and how they are going to share their resources, and how they are going to contribute to resources, because the country has been dwelling too much on the share of oil money without people working. They are stealing instead of working. No society can grow if all its members are bent on stealing, on taking away and putting nothing back. In every level of the Nigerian society that is what is happening, and so the nation is being torn apart. What we have now is a travesty; it has no future for the young, for the old or for anyone whatsoever.

You seem to be saying that the exploitation of Ogonis and other people of their type is the handiwork of the majority groups i.e. the Hausa-Fulani, Yoruba and Igbo. Now, how do you have a national conference of indigenous people to address these issues that are generally exploitation of the minorities when of course the majorities are there to win? It is to me like calling an Association of Landlords for the reduction of rents. It looks illogical.
That is not true because, basically, I am not convinced that it's all Yoruba people that want what is going on now to do so. Actually if you read Chief Obafemi Awolowo, for instance, who was a Yoruba, he would never have supported the kind of thing that is going on now. There are a lot of Yoruba people who are saying no to what is happening.

Beside these views from exploited minority people like you, what will you consider a good reason for a national conference at this time?
The reasons are obvious. Babangida, for instance, has turned

Nigeria into a unitary system of government against the wishes of the people. We voted for federalism. In fact when the Northern Region realised that General Ironsi was trying to practice the unitary system that Gowon and Babangida went on to do, there was a mutiny; Ironsi was removed as head of state. So, to have done that and actually turned round to drag the country back to a unitary system of government is wrong. Nigeria is a multi-ethnic state. There is no where in the world where a multi-ethnic state runs a unitary system of government. Even in Britain where you have a United Kingdom, you find that the Scottish people have their own home office with five ministers; the Welsh have theirs with a minister; the English decided not to carve themselves because they are 45 million to nine parliaments so that they can have as many parliaments as there are people in proportion with the Scots. So what is happening in Nigeria now is just robbery. This has happened so that Babangida can transfer the resources of the Delta to develop Abuja and incur debts which he will expect the Delta to pay in due course. It has also enabled him to give appointments to certain sections of the country which, if we were running a federal system or a confederal system which I think is better for Nigeria, will not happen. There is no reason whatsoever why the Ogoni people should not run their own government. The Hausa people theirs and Yoruba theirs, etc. We will meet at the centre to find out what we can do together and how everybody will contribute to that.

Chief Enahoro has called for eight federations that will later form confederation, what do you think of this?
That is brilliant, but I believe he is only suggesting that there should be eight federations. That is only a starting point. When we get to a sovereign national conference, he will have to show me why the Ogonis should not run a federation. When there are six kingdoms in Ogoni, each of them will be a part of the Ogoni federation and then we will want a proper representation as a unit at the centre. That's what I want to see. It's what I call erectism; ethnic autonomy, resolve and environmental control.

You are calling for what used to obtain in the former Soviet Union, where you have federated republics, autonomous areas and regions within the union.

Well, I am not even calling for that. I am calling for ethnic autonomy, resolve and environmental control. The only law to be in
Nigeria is: You are free to rule yourself, you're independent now, but
you must pay your bills, you will control all your resources, you
control your environment, run whatever government you like.
Those who have no men, since running a government is a matter of
human resources as well as material resources, to run the paraphernalia of a state can arrange with your neighbours and fashion a
new administrative structure which you all agree on. This will be
embodied in a constitution. Then you can move from here to the
centre; we will then know finally how federations exist in Nigeria or
if they are not federations, how many autonomous groups will
exist. But the point is that nobody is going to sit in Abuja and take a
pencil and say, "I cut Nigeria into 30 states, I cut it into 600 local
governments, we will share oil money." We are not talking about
who is going to contribute to what.

What kind of revenue allocation system will you therefore advocate?
I am not interested in revenue allocation. I am thinking on how we
are going to run the country. Because when you think of revenue
allocation in Nigeria everybody is thinking of how to share oil
money. Nobody is talking of how to contribute resources to the
centre so that we can share. If everybody has control over their
resources and the environment, all we will do in order to run the
country is to contribute to central services, centralised services such
as in this case, the future Nigeria of our dream, foreign policy of the
country and maybe currency, possibly rail lines, but not defence,
because there is nobody threatening Nigeria. One, the military
have not fought any external war.

*You seem to doubt the legitimacy of the Nigerian state. Do you want to
concede that the current Nigerian state is a legitimate successor to the precolonial states you say we should go back to? Do you think the current
Nigerian state is legitimate? If it is not, how can it turn around to uphold
justice?*
No, it cannot. It cannot uphold any justice.

What must be done to return legitimacy to the state?
You can only return legitimacy to the state when all the people who

have agreed to come together agree that they want to be together. They must do it by consent, not by force which the military has used in the past 32 years and the chicanery which they have used in the past 32 years. You can only return legitimacy to a government when all Nigerians are well taken care of and I postulate that nobody should take care of the other; let everyone care for himself. He should use his resources. It is true that some people are heavily endowed and that they will have to contribute to the others but it should be by consent not by force of arms.

Who is the Ogoni taking part in the presidential race?
I don't see any taking part at all. They will be foolish to do it. Why go to vote for somebody who is going to oppress and ruin you? The 1989 constitution is a complete disaster. With all the amendments, even the structure of the country is wrong. What has Nigeria got to offer Ogoni people except death under the 1989 constitution?

Can you draw a clear distinction between the 1979 constitution and the 1989 constitution?
They are the same. There is no difference except that Babangida has worsened the 1989 one by the quixotic experiment he is carrying on. Example, the Transitional Council and a lot of others one cannot even understand. No civilised man is going to accept that even in principle. How can one man sit there altering things which people have sat down to agree on? Even the Constituent Assembly was a ruse, because a third of the people were nominated. They were told certain areas were no-go areas. I cannot frankly understand how any group of people like Nigerians can sit down and take this load of rubbish.

Back to the legitimacy issue. Can't we say Rivers State represents the oil producing people of Rivers State?
It is not. Are all the people in Rivers State now willing to be in Rivers State? Is there a situation where an Ogoni man can become governor of Rivers State? No! The Egbeye man cannot be governor of Rivers State. It doesn't work where the Ijaws alone outnumber all the other groups put together, though they produce oil too. So let each of them go their separate ways if they want to. Why are they forcing them together, for what reason?

You are advocating ethnic autonomy in the Nigerian concept?
I am saying right now, an instrument of empowerment should be put in place so that the Yoruba with six states will be free from the Hausa/Fulani trap in which they fell. Because when you have those six states, it means there cannot be any overall Yoruba leader. There cannot be an overall Igbo leader either, whereas the Hausa/Fulani still look up at the Sokoto Caliphate where they still have their leadership. They have Hausa/Fulani people throughout the Sahel in the Sudan. They have assistance from the Arab world, from the Islamic states. Now, they believe the Yoruba people do not have a leadership neither do the Igbo; they can now dominate them. Chief Awolowo would never have allowed it because all the while, he wanted Yoruba in one state and all other people in various units. So I do not believe in Babangida's military-state creation exercise, right from 1967 when Gowon started bastardising the idea of state creation. Gowon started it by destroying physical federalism, then the Murtala/Obasanjo regime went into breaking the minorities into much smaller states so that the resources of the Delta minorities could be stolen. And Babangida has carried this to its utmost level of ridicule and exploitation. I am not involved in creation of states *a la* Babangida.

So what do you think of the people still canvassing for more states?
They are confused because that is not solving any of the problems we are asking after. The only people who deserve states in the country are the ethnic minorities which have been corralled into single states against the federal culture of the country. So the sort of states I would like to see is one Middle Belt state, one Hausa state, one Tiv state, Idoma state, Ijaw state, one Ogoni state. That is the state I would like to see; but you don't just get states. Do you have the resources to run the state? Are the states viable? If you are viable, yes; if not look for your neighbours and get into an agreement with them, because Switzerland is a very small country of three million people, but its federal constitution is more complex than that of the United States of America, which is a settler community. You cannot run Nigeria like that because there are a lot of indigenous people. So what is happening now is vampirism, and the military do it all the time because they all come from the big ethnic groups. They don't care for the minorities. The minorities produce all the resources.

Would you serve any state government now?
What state? If there is an Ogoni state, I can serve Ogoni people. Yes, I am serving them now even without them having to vote for me or anything; but that is because they are in trouble. They are going extinct. What you have there is an absolute disaster. But I do not want a situation where they contend with sitting there, paying the bills of six Yoruba states and governors, and eight Hausa-Fulani states. That is slavery.

Did the oil companies reply to your letter?
Not one of them at all. All I know is they would rush to the Nigerian government and get cover since they are running a 60 percent joint venture, and convince the government that if you don't have this oil, the government will collapse. Please send your troops. That has always been the attitude of the oil companies. They did not even acknowledge receipt of the letter. And all we saw was security operatives massing in Ogoniland. Don't forget what is going on is armed robbery in which the Nigerian government and oil companies are in league. I am sure they would have loved to give Ogoni people their own brand of awareness which we have already ruined. They have succeeded only through the collusion of the Nigerian government with its wretched army and police to frighten the Ogoni people to stop them from uniting to fight for their rights.

In canvassing the aspirations of the Ogoni have you ever come under governmental harassment?
No. As an individual I have not faced any harassment at all. So far, except last December, but even then that was not personal. I have never been invited for any chat anytime at all, except in 1974 when we asked for the creation of another Rivers State. That was the only time Diette Spiff got us locked up at the NPA wharf in Port Harcourt, in a room where they normally keep delinquents — criminals for about six hours. So that is the only time in my crusade, I have never been invited for a discussion or anything at all.

Apart from this crusade which other activities are you involved in?
I am involved in human rights and environmental activities across the world. On what is happening in Ogoni now, the UN is aware

particularly as regards ecological degradation. But I believe the rest of the world is beginning to know what is happening in Ogoni. We've been on Channel Four in England, and that has created a lot of awareness. I am still carrying on with broadening the frontiers of that awareness worldwide.

If you can work with international bodies in Europe and America, why not similar minority groups equally producing oil in Nigeria?
We are not shying from doing that. I have in fact called on all ethnic groups — Delta minorities to stand up and fight for their rights. I am available. We have the Ethnic Minority Group Rights of Africa. Our work is to assist each of these groups to come to the awareness of their problems.

What is the 'secret agenda' of the Ogoni?
(Prolonged laughter) We can't have a secret agenda, we have a Bill of Rights which we issued as a public document. There are no unexpressed things about the wishes of Ogoni people. These are not mere nightmares. We will continue to protest.

Should we expect a thunderstorm?
Well, I don't know about a thunderstorm. All I know is that the Ogoni people are determined; every man, woman and child will die before Nigerians will steal their oil any more.

NOTES
1   Excerpts of an interview with Ken Saro-Wiwa entitled "We Will Defend Our Oil With Our Blood." Originally published *in Tell*, 8 February 1993.

VII

Bibliography: Life and Works

Ken Saro-Wiwa: a Bio-bibliography
Abdul-Rasheed Na'Allah

It is difficult to write a detailed biography of a charismatic person, or compile everything that has been written by and on one who was not just a successful writer but a world renowned author, publisher, businessman, and an environmentalist; whose death was more controversial than his life. Eckhard Breitinger rightly describes Ken Saro-Wiwa as a "writer and cultural manager." Throughout his life, he demonstrated an unprecedented passion to write and to publish. He was so anxious for his views to get out to the people that he literally took over pages of Nigerian magazines and national newspapers, wrote and produced plays on television and published books covering all three major literary genres. Funso Aiyejina says of him, "Saro-Wiwa wrote like a man who knew he was living a borrowed life" (1995: 46). Within a short time, his works have made their way to different parts of the world. But even in the Nigerian and international socio-political scenes, Ken Saro-Wiwa greatly suited a person K. O. Mbadiwe would call a man of "timbre and calibre" to show the level of his attainment in society. Saro-Wiwa rose to the highest positions in all fields he ventured in. He was an administrator, an equivalent of a State Governor or Local Government Council Chairman (1967–68), President of the Association of Nigerian Authors (1990–94), President of the Ogoni Central Union (1989–95), President of the Movement for the Survival of the Ogoni People (MOSOP; 1993–95), President, Ethnic Minority Rights Organization of Africa (1992–95), and Vice-President, Unrepresented Nations and Peoples Organization (UNPO; 1993–95), a human rights group based in the Netherlands.

My intention in this paper is to present a short biography of Saro-Wiwa and also give bibliographies of his writings and criticism of his works. These should serve as resource materials for scholars and other people around the world who are interested in the life and works of the Ogoni writer.

KEN SARO-WIWA'S SHORT BIOGRAPHY

His full name was Kenule Beeson Saro-Wiwa. He was born on 10 October 1941, in Bori, Rivers State of Nigeria. He was educated at the Nigerian premier University, the University of Ibadan, where he graduated with a B. A. (Hon.) in 1965. Soon after graduation he took up a full teaching appointment at Government College, Umuahia, where he had a teaching job since 1962 while still a full time student at Ibadan. During the Nigerian civil war, between 1966 to 1970, Saro-Wiwa supported the federal government, and mobilized his people against the Biafran rebels led by the then Col. Odumegwu Ojukwu. They resisted the Biafrans because of the belief that the Ibos were out to dominate the tiny Ogoni population. From 1967 to 1973, Saro-Wiwa became an assistant lecturer at the Stella Maris College, Port Harcourt. In 1967 when the federal side liberated Bonny in the present Rivers State, General Yakubu Gowon, the then Head of State appointed Ken Saro-Wiwa as its Administrator. From 1968 to 1973, still on leave from his college, he became a commissioner (equivalent of a provincial Minister) and a member of the Rivers State Executive Council. During this time, Saro-Wiwa's interest in writing was very visible as he started writing short stories and his famous, *Basi and Company*, which later became a very successful television series in Nigeria. He wrote radio plays, *The Transistor Radio* and *Bride by Return* broadcast on BBC radio, in 1972 and 1973 respectively. His short story books, *Tambari* and *Tambari in Dukana* were written in 1973. So that when Saro-Wiwa decided later to establish a publishing company, it was clear that he had very many manuscripts waiting for publication and would no longer succumb to frustration from difficult publishers. As Breitinger submits, Saro-Wiwa reckoned that the only solution was to begin a publishing company himself. He started Saros International Limited in 1973, and became its Managing Director. He published volumes of his own poetry, short stories and novels and got them distributed to many parts of the world. Saros International has a branch in London which became the overseas headquarters of the company. Through it and many agents spread around the world, he was able to distribute his works around Europe and North America. His most successful novel, *Sozaboy: A Novel in Rotten English* (1985), soon put him on the same level with several popular Nigerian writers like Gabriel Okara and Amos Tutuola. Between 1991 and 1992, he turned out eleven new titles of his own. Eight of them were launched on a single day in 1991. The other companies that Saro-Wiwa published were Longman Nigeria (two books), in 1973, and Penguin, which published posthumously the prison diary, *A Month and A Day*, in 1995. Saro-Wiwa had columns in *Sunday Times*, called 'Similia', and in *The Vanguard Newspaper*. His many works are listed in the latter section of this paper.

Ken Saro-Wiwa's life as a public officer was also very exciting. Apart from being a former administrator and a Commissioner of Government as already mentioned, he was also appointed by President Ibrahim Babangida, between 1987 and 1988, as Executive Director of the Directorate for Social Mobilization, and between 1987 and 1992, as Director of the Nigerian Newsprint Manufacturing Company Limited. His time at the Directorate for Social Mobilization was particularly controversial. He soon became disgruntled with Babangida's transition agenda and resigned from the Directorate (see Breitinger and Schulze-Engler in this volume). Saro-Wiwa thenceforth dedicated his time and energy to business, to writing and to the emancipation of the Ogoni people. His role as president of MOSOP was however to cause his death. My introduction to this book, and many other articles printed here clearly enumerate Saro-Wiwa's peaceful strategies to bring the plight of his people to the world's attention. He was first arrested in 1993, after the June 12 Presidential election, for mobilizing his people to boycott the election and protest the unreadiness of government to listen to them. He was detained for a month and a day, an experience which he vividly recounted in his posthumously published book. He was arrested again in May 1994 for allegedly inciting the killing of four Ogoni Chiefs (See Na'Allah, "Introduction," Orage, and Boyd in this volume), and was put before a military special tribunal. On 2 November 1995, Kenule Saro-Wiwa was sentenced to death along with eight other Ogonis. He was hanged at Port Harcourt on 10 November, 1995. Thus Nigeria by its own very hand wasted one of its rare gems, a person who had laboured to keep the country together when it was almost disintegrated, and one who wanted peace, progress, justice and fair play for everybody.

Ken Saro-Wiwa's popularity in political and literary circles around the world is growing with an unprecedented speed. Already many critics have declared that he is next only to Wole Soyinka and Chinua Achebe in the amount of attention that his works have received in recent years.

To end this paper, therefore, I shall list to the best of knowledge and the available sources the many works he wrote, the critiques on his writings and the honors, and awards that people and institutions around the world bestowed on this literary giant.

BIBLIOGRAPHY OF SARO-WIWA'S WRITINGS
Books, Articles, Interviews and Critical Essays:
The Transistor Radio (radio play). British Broadcasting Corporation (BBC-Radio), 1972.

Bride by Return (radio play). BBC-Radio, 1973.

Tambari. Ikeja: Longman Nigeria, 1973.

Tambari in Dukana (for children). Lagos: Longman Nigeria, 1973.

Songs in a Time of War (poems). Port Harcourt: Saros International, 1985.

*Sozaboy: A Novel in Rotten English. Ewell: Saros International, 1985.

*A Forest of Flowers (short stories). Ewell: Saros International, 1986.

Basi and Company: A Modern African Folktale. Port Harcourt: Saros International, 1987.

'Planting Creative Writing in Schools'. *Vanguard.* 7 January 1988: 8–9.

Prisoners of Jebs. Port Harcourt: Saros International, 1988.

'The Odd, the Odious and Our Very Odia'. *Guardian.* 5 January 1989: 10.

'Odia and the Politics of Book Launching'. *Guardian.* 7 February 1989: 8.

Adaku and Other Stories. Port Harcourt: Saros International, 1989.

Four Farcical Plays. Port Harcourt: Saros International, 1989.

On a Darkling Plain: An Account of the Nigerian Civil War. Port Harcourt: Saros International, 1989.

'Pen Voice: Ken Saro-Wiwa'. *Daily Times.* 15 November 1989: 26; 22 November 1989: 22.

'Of Books and Bookmen'. *Sunday Times*. 27 May 1990: 7.

'Letter from Saro-Wiwa'. *Prime People*. 6 July 1990: 19.

Nigeria: The Brink of Disaster. Port Harcourt: Saros International, 1991.

Pita Dumbrok's Prison. Port Harcourt: Saros International, 1991.

Similia: Essays on Anomic Nigeria. Port Harcourt: Saros International, 1991.

The Singing Anthill: Ogoni Folk Tales. Saros International, 1991.

Genocide in Nigeria: The Ogoni Tragedy. Saros International, 1992.

'The Language of African Literature: A Writer's Testimony.' *Research in African Literatures*. 23.1 (1992): 154–58.

'Closing Statement to the Nigerian Military Appointed Special Tribunal'. Not Delivered. Unpublished. 2 November, 1995.

'Saro-Wiwa's 40-page Defence Statement'. *P.E.N. International*. 46.2 (1995): 109–10.

'Before I am Hanged'. *Association of Nigerian Authors Review*. November, 1995: 23.

A Month and A Day: A Detention Diary. London: Penguin, 1995.

'A Classic'. In Anon., *Everything about Basi & Co., the Most Hilarious Comedy on TV!* Lagos: Saros International Publishers, n.d.: 3.

'A Company is Born'. In Anon., *Everything about Basi & Co., the Most Hilarious Comedy on TV!* Lagos: Saros International Publishers, n.d.: 4–5, 7.

'Television Drama in Nigeria: A Personal Experience'. *African Literature 1988: New Masks*. Eds. Hal Wylie, Dennis Brutus, and Juris Silenieks. Annual Selected papers of the ALA, 14/1988. Washington, DC: Three Continents Press and the African Literature Association, 1990: 87–95.

'The Adventures of Mr. B' Series:

Mr. B. Ill. Pergrino Brimah. Port Harcourt: Saros International, 1987.

Basi and Company: Four Television Plays. Port Harcourt: Saros International, 1989.

The Transistor Radio. Port Harcourt: Saros International, 1989.

Mr. B Again. Ill. P. Brimah, Saros International, 1989.

Mr. B Goes to Lagos. Port Harcourt: Saros International, 1989.

Mr. B is Dead. Ill. P. Brimah. Port Harcourt: Saros International, 1991.

Segi Finds the Radio. Ill. P. Brimah. Port Harcourt: Saros International, 1991.

A Shipload of Rice. Ill. P. Brimah. Port Harcourt: Saros International, 1991.

Mr. B Goes to the Moon. Port Harcourt: Saros International, 1991.

Mr. B's Mattress. Port Harcourt: Saros International, 1992.

A Bride for Mr. B. Port Harcourt: Saros International, 1992.

Producer and writer, television series *Basi and Company*, NTA Network Service, Saros International Productions, 1958–90.

Editor, *Mellanbite*, 1963–64, *Horizon*, 1964–65, and *Umuahia Times*.

Member, editorial board, *Umuahian*.

Columnist, *The Vanguard Newspaper*. Lagos, 1979–1992.

Written in prison:

'Ogoni! Ogoni!' *Index On Censorship*. 4.5 (1994): 219.

'Corpses Have Grown'. Unpublished. 1993.

'Keep Out of Prison'. Unpublished. 1993.

Also published elsewhere:

*A Forest of Flowers: Short Stories. Burnt Mill, Harlow, Essex, England: Longman, 1995.

*Sozaboy: A Novel in Rotten English. Burnt Mill, Harlow, Essex, England: New York, USA: Longman, 1994.

BIBLIOGRAPHY OF CRITICAL WORKS ON SARO-WIWA'S WRITINGS:

Abu, Bala Dan. 'Saro-Wiwa is no friend of the Igbos — Chief Ahanonu'. *Quality*. 16 August 1990: 13, 15.

Abu, M.A.I. 'A Stylistic Analysis of Ken Saro-Wiwa's *Sozaboy*'. Master's thesis, University of Lagos, 1990.

Abuah, Valerie. 'At Ken Saro-Wiwa's Launch, it was Book, Talk and Art'. *Vintage People*. 25 October 1991: 14–15.

Adeda, Ediri Unurowho. 'Media Drama (Radio and Television) in English and the Nigerian Society: A Case Study of Basi and Company and the Adventures of Sunny Sunny'. Master's thesis, University of Ibadan, 1990.

Adinuba, C. Don. 'To Cheer and Challenge'. *African Concord*. 27 February 1989: 32.

Agbor, Ajan, Soji Olaitan and Stella Oyibo. 'A Giant at 50'. *Tell*. 28 October 1991: 38.

Aiyejina, Funso. 'Ken Saro-Wiwa: A Pebble for Our Sling-Shot'. *Trinidad Guardian*. 19 December, 1995: 45–8.

Ajayi, Sesan. 'Saro-Wiwa and the National Question'. *Guardian*. 24 November 1991: B4; 8 December 1991: B7; 22 December 1991: B5; 29 December 1991: B7.

Ajibade, Kunle. 'A Pen Merchant'. *African Concord*. 5 March 1990: 52.

———. 'Kick Nigeria out of UNO: Conversation with Ken Saro-Wiwa'. *Weekend Concord*, 21 July 1990: 7, 18.

———. 'Tempestuous Ken'. *African Concord*, 30 July 1990: 57.

Aka, S.M.O. 'Open Letter to Ken Saro-Wiwa'. *Guardian*. 13 December 1989: 19.

Akanni, Tunde. 'Ken Saro-Wiwa at 50'. *Mid-Week Concord*. 17 October 1991: ii.

Akaraogun, Olu. 'A Lone Voice Crying in the Delta Region'. *Sunday Times*. 6 October 1991: 9.

Akindoyo, Dele. 'Be Warned'. *Classique*. 30 September 1991: 24–5.

Akinpelu, Mayor. 'The Untold Story of *Basi and Co.* Palaver'. *Prime People*. 8 January 1988: 14–5, 23.

Akinsola, 'Biyi, Sola Osofisan, and Kayode Ogunfeyetimi. 'Ken Saro-Wiwa'. *Crown Prince*. October 1991: 26–30, 44, 51, 58.

Akpederi, Joni. 'An Impressive Sitcom'. *African Guardian*, 23 April 1987: 26.

———. 'Reaching Out'. *African Guardian*. 29 October 1987: 22.

Akwei, Adotei. 'And Justice for All? The Two Faces of Nigeria'. *Ogoni's Agonies: Ken Saro-Wiwa and the Crisis in Nigeria*. Ed. Abdul-Rasheed Na'Allah. Lawrenceville: Africa World Press, 1998: 39–40.

Alabi, Adetayo. 'Saro-Wiwa and the Language of Politics in African Literature'. *Ogoni's Agonies: Ken Saro-Wiwa and the Crisis in Nigeria*. Ed. Abdul-Rasheed Na'Allah. Lawrenceville: Africa World Press, 1998: 307–318.

Alibi, Idang. 'Saro-Wiwa: A Short Giant'. *Sunday Times*. 25 June 1989: 20.

———. 'Ken Saro-Wiwa'. *Daily Times*. 29 May 1990: 13; 5 June 1990: 13.

Anikwe, Ogbuagu. 'Behind Ken Saro-Wiwa's Humour'. *Guardian*. 8 April 1990: 9.

Anim, Etim. 'Prose of an Underdog'. *Newswatch*. 9 April 1990: 43–54.

Anon. '*Basi and Company* Goes International'. *Sunday Times*. 18 October 1987: 20; 25 October 1987: 20; 1 November 1987: 20.

Anon. 'We Will Defend Our Oil with Our Blood'. *Tell*. 8 February, 1993: 28–33.

Anon. 'They Are Killing My People'. *The News*. 17 May, 1993: 22–7.

Anon. *Everything About Basi & Co., The Most Hilarious Comedy on TV!* Lagos: Saros International, n.d.

Anon. 'Ken Saro-Wiwa (Creator and Producer)'. *Everything about Basi & Co., The Most Hilarious Comedy on TV!* Anon. Lagos: Saros International: 11.

Alibi, Idang. 'Saro-Wiwa: A Short Giant'. *Sunday Times*. 25 June 1989: 20.

———. 'Ken Saro-Wiwa'. *Daily Times*. 29 May 1990: 13; 5 June 1990: 13.

Apter, Andrew. 'Death and the King's Henchmen: Ken Saro-Wiwa and the Political Ecology of Citizenship in Nigeria'. *Ogoni's Agonies: Ken Saro-Wiwa and the Crisis in Nigeria*. Ed. Abdul-Rasheed Na'Allah. Lawrenceville: Africa World Press, 1998: 121–60.

Avwarute, Agboro James. 'Some Prevalent Themes in Modern Nigerian Short Stories'. Master's thesis, University of Lagos, 1990.

Bello, Remi. 'Why I wrote *Prisoners of Jebs*'. *Vanguard*. 14 December 1988: 8–9.

Boyd, William. 'Saro-Wiwa: Smile on the Face of the Niger'. *Times* (London). 15 December 1990; *Daily Times*. 23 March 1991: 12.

———. 'Death of a Writer'. *The New Yorker*. 27 November, 1995: 51–5.

———. 'Death of a Writer'. *Ogoni's Agonies: Ken Saro-Wiwa and the Crisis in Nigeria*. Ed. Abdul-Rasheed Na'Allah. Lawrenceville: Africa World Press, 1998: 49–55.

———. 'Introduction'. *A Month and A Day: A Detention Diary*. Ken Saro-Wiwa. London: Penguin, 1995.

Breitinger, Eckhard. 'Ken Saro-Wiwa: Writer and Cultural Manager'. *Ogoni's Agonies: Ken Saro-Wiwa and the Crisis in Nigeria*. Ed. Abdul-Rasheed Na'Allah. Lawrenceville: Africa World Press, 1998: 241–53.

Brooke, James. '30 Million Nigerians Are Laughing at Themselves'. *New York Times*. 24 July 1987, 1: 4.

Edafioka, Veronica, Abiola Oloke, and Sam Smith. 'Newsliners'. *Newswatch*. 28 November 1988: 38.

Egbe, Nkanu. 'Our Country is Anti-Art — Ken Saro-Wiwa'. *Top News*, 11 January 1989: 12–4.

Ehling, Holger G. 'Ken Saro-Wiwa (Nigeria)'. *Literaturnachrichten*. 17, 1988: 15–6.

Emereole, Olisaemeka. 'Ken Saro-Wiwa's Literary Harvest'. *Guardian*. 14 October 1991: 33.

Ette, Mercy, and Josephine Akarue. 'Newsliners'. *Newswatch*. 28 October 1991: 43.

Ezenwa-Ohaeto. 'Interview: Ken Saro-Wiwa'. *Daily Times*. 29 July 1989: 20; 12 August 1989: 9.

———. 'The Culture Imperative in Modern Nigerian Drama: A Consolidation in the Plays of Saro-Wiwa, Nwabueze, and Irobi'. *Neohelocon: Acta Comparationis Litterarum Universarum*. 21.2, 1994: 207–20.

Fashomi, Dele. 'Ken Saro-Wiwa and the Nigerian Polity'. *National Concord*. 3 October 1991: 7.

Fayemi, O.O. 'Origins and Evolution of the Short Story Genre in Nigeria: An Analytica Survey'. Ph.D. dissertation, University of Ibadan, 1990.

Feuser, Willfried F. 'The Voice from Dukana: Ken Saro-Wiwa'. *Matatu: Journal for African Culture and Society*. 1.2, 1987: 52–66; *Literary Half Year*. 29.1, 1988: 11–25.

Fiofori, Tam. 'Faces and Voices of Wars'. *Times International*. 16 March 1987: 29.

———. 'Saro-Wiwa's Words and Music'. *Vanguard*. 18 January 1990: 8–9.

———. 'Conversation with Saro-Wiwa'. *Vanguard*. 5 April 1990: 8–9.

Garuba, Harry. 'Ken Saro-Wiwa's Sozaboy and the Logic of Minority Discourse'. *Ogoni's Agonies: Ken Saro-Wiwa and the Crisis in Nigeria*. Ed. Abdul-Rasheed Na'Allah. Lawrenceville: Africa World Press, 1998: 229–39.

George, Karibi T. 'Myth and History in Ken Saro-Wiwa's *Basi And Company: A Modern African Folktale*'. *African Literature and African Historical Experiences*. Eds. Chidi Ikonné, Emelia Oko, Peter Onwudinjo, and Ernest N. Emenyonu. Calabar Studies in African Literature, [6]. Ibadan: Heinemann Educational Books Nigeria, 1991: 107–15.

Gibbs, James. 'Ola Rotimi and Ken Saro-Wiwa: Nigerian Popular Playwrights'. *Signs & Signals: Popular Culture in Africa*. 6, 1990: 121–35.

Igwe, Dimgba. 'The Day Professor Osofisan, a Socialist, was Happy in the Company of Capitalists'. *Sunday Concord*. 5 April 1987: 17.

———. 'Saro-Wiwa: 120 Minutes of Critical X-ray'. *Sunday Concord*. 15 January 1989: 8, 13.

———. 'Writers War on Book Launches'. *Sunday Concord*. 15 January 1989: 8, 13.

Ikandu, Hakeem. 'Enter New Mr. B: Soldier Go, Soldier Come, Says Creator Ken Saro-Wiwa'. *Vanguard*. 2 September 1987: 7.

Ike, Osita. 'A Chat with Ken Saro-Wiwa'. *National Concord*. 17 December 1987: 5.

Ilagha, Nengi. 'Seven-Up for Saro-Wiwa'. *EKO*. 12 October 1991: 15.

Ilesanmi, Obafemi. 'An Agenda for Saro-Wiwa'. *Daily Times*. 29 December 1990: 11.

Inyama, Nnadozie. 'Point of View in Saro-Wiwa's Sozaboy'. *Critical Essays on Ken Saro-Wiwa's Sozaboy*. Ed. C. Nnolim. Port Harcourt: Saros International, 1992: 102–7.

Irele, Abiola. 'The Fiction of Ken Saro-Wiwa'. *Guardian*. 17 January 1987: 13; 24 January 1987: 13.

———. 'Ken Saro-Wiwa'. *Perspectives on Nigerian Literature: 1700 to The Present*. Vol. II. , Ed.Yemi Ogunbiyi. Lagos: Guardian Books Nigerian Limited, 1988, 333–44.

———. 'Ken Saro-Wiwa'. *Ogoni's Agonies: Ken Saro-Wiwa and the Crisis in Nigeria*. Ed. Abdul-Rasheed Na'Allah. Lawrenceville: Africa World Press, 1998: 255–67.

Iserhime, Emu Dorcas. 'Nigerians are Vulgar, says Ken Saro-Wiwa'. *Prime People*. 3 April 1987: 16.

Ivbijaro, Monica. 'Why *Basi and Co.* is in the Cooler'. *Vanguard*. 4 May 1988: 12–3.

Joseph, P.A. Curtis. 'Fall Outs from *On A Darkling Plain*'. *Guardian*. 29 June 1990: 11.

Kassim, Omolulu. 'The Story of *Basi And Company*'. *National Concord*. 17 December 1987: 5.

King-Aribisala, K. '*Basi & Co.* and *WAI*'. *Everything about Basi & Co., The Most Hilarious Comedy on TV!* Anon. Lagos: Saros International, n.d.: 8.

Kirk-Greene. 'A Review, *A Month and a Day: A Detention Diary*, by Ken Saro-Wiwa'. *African Affairs*. 95.379, 1996: 294–5.

Koroye, Seiyifa. 'Sozaboy: First Person Narration and Mene's "very bad dream"'. *Critical Essays on Ken Saro-Wiwa's Sozaboy*. Ed. C. Nnolim, Port Harcourt: Saros International, 1992: 82–101.

Lawal, Sola. 'Writers Also Speak'. *Hotline*. July 1991: 34–6.

* Lindfors, Bernth. *Black African Literature in English, 1987–1991*. London: Hans Zell Publishers, 1995: 447–83.

———. 'Ken Saro-Wiwa — in Short, a Giant'. *Ogoni's Agonies: Ken Saro-Wiwa and the Crisis in Nigeria*. Ed. Abdul-Rasheed Na'Allah. Lawrenceville: Africa World Press, 1998: 195–7.

Loimeier, Manfred. *Zum Beispiel: Ken Saro-Wiwa*. Göttingen: Lamuv Verlag GmbH, 1996.

Mair, Christian. 'The New Englishes and Stylistic Innovation: Ken Saro-Wiwa's *Sozaboy: A Novel in Rotten English*'. *Us/Them: Transla-*

tion, Transcription and Identity in Post-Colonial Literary Cultures. (*Cross/ Cultures 6*). Ed. Gordon Collier. Amsterdam/Atlanta: Rodopi, 1992: 277–87.

McGreal, Chris. 'A tainted hero'. *The Guardian Weekend* (London), 23 March 1996: 25–8.

Meier, Didi. 'The Man Inside Mr. Basi'. *New African.* October 1988: 41.

Mofe-Damijo, Richard, Prince Emeka Obasi, and Dozie Arinze. 'A Voice for the Minority'. *Classique.* 23 April, 1990: 27–8, 31–3.

Momoh, Siaka. 'The Return of *Basi and Company*'. *Vanguard.* 9 July 1988: 9.

———. "Saros' Unique Launch." *Vanguard.* 30 November 1989: 9.

Na'Allah, Abdul-Rasheed. 'Ken Saro-Wiwa: A Bio-Bibliography'. *Ogoni's Agonies: Ken Saro-Wiwa and the Crisis in Nigeria.* Ed. Abdul-Rasheed Na'Allah. Lawrenceville: Africa World Press, 1998: 363–77.

———. Ed. *Ogoni's Agonies: Ken Saro-Wiwa and the Crisis in Nigeria.* Lawrenceville: Africa World Press, 1998.

New African 'Persecution of Ken Saro-Wiwa'. 330, May 1995: 18.

Ngene, Charles Emeka. 'A Critical Study of the Language of Ken Saro-Wiwa's *Songs In A Time Of War*'. Master's thesis, University of Lagos, 1991.

Nixon, Rob. 'Pipe Dreams: Ken Saro-Wiwa, Environmental Justice, and Micro-Minority Rights'. *Black Renaissance Noire.* 1.1, 1996: 39–56.

Nnolim, Charles. Ed. *Critical Essays on Ken Saro-Wiwa's Sozaboy.* Port Harcourt: Saros International, 1992.

Nnoru, Joe. 'Interview with Ken Saro-Wiwa'. *Guardian.* 21 December 1988: 15.

Nwabueze, Goddy. 'Ken's National Project: The Guilty Tribes'. *Sunday Times.* 25 November 1990: 7.

Nwangbu, Chido. 'Ken Saro-Wiwa's Wars'. *National Concord.* 10 May 1990: 7.

Nwiadoh, Deebi. 'Saro-Wiwa is not a tribalist'. *Daily Times.* 13 July 1990: 13.

———. 'Saro-Wiwa at 50'. *Daily Times.* 21 September 1991: 17; *Association of Nigerian Authors Review.* 6.8, 1991: 30.

Obi, Chioma. '*Basi & Co.* May Go Off the Screen'. *Vintage People.* 20 July 1990: 23.

Obaigbo, Aoiri. 'How Saro-Wiwa Made the Million Naira that Got *Basi & Co.* to the Screen'. *Vintage People.* 8 December 1989: 18, 22.

Obasi, [Prince] Emeka. '*Basi and Company* has caught the imagination of Nigerians'. *Guardian*. 5 November 1988: 9.

Obiagwu, Kodilinye. 'Let's Launch This Book'. *Times International*. 26 December 1988: 34.

——— and Dapo Olasebikan. 'Popular TV Comic-serio Series'. *Times International*. 16 November 1987: 33.

Obijiofor, Levi. 'Writers Against Writers'. *Guardian*. 14 January 1989: 11.

Odugbemi, Sina. 'The Tales of Saro-Wiwa'. *Vanguard*, 5 March 1987: 9.

———. 'Saro-Wiwa Threatens Your Ribcage'. *Vanguard*. 10 December 1987: 9.

Ofeimun, Odia. 'Steak for *Prisoners of Jebs*'. *Guardian*. 14 December 1988: 13; *Association of Nigerian Authors Review*. 4.6, 1989: 23.

———. 'Saro's Sour Logic'. *Guardian*. 11 January 1989: 11.

———. 'Come Down to Earth, Writer'. *Guardian*. 15 February 1989: 13.

Ogbowei, G. 'Ebinyo and Ibiere Bell-Gam. 'Sozaboy: Language and a Disordered World'. *English Studies in Africa*. 38.1, 1995: 1–17.

Offoara, Chinedu. 'Saro-Wiwa, Alibi and Tribalism'. *Daily Times*. 14 June 1990: 13.

Ogbuanoh, Jossey. 'The People's Entire Mentality Should Change'. *Probe*. 29 December 1988: 50–2.

Ojo, Damilola. 'Saro-Wiwa, a Sad and Funny Guy, Talks of Nigeria's Vulgar Book Culture'. *Daily Times*. 3 December 1988: 12.

———. 'Mirror of Our Time'. *Daily Times*. 16 December 1988: 7.

Okediran, Wale. 'Ken Saro-Wiwa at 50'. *Guardian*. 19 October 1991: 11.

Okere, Augustine. 'Patterns of Linguistic Deviation in Saro-Wiwa's *Sozaboy*'. *Critical Essays on Saro-Wiwa's Sozaboy*. Ed. C. Nnolim. Port Harcourt: Saros International, 1992: 9–15.

Okome, Onookome. 'Saro-Wiwa: "Not Right to Judge Yet".' 4 September 1991: 22.

Okonedo, Tony, Boye Ola, and Debo Fatiregun. 'Saro-Wiwa Comes Back Smoking'. *Vanguard*. 6 May 1988: 8.

Okonta, Ike. 'A Writer's Vision'. *Citizen*. 21 October 1991: 46.

———. Bolaji Adebiyi, Aluko Akinyele, Nkechi Attoh, Samson Ojo, and Clifford Amadi. 'Ken Saro-Wiwa: Create Ethnic States'. *Citizen*. 12 August 1991: 16–21.

Okpewho, Jerome. 'Content and Style in Ken Saro-Wiwa's Works'. *Muse*. 20, 1990: 40–3.

Ola, Boye. 'At the Real Launch'. *Sunday Concord*. 1 April 1990: 3.

——. 'How I write Saro-Wiwa'. *Sunday Concord*. 1 July 1990: 14.

Olafioye, Tayo. 'Ken Saro-Wiwa Echo'. *Ogoni's Agonies: Ken Saro-Wiwa and the Crisis in Nigeria*. Ed. Abdul-Rasheed Na'Allah. Lawrenceville: Africa World Press, 1998: 179–86.

Oloruntoba-Oju, Taiwo. 'The Writer and the Junta'. *Ogoni's Agonies: Ken Saro-Wiwa and the Crisis in Nigeria*. Ed. Abdul-Rasheed Na'Allah. Lawrenceville: Africa World Press, 1998: 187–94.

Olugbile, Femi. 'The Writer as a Protagonist'. *Vanguard*. 7 June 1990: 9.

Oluwajuyitan, Jide. 'Saro-Wiwa's Misplaced Aggression'. *Guardian*. 28 August 1990: 11.

Omoifo, Isi. 'Humour as Mask'. *African Guardian*. 19 December 1988: 36.

Omotoso, Kole. 'In the Company of *Basi And Company*'. *West Africa*. 28 September 1987: 1919.

——. 'Ken Saro-Wiwa — Writer Extraordinaire'. *West Africa*. 19–25 March 1990: 454.

Onuorah, Madu, and Kehinde Latunde-Dada. 'Literary Novels Give Only Fame'. *ThisWeek*. 30 January 1989: 31.

[Onwenu], Onyeka. 'Remembering Papa'. *Prime People*. 27 April 1990: 19.

——. 'Letter from Saro-Wiwa'. *Prime People*. 6 July 1990: 19.

Opara, Chioma. 'Magical Effect in Magic Land: The Pain of the Game in Ken Saro-Wiwa's *Prisoners of Jebs*'. *Review of English and Literary Studies*. 7.1, 1990: 11–7.

Orage, Desmond Lera. 'The Ogoni Question and the Role of the International Community in Nigeria'. *Ogoni's Agonies: Ken Saro-Wiwa and the Crisis in Nigeria*. Ed. Abdul-Rasheed Na'Allah. Lawrenceville: Africa World Press, 1998: 41–8.

Oriaku, R.O. 'Ken Saro-Wiwa's War Songs'. *Review of English and Literary Studies*. 2.1, 1985: 57–64.

Osaghae, E. Eghosa. 'The Ogoni Uprising: Oil Politics, Minority Agitation and the Future of the Nigerian State'. *African Affairs*. 94.376, July 1995: 325–44.

Osewele, Nat Beifoh. 'Ken Saro-Wiwa, a Baby at 50'. *National Concord*. 10 October 1991: 5.

Oshuntokun, Bisola. 'Ken Saro-Wiwa Writes Children's Book on Late Papa Awo'. *Aura*. 22 July 1991: 19–21, 37–9.

Osundare, Niyi. 'Not an Internal Affair'. *Ogoni's Agonies: Ken Saro-Wiwa and the Crisis in Nigeria*. Ed. Abdul-Rasheed Na'Allah. Lawrenceville:

Africa World Press, 1998: 105–8.

Oti, Sonny. 'Good Theatre for the Screen and Stage'. *Everything about Basi & Co., The Most Hilarious Comedy on TV!* Anon. Lagos: Saros International, n.d.: 9.

Quayson, L. Ato. 'Anatomizing a Post-Colonial Tragedy: Ken Saro-Wiwa and the Ogonis'. *Journal of Performance Research*. 1.2, 1996: 83–92.

———. 'For Ken Saro-Wiwa: African Post-Colonial Relations Through a Prism of Tragedy'. *Salt*. 9, 1996: 157–76.

———. 'For Ken Saro-Wiwa: African Post-Colonial Relations Through a Prism of Tragedy'. *Ogoni's Agonies: Ken Saro-Wiwa and the Crisis in Nigeria*. Ed. Abdul-Rasheed Na'Allah. Lawrenceville: Africa World Press, 1998: 57–80.

Raji, Wumi. 'Oil Resources: Hegemonic Politics and the Struggle for a Re-invention of Post-Colonial Nigeria'. *Ogoni's Agonies: Ken Saro-Wiwa and the Crisis in Nigeria*. Ed. Abdul-Rasheed Na'Allah. Lawrenceville: Africa World Press, 1998: 109–20.

Sachs, Aaron. 'Dying For Oil'. *World Watch*. 9.3, 1996: 10–21.

Saseun, Segun, and Simi Awosika. 'Saro-Wiwa's Vision'. *African Guardian*. 4 November 1991: 37.

Schulze-Engler, Frank. 'Civil Critiques: Satire and Politics of Democratic Transition in Ken Saro-Wiwa's Novels'. *Ogoni's Agonies: Ken Saro-Wiwa and the Crisis in Nigeria*. Ed. Abdul-Rasheed Na'Allah. Lawrenceville: Africa World Press, 1998: 285–306.

Schmied, Josef J. *English in Africa: An Introduction*. London and New York: Longman, 1991.

Soyinka, Wole. 'The Self-Expression in Style'. *Daily Times*. 18 June 1990: 28ff.

———. *The Open Sore of a Continent: A Personal Narrative of the Nigerian Crisis*. Oxford: Oxford University Press, 1996.

Tella, Yinka. 'People'. *Citizen*. 17 June 1991: 51.

Udenwa, Onuora, and Chinwude Onuwuanyi. 'Interview with Ken Saro-Wiwa'. *Quality*. 15 December 1988: 36–8, 41–4.

Usuhor, U.J. 'Satire in Nigerian Prose'. Master's thesis, University of Ibadan, 1990.

Uzoatu, Uzor Maxim. 'A Celebration of Talent'. *Timesweek*. 28 October 1991: 40.

Vincent, Theo. 'The Mirror of Our Times'. *Daily Times*. 23 December 1988: 13.

Ward-Allen, Rosalind. 'Ken Saro-Wiwa — Writer, Human Rights Campaigner, and Environmentalist'. *Wasafiri*. 23, 1996: 53–5.

Yakubu, Ikhazs. 'Saros' Unique Launch'. *Vanguard*. 30 November 1989: 9.

———. 'Ken Saro-Wiwa: "Not right to judge yet".' *Daily Times*. 28 August 1991: 26.

Zabus, Chantal. 'Under the Palimpsest and Beyond: The 'Original' in the West African European Novel.' *Crisis and Creativity in the New Literatures in English. Cross/Cultures: Readings in the Post/Colonial Literatures in English,* 1. Eds. G. Davis and Hena Maes-Jelinek. Amsterdam and Atlanta, GA: Rodopi, 1990.

———. 'The African Palimpsest: Indigenization of Language in the West African Europhone Novel'. *Cross/Cultures*, 4. Amsterdam and Atlanta, GA: Rodopi, 1991.

———. 'Ken Saro-Wiwa'. *Post-War Literatures in English: A Lexicon of Contemporary Authors*. Eds. Hans Bertens, Theo D'haen, Joris Duytschaever, and Richard Todd. Houten: Bohn Stafleu Van Loghum; Groningen: Wolters-Noordhoff, 14, 1991: 1–15, A1–2, B1–5.

AWARDS AND HONORS:

- African Theatre Prize, British Broadcasting Corporation, 1972 (for radio play, *The Transistor Radio*).
- Poetry Prize Runner-up, Association of Nigerian Authors, 1985 (for *Songs in a Time of War*).
- Commonwealth Writer Prize, 1987 (for *A Forest of Flowers*).
- Association of Nigerian Authors' Prize, 1990 (for *Four Farcial Plays*).
- Right Livelihood Award, 1994 ($250,000).
- Fonlon-Nichols Award, 1994 (from the Research Institute for Comparative Literature, The University of Alberta, Edmonton, Canada for excellence in creative writing and contributions to the struggle for human rights).
- Nominee for Nobel Peace Prize, 1995.
- Goldman Environmental Prize, 1995 ($75,000).
- Amnesty International Prisoner of Conscience, 1995.
- Bruno Kreisky Human Rights Award, 1995.

NOTES
* Many of the bibliographical entries here are from Lindfors, 1995.

Notes On The Contributors

Pius Adesanmi, born in 1972, obtained a First Class Honors in French from the University of Ilorin in 1992. Currently pursuing a post-graduate programme in the same discipline at the University of Ibadan.

Adotei Akwei, a Ghanaian, is the Government Program Officer for Africa with Amnesty International USA. Before joining AIUSA, Mr. Akwei served as Africa Program Director for the Lawyers Committee for Human Rights in New York.

Adetayo Alabi, a Lecturer of English at the University of Maiduguri, Nigeria, is currently on study-leave at the English Department, University of Saskatchewan, Canada. He has contributed to the *Routledge Encyclopedia of Post-Colonial Literatures* and the *Oxford Companion to African Literatures*, and his papers have appeared in *Liwuram* and *In-Between*.

Andrew Apter teaches in the Anthropology Department at the University of Chicago. His recent publications include "Notes on Orisha Cults in the Ekiti Yoruba Highlands' (*Cahiers d'Études Africaines* 138-9 [1995]: 369–401) and *Black Critics and Kings: The Hermeneutics of Power in Yoruba Society* (Chicago: University of Chicago Press, 1992). After finishing a book on oil-capitalism and national culture in Nigeria, he plans a second Yoruba volume, *The Blood of Mothers*, and a study of Santeria and the state in Cuba.

Oluwatoyin A. Asojo, a Nigerian, holds a Ph.D. in Chemistry and is also a poet.

Sonia Atwal, an East-Indian Canadian, is working on her Ph.D. at the Department of Modern Languages and Comparative Studies, University of Alberta, Canada. She is interested in postcolonial literatures and is doing her dissertation in South Asian Women's Studies.

Ronke Luke Boone is from Sierra Leone, West Africa. He writes poetry that reflects on the conditions in Africa.

William Boyd is a British novelist.

Marcielle Brandler was born in Riverside, California. She currently works with International PEN's Writers in Prison Campaign and also directs poetry workshops in schools and universities. Her poems have been translated into Spanish, Castillano, Czech and French.

Eckhard Breitinger, Editor of *Bayreuth African Studies*, teaches at the Universität Bayreuth Institut für Afrikastudien, Bayreuth, Germany.

Charles Burmeister was born in San Antonio. His first novel, *Strike the Stone*, was set in pre-historic Africa. He is currently a James A. Michener Fellow at the Texas Center for Writers at the University of Texas at Austin, USA.

Eze chi Chiazo, a published poet from Eastern Nigeria, lives at Schlossbergleinz, Bayreuth, Germany.

Femi Dunmade has a Master's degree in English and teaches at the University of Ilorin, Nigeria.

Ezenwa-Ohaeto, a Nigerian obtained B.A. and M.A. degrees in English from the University of Nigeria, Nsukka and a Ph.D. in English from the University of Benin. He is presently at the University of Bayreuth, Germany. He is the author of the poetry collections *Songs of a Traveller* (1986), *I Wan Be President* (1988), *Bullets for Buntings* (1989) and the critical studies *Longman Examination Guide: Zaynab Alkali's The Stillborn* (1991) and *Chinua Achebe, The Life:*

Facing the Frontiers (1997). He has won a first prize for short stories in 1978, BBC Arts and Africa Poetry Award 1981, Orphic Lute Poetry Prize 1985 and the Humboldt Prestigious Research Fellowship 1993. His works have been translated into Russian, French and Italian.

Harry Garuba, author of *Shadow Dream and Other Poems*, is a Senior Lecturer in the Dept. of English, University of Ibadan, Nigeria, where he teaches creative writing, literary theory, and the literature of Africa and the African Diaspora. He is also a writer and a member of the Association of Nigerian Authors (ANA), and Managing Editor of the Association's journal, the *ANA Review*.

Doris Hambuch is doing a Ph.D. at the Department of Modern Languages and Comparative Studies, University of Alberta, Canada, and working on Caribbean literatures.

Jonathan Hart is Professor of English and Adjunct Professor of Comparative Literature at the University of Alberta, Canada, and a Visiting Fellow at Cambridge, Harvard and Toronto. Some of his most recent works are on the relation between exploitation of the land in colonial and postcolonial history and literature, from 1942 to the present. His poetry has appeared in *Harvard Review*, *Mattoid* (Australia) and *Quarry* (Canada). From July, 1998, Hart assumes duty as Editor, *Canadian Review of Comparative Literature*.

Ikhide R. Ikheloa was born in Lagos, Nigeria in 1959. He attended Benin and Mississippi. He is currently the School System Administrator, Montgomery County, Maryland.

Abiola Irele, Professor of African Comparative Studies at Ohio State University, Ohio, is the current editor of *Research in African Literature*.

Andre Karl studies at the University of Alberta, Canada.

Bernth Lindfors is former Editor of *Research in African Literatures*. He is the author of *Early Nigerian Literature* and *Popular Literatures in Africa*, among others.

Lisa Mahoney is the Area Coordinator in Los Angeles and a trainer and member of the District 16 Refugee Team (Southern California) of Amnesty International. He is also a Campaign Coordinator for Amnesty's Nigeria/Kenya Campaign for Group 92 in Sherman Oaks, California, USA.

Kofi Mensah, a Ghanaian, teaches at the University of Botswana, Southern Africa.

Felix W.J. Mnthali, a well-known African poet, was born in Zimbabwe of Malawian parents. He was educated in Zimbabwe, Malawi, Lesotho and Canada. He has taught at the Universities of Malawi, Ibadan and Botswana.

Haba G. Musengezi is a novelist and playwright from Zimbabwe. Some of his poems have appeared in *Kalahari*, a journal of Southern African literatures.

Abdul-Rasheed Na'Allah is the co-author of *Introduction to African Oral Literature*. He presented a literary and current affairs discussion program, 'Focal Point', on Radio Kwara, Ilorin, Nigeria, from 1986 to 1993, taught African literature, English and oral literature at the Department of Modern European Languages, University of Ilorin, Nigeria, and is now a Ph.D. candidate at the Department of Modern Languages and Comparative Studies, University of Alberta, Canada. His works have appeared in *Nigeria Magazine, Frankfurter Afrikanistische Blätter, Language Learning Journal, Canadian Journal of African Studies* and *Canadian Review of Comparative Literature*, among others. He is a member of the Ilorin Writers Unlimited, the African Literature Association, the Canadian Comparative Literature Association, and the Canadian Association of African Studies.

Olu Obafemi, a popular Nigerian dramatist, is professor of English at the University of Ilorin, Nigeria. His drama works include *The Suicide Syndrome, Nights of a Mystical Beast* and *Naira Has No Gender*. He is also a co-author of *The Rising Voices: an Anthology of New Nigerian Poetry*, where all his poems published in this book first appeared.

Tanure Ojaide is a Nigerian poet and scholar. He was educated in Nigeria and the United States, where he received an M.A. in Creative Writing (1979) and Ph.D. in English (1981) from Syracuse University. He is a Fellow in Writing of The University of Iowa; has been inducted into the Ahmadu Bello University Creative Writers' Club's Roll of Honor; and is a member of the Association of Nigerian Authors (ANA). He was Africa Regional Winner of the Commonwealth Poetry Prize in 1987; Winner of the All-Africa Okigbo Prize for Poetry in 1988; and also the 1988 Overall Winner of the BBC Arts and Africa Poetry Award. His publications include: *The Fate of Vultures* (1990), *The Blood of Peace* (1991) and *Poetic Imagination in Black Africa* (1996), *Great Boys: An African Childhood* (1997). Tanure Ojaide currently teaches at the University of North Carolina at Charlotte.

Tayo Olafioye, critic, novelist, poet, teaches at the University of California St. Marcos. His contributions in this book are from his new anthology of poems, *The Anthology of Agony*. Among his other books are *The Saga of Sego, Politics in African Poetry* and *Sorrows of a Town Crier*.

Taiwo Oloruntoba-Oju, a poet and dramatist, teaches English at the University of Ilorin, Nigeria. He is currently the General Secretary of the Association of Nigerian Authors, Kwara State Branch, and the Vice-Chairman of the Academic Staff Union of Nigerian Universities (ASUU), University of Ilorin.
Jacqueline Onyejiaka was born in Nwerre LGA in Imo State, Nigeria. She is currently working on her first book of poetry, 'Milk, Tears and Blood'.

Desmond Lera Orage is the eldest son of one of the four Ogoni Chiefs, Chief Samuel Orage, whose murder on May 21, 1994, raised a lot of controversies. He currently lives in Los Angeles, California.

Niyi Osundare, the foremost of the new generation of Nigerian poets, is the joint winner of the Commonwealth Poetry Prize in 1986 and the winner of the Association of Nigerian Authors Poetry

Prize in 1986, the Cadbury Poetry Prize in 1989 and the NOMA award in 1991. His books of poetry include *Village Voices*, *The Eye of the Earth*, *Moonsongs*, *A Nib in the Pond*, *Selected Poems* and *Mildlife*. He is a columnist with *Newswatch*, a Nigerian news magazine, and currently the Chair of English at the University of Ibadan, Nigeria.

Ato Quayson teaches Commonwealth Literature and Postcolonial Theory at the Faculty of English and is a Fellow of Pembroke College, University of Cambridge. His book on Nigerian literary history is in press and he is currently working on a critical introduction to Postcolonial Theory.

Wumi Raji, a book prize winner in the 1988 BBC Arts and Africa Poetry competition, teaches English at the University of Ilorin, Nigeria. He is a co-editor of *Rising Voices: An Anthology of New Nigerian Poetry*.

Frank Schulze-Engler, wrote his Ph.D. thesis on East African Literature and currently teaches at the Institute for English and American Studies at J.W. Goethe University, Frankfurt/M. He has published a number of articles on African literature, comparative approaches to the new literatures in English and postcolonial theory.

Joseph Ushie teaches at the Department of English, University of Uyo in Akwa Ibom State, Nigeria, and is currently doing his Ph.D. at the English Department of the University of Ibadan.

INDEX